A.D.R. Student Simplified

JAVA
Simplified

For
Students and Beginners

By

Adam Shaw

A.D.R. (London) Limited
2-4 Wellington Road
Bridlington
YO15 2BN
England

A.D.R. Student Simplified Text Series

JAVA Simplified
Latest Version

Acknowledgements

I would like to thank Robin Taylor for his encouragement and support during the writing of this book, and David Dunn for his very helpful comments and advice on its drafting.

Copyright

© A . D . R . (London) Limited 1999

British Library Cataloguing in Publication Data

A catalogue record for this book is available from the British Library

ISBN 190 1197 88 3

Trademarks and registered Trademarks & Acknowledgements

Computer hardware and software names mentioned in this book are protected by their respective trademarks and are acknowledged as being the property of their owners. ADR cannot guarantee the accuracy of information. **Java** is a trademark of Sun Microsystems, Inc. Thanks are due to Sun Microsystems , the owners of Java Language for their permission to use the Java Development Kit.

Warning and Disclaimer

Every effort has been made to make this book as complete and as accurate as possible, but no warranty or fitness is implied. The information given in this book, is on an "as is " basis. The author and the publisher shall have neither liability or responsibility to any person or entity with respect to any loss or damages arising from the information contained in this book or from the use of the Web site or programs in it.

Direct Order

In case of difficulty, you can obtain this copy from the publisher.

A . D . R . (London) Limited
2-4 Wellington Road
Bridlington
YO15 2BN
England

Tel: 01262 605538
Fax: 01262 605538 & 400851
e-mail: ADRLONDON @ aol.com

Printed in Great Britain.

Preface

Java is the programming language for the new millennium and, as such, is much in demand by prospective Java Programmers. This book is designed for both students and beginners who wish to acquire knowledge of Java and practise what they have learnt through worked examples.

A reader who is self-motivated and persistent will undoubtedly benefit from this book. The only other requirement is that you must have access to a modern computer system with the Java Development Kit installed for Windows. The latest version is called Java 2.

The book introduces Java programming by means of solved practical examples which may appear to be simple at first but they demonstrate the application of Java language. The book does not claim to cover all aspects of the language. It is a practical book and thus covers those topics for which space was available to demonstrate their application. The emphasis is on learning from experience.

The book is filled with examples which are coded and explained. For testing each applet, the html document is also written for testing the applet with the appletviewer Java tool. Each applet is tested successfully and the result of the test is shown as screen capture. For each example, the code and program output are listed in a diagram or a number of diagrams. The output is an important part of an example as it will enable you to learn the programming technique introduced. You are advised to try these out on your computer as you progress through the book. Programming is best learnt by a hands-on approach, therefore it is recommended that you work through these examples, and also produce answers to exercises given at the end of each chapter. A suggested solution is given for each exercise in Chapter 15. Try not to read the solutions until you have attempted the exercises.

The book will enable you to achieve your objective to write workable practical programs. It will lay the foundation for advancing your Java programming skills, and help you to become a professional Java programmer. I hope you derive as much pleasure and satisfaction from it as I enjoyed in its writing. Good luck!

Adam Shaw
Bridlington
England

August 1999

Contents

****

Preface

Chapter 1 Towards Understanding Java Language 1

Vi

Chapter 5 Conditions Testing 79

Chapter 6 Working with objects and classes 100

Viii

Chapter 7 Applets Basic understanding 123

Chapter 8 Fonts and colours 140

Chapter 9 The graphical user interface - UGI 157

Chapter 10 Event Handling 197

Chapter 11 Drawing Shapes 207

Chapter 12 Drawing Shapes using 2D Graphics 232

X

Chapter 13 Animation and Threads 252

Chapter 14 Exception Handling 269

Chapter 15 Suggested Solutions 276

Chapter 1

Towards Understanding Java Language

Before you can start writing a Java program, it is necessary that you understand this chapter. It will lay the foundation for applying some of the basic concepts of Object Oriented Programming. The purpose of this chapter is to serve as an introduction. These ideas are developed further elsewhere in this book.

Introduction

The Java programming language was developed from 1990 at Sun Microsystems. It looks like C++ from which it has borrowed a lot. It has been growing in popularity since 1995. It has taken the Computer Industry by storm with the promise of "Write once. Run anywhere." Java is often linked to World Wide Web (WWW), Internet, applets, applications and beans programs that are written in this language.

Amongst other things, it has been described as object oriented, portable, multithreaded and dynamically-linked programming language. C++ is also object oriented programming (OOP) language. The similarities between Java and C++ make it easy for anyone with C++ experience. For the meaning of portable, multithreaded and dynamically-linked, see the last paragraph of this chapter.

A justification for a programming language

A **computer** is a machine. It has to be instructed by human beings in the same way as one person instructs the other person in a language that is understood by both the instructor and the person to whom instructions are given. For instance, if you ask a police officer to direct you to the Houses of Parliament in London, you have to ask the officer in English. This is due to the fact that English is the language spoken in London. The officer will direct you using the English language. Let us assume that the officer gave you precise directions and that you were able to understand and follow the route until you reached your destination. In this case, we can say that the police officer programmed you using the English language by giving you a set of instructions (directions), and you were able to complete the task (reached your desired destination) successfully.

In the above example, we have assumed that the police officer and the enquirer communicated with each other using the English language. Of course, being human, both are able to think, remember and recall. In fact, a computer can perform tasks not only so simple, but much more complicated, providing someone has already thought out **instructions**, and the **sequence** of these instructions for the computer. From this illustration, you can see that a set of instructions arranged in sequence for a computer, is known as a **program**.

A program

It tells the computer what to do and how to carry out a task step-by-step. The set of instructions that makes up the program has to be given in a particular programming language, that a computer can understand. Indeed, a computer can solve most of our day-to-day problems, if we can relay these to it in a particular programming language such as **Java**.

Languages spoken by people tend to be ambiguous and metaphorical. Our phrases can mean different things to different people. We may use words to confuse other people. Therefore, programming languages have been developed to remove such difficulties. They have precise **syntax rules** governing arrangements of words, and are concise in their meanings.

Classification of programming languages

For simplicity, these computer programming languages can be broadly classified as **Low** and **High Level Languages**.

Low Level Languages

These languages use binary codes. These codes are complex and cannot be easily transferred from one computer to another. It is not so easy to learn a low level language. One very important advantage of these languages is their speed. A program written in a low language hardly requires any translation into machine codes. Therefore, a Low Level Language program operates faster than a High Level Language program. These languages are machine-based.

High Level Languages

High Level Languages such as C, C++, COBOL, and Pascal use English-like words. This makes computer programming easier to learn. They are not machine-based, and therefore can be used on most computers. The program written by you (programmer) in any of these languages is known as **source program**, that contains **source code**. Before a High Level Language source program can be run, it has to be translated into the **object program**, that contains machine code. Yes indeed, the compiler is also a program, which checks the source code for syntax errors. When it finds such errors, it displays these for the programmer to correct them. It is the object program that the computer can understand, as it is in machine code. It is now an executable program.

How is this done?

In accordance with the well established traditional programming approach (see next page), this is achieved by means of interpreters and compilers. These are program translating systems (software). Their main features are listed below.

A Foot Note

Every computer needs an **operating system** to organise its operations. Usually, the operating system is stored in RAM(Random Access Memory). Microsoft Windows 98 is an operating system. An operating system itself is a large program. It manages the memory, interprets the user's keyboard operations, operates the screen, allows the user to create, delete move, print, read and write on disk, run other programs and so on.

Interpreter

. Translates and carries out the instruction immediately line by line as it meets each line.
. Source code and the interpreter are together in memory.
. Memory space for data is reduced due to the presence of the interpreter in the memory.
. Speed of translation and run is slower than that of the compiler.

Compiler

. It translates the <u>whole</u> source program into a self-contained program.
. The self-contained program can be run independently, immediately or at a later stage.
. During the run neither the source program nor the compiler has to be in memory.
. Efficient use of memory space for data.
. Speed of translation and run is faster than that of the interpreter.

Traditional approach

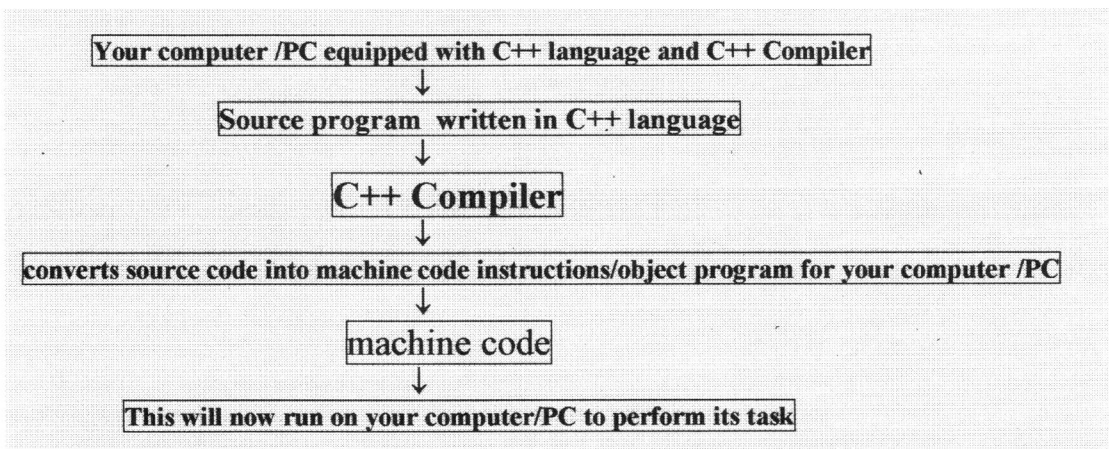

The source program written say in C++ or any other high level language has to be translated into the machine code so that it can perform its task. The following diagrams illustrate the stages of running a program by well established traditional approach.

Traditional approach

Your computer /PC equipped with C++ language and C++ Compiler
↓
Source program written in C++ language
↓
C++ Compiler
↓
converts source code into machine code instructions/object program for your computer /PC
↓
machine code
↓
This will now run on your computer/PC to perform its task

Diagram 1

. Will a High Level Language program run on a different machine (different platform)?

. Will a High Level Language program run with a different operating system ?

In theory, the answer is yes; but in practice, if you wish to run it on another platform, you have to make some adjustments to your program by way of re-writing some of its segments. It is due to the fact that each different platform has its own way of working. Thus, in practice, a program written in a High Level Language is machine-dependent.

• How do we overcome the problem of platform dependency?

Well, this is where Java comes in to play. A program written in Java language can be run on a different platform, providing the different platform has installed the **Java Virtual Machine (JVM)**.

The Java Development Kit

Before we proceed any further, you must know that if you want to develop and run Java programs, you must have access to the Java Development Kit (JDK), if possible the latest version, or any graphical Integrated Development Environment (IDE). There are several commercially available IDE packages on the market. The IDE incorporates a version of JDK You can download your copy of JDK from Java soft at:

http : // java . sun . com / products / jdk1.2/

The main Java Web site is at   **http: / /java.sun.com/**

There are some other sites concerning online information and help for Java users. The site at

http://www.gamelan.com/

is of particular interest for development resources. It contains many sample codes, applets, applications, and guidelines for Java language and development.

There have been many fast developments leading to a number of JDK's versions, and undoubtedly there will be some more soon. So far, JDK's versions are JDK 1.0.2, JDK 1.1.1, JDK 1.2. Each version has more features and is bigger in size than its predecessors. The JDK has numerous tools, documents and help pages. See also page 20.

Installing the JDK

If you are a student at an institution, it is highly likely that JDK has already been set up by the institute for teaching purposes. However, it may be that you wish to download it on your own home or office computer in order to learn it. Once you have downloaded it successfully on your machine, say in a temporary folder or in a briefcase, the next step is to install it. In fact, Sun's own **Installation Instructions** for Microsoft Windows 98/95/NT is a very helpful document, which you should download, and read before the JDK installation. This installation document gives concise practical information which can save your time and efforts when trying to install the JDK by trial and error.

JDK's Essential Tools

Some of its most important tools are as follows:

• **javac.exe** - the **compiler** for converting the source code into Java **bytecode** (described below).

•**java.exe** - the **interpreter** to execute the bytecode of a Java application (described below).

•**appletviewer.exe** – the **appletviewer** to view an HTML page which contains an applet. The HTML is briefly outlined in this chapter.

• **javap.exe** – the **decompiler** to convert the compiled program into a Java file. It is useful when you wish to find out how an applet was written.

Running a Java program

A program written in Java language is machine independent at the source and binary levels.

What does it mean?

Now let us examine how a Java program is executed and run.

• The programmer writes the program. This is your source program or source code. Java source program is first handled by the Java compiler – **javsc.exe**. The **javac.exe** is one of a number of Java tools, which come with JDK.

• **Compiler converts the source code into bytecode**, which is an intermediate code. This is **not** machine code, and thus compilation does not produce machine code in the same way as say, C++ compiler will do. The bytecode resembles machine code, and is not specific to one particular processor. The source program at this stage is not an executable file yet. Bytecode instructions are not specific to any particular processor. They look like machine code instructions; but you can think of them as "half-way machine" code instructions.

•**The bytecode has to be interpreted by the bytecode interpreter** (also called Java runtime interpreter). The Java interpreter is also known as **Java Virtual Machine (JVM)**. It is another part of the Java development environment, that translates the bytecode into the **native machine code** and then runs it. Here, by native, it means a particular system. For example, your own computer system is a native system. If a machine, say your PC has already installed the **JVM** which is a piece of software, such as Netscape 3.0, then this JVM will read the bytecode and convert it into machine format and run it.

If you wish to run your Java program on a different platform that is equipped with the JVM, your Java program will be executed and run as required. It does not have to be the same JVM as it is on your own machine. Certainly, the JVM is an integral part of a web browser (for short browser). As long as the other platform has a Java-enabled browser, you can run your Java program on it.

Are there any likely disadvantages?

. Yes indeed, you may run into some difficulties if you use a browser that handles the old version of Java. There are several versions of Java, and probably there will be some more due to its continuing development. This book concentrates on Java 2.

Java approach

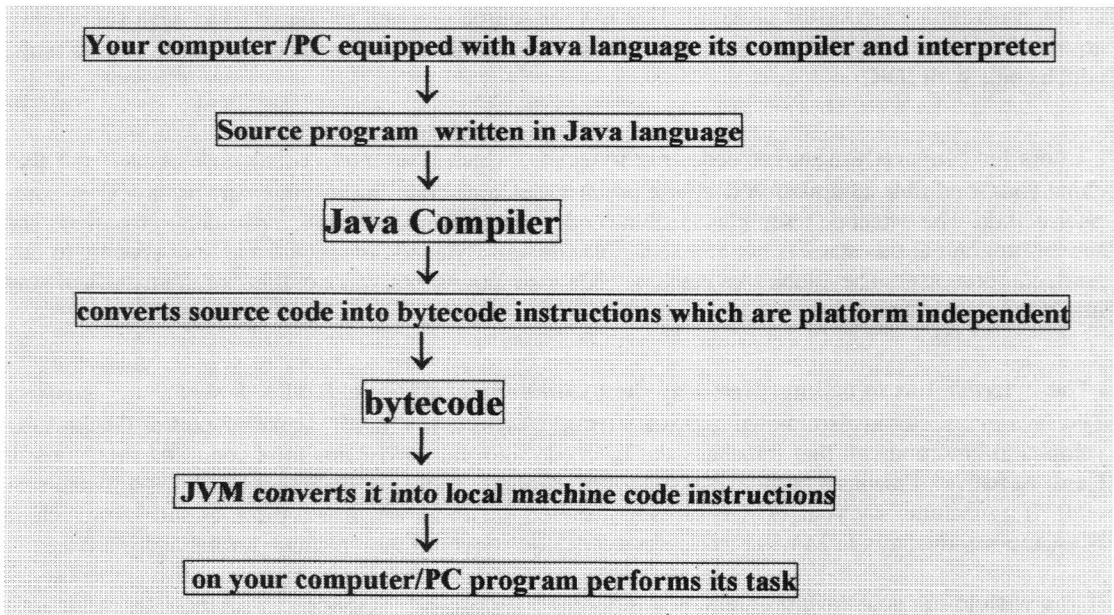

I have called the old established approach the traditional approach in order to distinguish it from the Java approach. The Java approach is depicted in Diagram 2, so that you can compare and contrast these two approaches to developing and running a program.

Types of Java programs

A Java program can be:

        . applications   **. applets**   **or**   **. beans**.

These are outlined on the next page.

Java Approach

Your computer /PC equipped with Java language its compiler and interpreter

↓

Source program written in Java language

↓

Java Compiler

↓

converts source code into bytecode instructions which are platform independent

↓

bytecode

↓

JVM converts it into local machine code instructions

↓

on your computer/PC program performs its task

Diagram 2

Applications

These are stand-alone programs. Any program that is designed for any business purpose or maintaining personal finance, can also be developed in Java. Like C++, Java is a programming language for all programming solutions.

A program that is designed simply as an application <u>does not</u> need any Java-enabled **Web browser** (see below) to run it. It can be added at this stage, that a program can be both an applet and application. <u>The distinction between an applet and application can be made on the basis of their purposes, sizes, capabilities and program development methods.</u>

Applets

These are small programs in fact, often smaller than applications. They are designed specifically to run by a Java-enabled **Web browser (or just browser)**, such as Netscape Navigator, on the **World Wide Web (WWW)**. You can also run applets by using Microsoft's Internet Explorer. Applets are embedded into the **HTML Web pages** (see below). They are, in fact, small networked applications that are designed to be dynamically downloaded across the Internet. It is fair enough to say that applets have made Java world wide famous in such a short space of time since 1995.

It is worth mentioning here that **WWW** is a distributed information service. It was developed, in the early 1990s, at CERN, the European Centre for Practical Physics. In short, the **Web** is the most exciting and popular part of the **Internet**, that is a computer communications network system. It was developed during the 1970s in the USA. It is now a huge collection of computer networks linked together world wide. Even you can link loosely your own PC system to the Internet.

Web Server

Nothing is possible on the internet without the Web server. For instance, your HTML document (see below) is accessed by other internet users on their computers through the Web server. A Web server is a computer system on a network that provides a service to other systems connected to the network. There are many commercial Web Server service providers to allow you to use the internet.

What is HTML?

HTML is an abbreviation for **Hypertext Mark-up Language**, which is used for presenting documents within the Web pages. You have to use it in order to create a Web page that contains your applet with the **<APPLET>tag** within the Web pages. Thus, it is essential to learn HTML, so that you can write HTML pages. It is not considered as a programming language, but **markup-language**. You can create and edit HTML documents by using any editing tools. You can use Microsoft Word for this purpose.

Whenever, you access a **Web** document, follow the hyperlinks by using your mouse pointer, see animated images on your screen, and so on, all these things are created by using the HTML language. The HTML enable you

- **to create pre-formatted text**.

- **to format document** - you can choose numerous typeface styles.

- **to create hyperlinks** – the hyperlinks allow you to point to such things as multimedia files, other
  Web documents.

- **to create tables**.

- **to create graphical images and link these to other documents** – you can link these to
  other documents all over the internet.

- **interactive tasks** – a user can perform various tasks. For example, form completion.

- **other features** – such as downloading and running of Web pages on your system.

The HTML language has its own set of symbols and rules. The **HTML** language is a part of **http**
which is also briefly outlined below for your benefit.

What is a Browser?

It is a piece of software that enables a user to explore the Internet. Two well-known WWW browsers
are **Netscape Navigator** and **Microsoft Internet Explorer**. Web browsers communicate over the
network with **Web Servers** by means of the:

Hyper Text Transfer Protocol which is widely known as **http**. It is also known as:

> . Transmission Control Protocol – **TCP** and

> . Internet Protocol – **IP**

The network protocol is a set of agreed symbols and rules that allows communication between computers in the network.

Are there other protocols used on the network?

Yes, there are many other protocols used on the network. These protocols have their own rules and
symbols. One example of such a protocol is the **Electronic Mail**. It is also called file transfer. These
protocols have a specific purpose.

It should be noted that the **http protocol** incorporates numerous network protocols, and thus it is the
multi-purpose protocol. The Web browsers speak the **http** protocol. The **http protocol** enables the
user by means of browser to access all kinds of services on the Internet.

What is Browsing?

In order to locate and retrieve information from a large information database set, you have to **dip** into
that area of the **WWW** that interests you on the Internet. This **dip** which is in fact a searching method

is called **browsing**. It is also known as **surfing**. A browser that supports Java applets is a **Java-enabled** browser. Netscape is a Java-enabled browser. Java applets are downloaded via a Java-enabled browser.

The relationship between the Browser, HTML, http and Web Server is shown below in the same order as it happens. It is a simplification to illustrate their working together

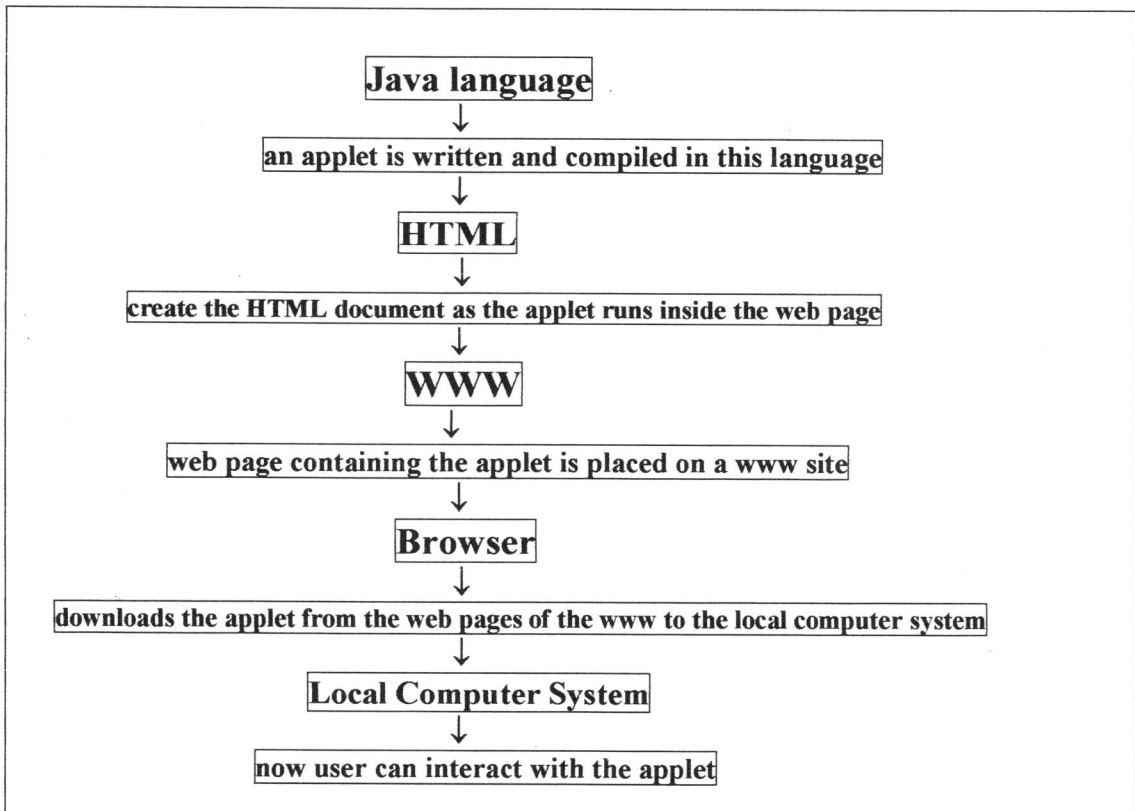

```
                    Java language
                         ↓
        an applet is written and compiled in this language
                         ↓
                        HTML
                         ↓
     create the HTML document as the applet runs inside the web page
                         ↓
                        WWW
                         ↓
        web page containing the applet is placed on a www site
                         ↓
                       Browser
                         ↓
   downloads the applet from the web pages of the www to the local computer system
                         ↓
                Local Computer System
                         ↓
            now user can interact with the applet
```

Diagram 3

Beans

Java beans are re-useable software components. These beans can enable programmers to design applications, create beans and to write interfaces in order to manipulate beans. Java beans technology is rather new, but promises comprehensive software components that can be used across platforms world

Wide. Already there are a number of commercial programs on the market, which can enable you to develop beans for using them in your own programs. Examples of these programs are Borland Jbuilder and Symantec Visual Café.

Object Oriented Programming

Object Oriented Programming (OOP) is not new. What is new is the application of its concepts in modern programming languages such as C++ and Java. So, this raises a simple question:

•What is the basic thinking behind it which has made it so popular in recent years?

The straightforward answer to this question is that in OOP a given situation is considered in the same way as one would see it in the real world. Let us expand this idea by way of thinking of the real world around us. In this real world, there are unlimited objects. For instance, a train is an **object**. Therefore, an aeroplane is also an object like other countless objects in this world. These objects may be simple or complex which are made of many other, smaller objects. These objects may interact with some other objects. These objects may have one or more objectives to achieve, and display similar characteristics. We can apply this basic idea to the programming field. The concept **object** is very important indeed in OOP.

Let us further consider the science and technology library of a large national public library where a very large number of books on all aspects of technology and science are kept and are available to its readers. The library is divided into many sections, where books are kept on shelves in accordance with a particular classification used in a public library. The two major categories under which books are arranged on shelves are science and technology. These two categories are further sub-divided into many sub-categories in such a way that an individual item on a shelf can be located without any unnecessary waste of time.

For example, **Java Simplified** (object) is one particular book that belongs to a broad category of books called computer literature. All computer literature books share some common characteristics. For instance, all computer books are sources of information on many aspects of computer systems. Whether a book from a computer literature is on a particular programming language, or on types of computers, or on systems design, the fact is that all three books are about the computer world. Thus, in this example, all three books are **members** of the same category of books. In OOP terminology this category is called a **class** . In OOP, **class** is the most important idea.

In this example, science and technology library, social sciences library and other specialist libraries within this national public library contain many different classes of objects in each class (books, magazines, maps, etc.) which are kept together in pre-defined **methods** for this large national public library system. Thus, each library is a **self-contained large object**, and has scores of classes of many different objects. Furthermore, each library **interacts (or communicates)** with each other library in order to meet the **objectives** of the national public library as a whole system. You can imagine the complexity of this national library system, where a very large number of different objects are kept together. The idea of putting together or **combining objects** into **classes** is also at the heart of OOP. A **Class of objects** means a group of objects which have some similar features. For instance, all computer programming books have the same common aim which is to enable readers to learn computer programming.

- When designing a computer program, the programmer can think of a program in terms of:

- different objects

- how to create these objects

- how to combine them into relevant classes of objects

- how to use them for the purpose for which the program is designed

- how these objects communicate with each other in some pre-defined methods

These are some of the basic concepts of object oriented programming which are also applied in Java programming. In a well equipped academic or public library you can find some books dealing in depth with both the theory and application of object oriented programming.

Classes

The essence of a class is that it embodies all the features of all objects in it.

• What does it mean in practice?

Now we consider a particular class called **car class. car class** is a template for millions of cars in the real world. It is thus an abstract idea. So, this idea leads to the following important question?

• Which common features cars have to be a class of their own?

One can think of all cars sharing the following **intrinsic** features:

. **cars are designed**
. **cars are built**
. **cars have body shapes**
. **cars have engines**
. **cars have speeds**
. **cars have colours**
. **cars have speedometers**
. **cars are driven**

The idea or concept **'car'** is useful as it enables us to think of a car which has the above features. But, it leads to further question:

• How to identify a car to be able to see its features ?

In order to be able to identify it, you have to have at least one car available. Thus, you have to **create** a specific **instance** of an object (car) of a car class. In OOP terminology, you have to **instantiate** it.

But, you must know that if you have a car class, you can create many **different instances** of car. Furthermore, each different instance (car) will have different features.

- **How?** Just imagine:
- **How cars differ from each other?** For instance:
- different body shapes
- different colours
- different maximum speeds
- different engines
- etc.

Despite these apparent differences, you can still create instances (objects) of a car class. **Why?**

Yes indeed, each car is different, but as a class, cars have some **intrinsic values or properties**. These intrinsic properties are the essential requirements in any definition of a class of objectives. This is the prime reason that you can create instances of a class.

- **Is there any difference between an object and an instance of a class?**

There is no difference between an instance and an object. Both words mean the same thing which is in reality an object. This object has some distinguishable attributes.

Attributes, methods & data

In the above example of a **car class**, you can differentiate one car from another car, yet all cars belong to the same **class of objects** (cars).

- **How do we differentiate one object from another object?**

We look for specific items of information that tell us enough about the object in terms of its attributes.

- **What do we mean by attributes ?**

An attribute is a property of an object. An object can have several attributes as illustrated by the following example.

Example

Class employee is a class of objects called employees. It has x number of employees (**objects**), and each employee has the following **attributes**:

• surname	• employee number
• other names	• national insurance number
• date of birth	• tax code
• age	• Job title
• place of birth	• annual salary
• marital status	• some other attributes

In any organisation, some of these attributes (values or variables) are used with other relevant information in order to:

• calculate net monthly salary for each employee

• calculate tax and national insurance payable by each employee

• produce relevant information for transferring each employee's monthly payable salary into his/her bank account

• produce relevant payroll information for the internal administrative purposes

• generate relevant tax and national insurance information for the appropriate Central Government Agencies

• How can it be achieved?

Each attribute is given a **value,** which in reality, is a **data** item. For instance, each employee has a tax code, which is one data item. Let's assume that

• total number of employees = 100

• total number of relevant attributes = 10

• therefore total number of data items = 100 x10 = 1000

Thus, **1000** data items are subjected to some methods of calculations and information production in the appropriate required formats (payslips, bank transfer information sheets and other required information). This example clearly demonstrates that **data items** are subjected to certain **methods** in order to prepare the monthly payroll and all the relevant required information.

If you are familiar with C++, you already know about functions. In Java, there are no functions, but methods. These methods perform the same pre-defined operations or tasks as functions do in C++. For instance, calculate monthly tax deduction by applying the rules (Pre-defined) laid down by the Central Government Tax Department, for each married employee who has two children.

It is necessary to emphasise that for all purposes, these methods are functions. The important point to remember is that methods are defined **inside** a class together with objects. (In C++ functions are outside with operators.) This will soon become clearer, when programming examples are discussed.

Definitions of a class and an object

What you have learnt so far is sufficient for our purpose to arrive at a working definition of a class and an object, so that we can use these in our practical work. This book is not about Object Oriented theory, but its application in Java programming, and our following definitions reflect it.

. **A class contains both objects and methods. These methods operate on objects**.

. **An object has to be Instantiated. It encapsulates (contains) its own data and methods.**

Inheritance & Class Hierarchy

At this stage, you must also understand the meaning of inheritance. It is another vitally important idea of OOP that is applied in Java programming. Inheritance is concerned with an object's relationship in a hierarchical manner in a class, and it enables us to know how a class differs from another particular class. It is in fact more than deriving a class from another class as demonstrated below.

Example 1: The train inheritance hierarchy

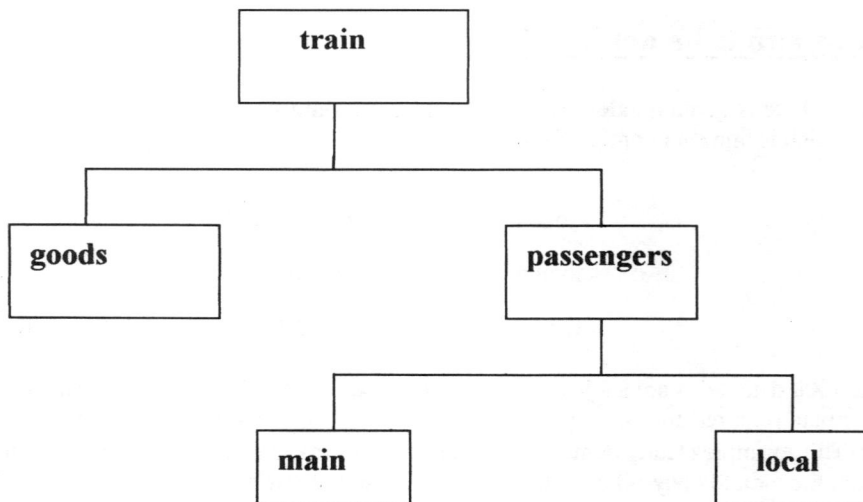

Diagram 4

In this example, **class train** is an **abstract** class. It is also known as **superclass**. This superclass contains some data items and methods that operate on the data. Let's assume that class train is a database which is designed to store all relevant data items on trains together with methods that are used to store, process and retrieve data. The data items are as follows:

- type
- minimum length
- place of manufacture

- engine power
- maximum length
- interior design

- speed per hour
- date of manufacture
- mileage completed

In this illustration, from the class train, two objects are **instantiated**. These are **goods** and **passengers**. Both these objects inherit the basic characteristics/ properties of train which are shown above; but they also have their own following set of data and methods that operate on them:

passenger data items

- total number of first class carriages

- total number of second class carriages

- restaurant for first class passengers

- total number of first class seats

- total number of second class seats

- café for all passengers

goods data items

- total number of open carriages for vehicles

- total number of covered carriages for other goods

- total number of carriages for Royal Mail

Although these two objects differ from each other, they **inherit** data and methods of our superclass train. In fact, these are subclasses derived from this superclass train.

From the **subclass passenger** two objects are **instantiated**. These are **main** and **local**. These two objects are shown in diagram 4 in class hierarchy.

Diagrams 4 and 5

•Diagrams 4 and 5, contain examples of inheritance. In these diagrams classes are arranged in strict class hierarchy, which is the hallmark of class hierarchy and inheritance.

• These diagrams show that each class has a superclass – a class which is above it in the hierarchy.

• These diagrams and table 1 reveal that a class can have several subclasses – classes which are below it in the hierarchy.

•The inheritance implies that subclasses inherit arguments (variables) and behaviour (methods) from their superclasses. This property of inheritance means that if a superclass has for instance a particular variable, which the subclass requires, this subclass has an access to this particular variable. This facility eliminates the need to re-define those variables and methods that are already available in the super-class, and can be accessed by any class in the class hierarchy.

. This feature of inheritance means that a subclass has access to both variables and methods of its su-perclass, that superclass also has access to its own superclass , and so on, right to the top of the class hierarchy. In this way, a class has access to all arguments and methods of the classes, which are above it in the class hierarchy.

Example 2: A class hierarchy

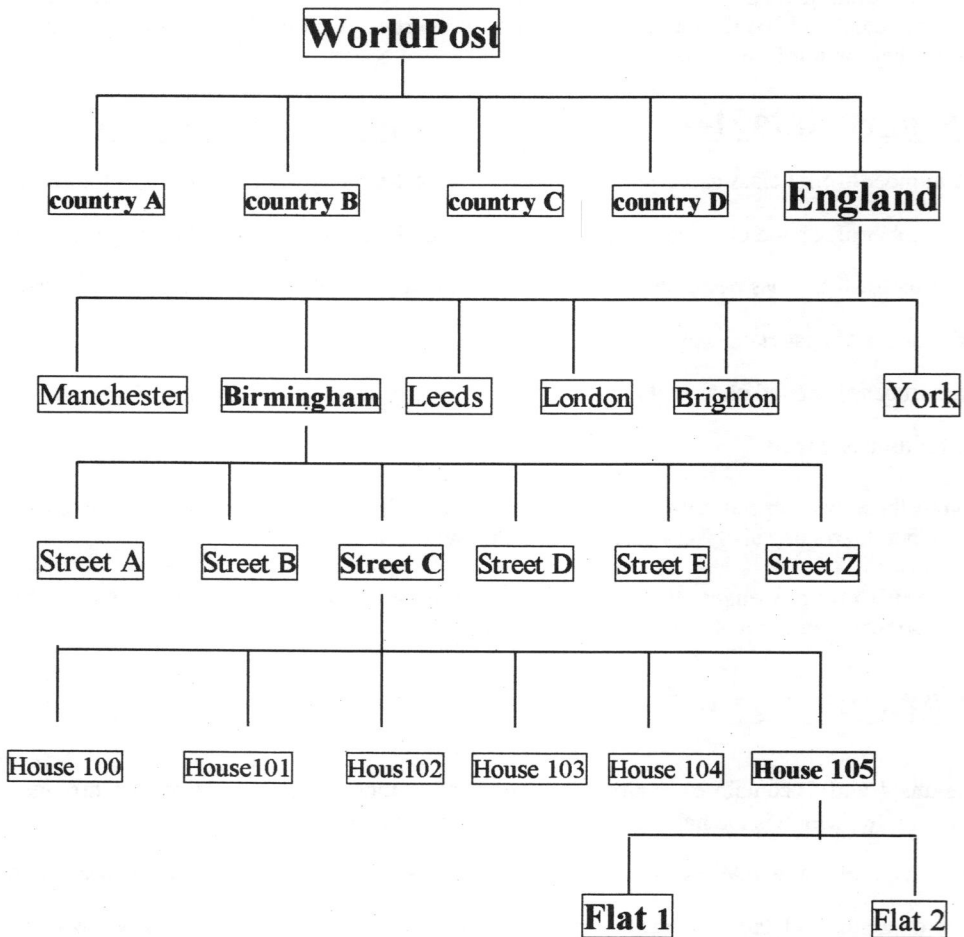

```
                          ┌─────────────┐
                          │  WorldPost  │
                          └─────────────┘
     ┌───────────┬───────────┬───────────┬───────────┐
 ┌─────────┐ ┌─────────┐ ┌─────────┐ ┌─────────┐ ┌───────────┐
 │country A│ │country B│ │country C│ │country D│ │  England  │
 └─────────┘ └─────────┘ └─────────┘ └─────────┘ └───────────┘
      ┌──────────┬──────────┬──────────┬──────────┬──────────┐
 ┌──────────┐┌──────────┐┌──────┐┌────────┐┌─────────┐  ┌──────┐
 │Manchester││Birmingham││Leeds ││ London ││ Brighton│  │ York │
 └──────────┘└──────────┘└──────┘└────────┘└─────────┘  └──────┘
      ┌─────────┬─────────┬─────────┬─────────┬─────────┐
 ┌────────┐┌────────┐┌────────┐┌────────┐┌────────┐┌────────┐
 │Street A││Street B││Street C││Street D││Street E││Street Z│
 └────────┘└────────┘└────────┘└────────┘└────────┘└────────┘
    ┌─────────┬─────────┬─────────┬─────────┬─────────┐
┌─────────┐┌─────────┐┌────────┐┌─────────┐┌─────────┐┌─────────┐
│House 100││House101 ││Hous102 ││House 103││House 104││House 105│
└─────────┘└─────────┘└────────┘└─────────┘└─────────┘└─────────┘
                                             ┌────────┬────────┐
                                        ┌────────┐      ┌────────┐
                                        │ Flat 1 │      │ Flat 2 │
                                        └────────┘      └────────┘
```

Diagram 5

- By applying these features of class inheritance hierarchy to diagram 5 you can say that:

  - **class Flat 1** has access to information in its superclass **House 105**.

  - **superclass House 105** has access to information in its superclass **Street C**.

  - **superclass Street C** has access to all information in its superclass **Birmingham**.

  - **superclass Birmingham** has access to information in its superclass **England**.

  - **superclass England** has access to information in its superclass **WorldPost**.

Table 1: Relationship between superclass and its subclasses

super class	subclasses of a superclass
• WorldPost	country A, country B, country C, country D, **England**
• England	Manchester, **Birmingham**, Leeds, London, Brighton, York
• Birmingham	Street A, Street B, **Street C**, Street D, Street E, Street Z
• Street C	House 100, House 101, House 102, House 103, House 104, **House 105**
• House 105	**Flat 1**, Flat 2

. Java Class Libraries and Packages

Java's strength lies in its extensive libraries. These libraries contain more than 150 classes. The class libraries in the JKD are in the **package** called Java. The Java package contains other packages for classes. The base Java language package is called **java . lang**. It is the package to which by default, your Java classes have access. This is the foundation package for the Java programming. How to use a package or a class within a particular package will be discussed soon. It is not possible here to describe in any reasonable detail Java Class libraries. In fact, it will take many hundreds of pages to outline these classes briefly. A package contains related classes and interfaces. If it helps, you can visualise it as a collection of related classes and interfaces. Some of the packages that are available to you are as follows:-

. java . applet – this package contains the superclass of all all Java applets. **Japplet** is a subclass of Applet class. When you create your own applet, the first thing you have to do is to make your applet a subclass of **Japplet**. It is a part of **com . sun . java swing** package.

. java . awt - **the Abstract Windowing Toolkit**. It contains the basic classes, which provide you with the facility for graphical user interface (GUI). It has been extended by the Swing Windowing classes. Some examples of graphical user interface components are menus, scrollbars, and buttons.

. Java . awt . event – it deals with different types of events.

. java . awt . font – it has classes for fonts.

. java . io – classes for input and output streams and files.

. java . math – classes for dealing with numbers and sizes.

. java . net – classes for network communication.

. java . util – utility classes. It includes things like random numbers.

The classes you will write for your programs can also be grouped into your own packages. Your classes will also follow the same pattern and use the same OOP concepts.

Some core features of class hierarchy

• When a program contains many classes, the class hierarchy diagram can enable you to identify the relationship between classes. This helps to develop the program efficiently.

• Each class has only one superclass. For instance **Street Z** in the above diagram has only one super-class called **Birmingham**.

• A class inherits variables (arguments) and behaviour (methods) from its superclass, and all its super-classes, up to the top superclass for the whole chain of hierarchy. Variables and behaviour are collectively known as information.

• Java has single class hierarchy inheritance. This technique has the advantage of making relationships between the classes easy to understand.

• In order to overcome single class hierarchy major drawback, Java has the technique called **interfaces**.

• By applying the technique of interfaces, it eliminates the difficulty faced when your program is attempting to duplicate the information across the branch of the class hierarchy. At this stage, suffice to say that interfaces do not have definitions (methods and arguments) except methods names. The idea is to keep methods' names only in one place. When classes require these methods then these can be made available to them. These basic OOP's ideas are further discussed in this book, when some more tools for OOP programming with Java are discussed with examples.

• **What do we mean by portable, multithreading and dynamically-linked language?**

At the beginning of this chapter, these words were used to describe some of the widely publicised attributes of Java language. Before we proceed to the practical aspects of developing Java program in our next chapter, it is wise to know the meaning of these technical words.

Portable

When software can be transferred from one type of machine to another type of machine, it is termed as portable. Since Java programs are compiled into **neutral bytecode** format, which is not dependent on the machine on which it was compiled, it can be run on another type of machine, as long as it has installed the JVM. This has made Java popular, because a Java program can be transferred over the internet to another platform and run on that machine, providing it has installed JVM. Another advantage of portability is that commercial software developers can design their applications packages, which can run on a variety of Personal computers and workstations. For instance, if you develop an application on a PC under Windows 95, you can run it on another PC, which is running under UNIX, providing this PC has installed JVM. However, the current trend of Java Popularity points to the near future when new modern PC's will be supplied with JVM.

Multithreaded & Multithreading

Just imagine that there are a number of jobs to be done. One job must be first completed before the second job can be started. Now assume that a program can perform more than one task, but at one time, it can only perform one particular task. This sort of program is called a **single threaded** program.

Now assume that a program has a number of parts. Each part is designed to carry out a different job. When this program runs, it allows its several parts to perform their respective tasks concurrently, without interfering with each other. Such a program is called a **multithreaded** program. Each part of such a program is termed as **thread**.

A program design technique, which uses this idea of running different parts of the same program at the same time, without interfering with each other, is known as **multithreading**. The **Java. lang** package has a thread class that supports multithreading. In addition, Java language has built-in language support for multithreads.

Dynamically-linked

In Java, you can:

- load a Java class when the interpreter is running

- instantiate the loaded class

- get information about the class which is currently running

- load libraries when the interpreter is running

This is why it is often described as a dynamically-linked language.

Distributed Language

Often Java is called distributed language. This property of Java is well publicised due to its support for the networking. Java has the **Java . net** package which contains classes that can enable you to retrieve a file over the network which is at the other end of the continent and read it as it is in your office. For instance, the dynamic and distributed powerful tools make it possible for the Java interpreter to download a file over the internet and run .it.

Keywords

Keywords in Java are reserved words as in C++. These are pre-defined and each of them has a specific meaning to the compiler. These are written in lowercase. These words cannot be used as variable names. When a Keyword is used in programming, it performs a specific function within the program.

List of Java Keywords

abstract	boolean	break	byte	case	catch	char	class	continue
default	do	double	else	extends	false	final	finally	float
for	if	implements	import	instanceof	int	interface	long	native
new	null	package	private	protected	public	return	short	static
super	switch	synchronized	this	throw		throws	transient	true	try
void	volatile	while						

Reserved but not yet implemented

byvalue   cast   const   future   generic   goto   inner   operator   outer   rest   var

The meaning of a keyword and its use will become clear to you when you meet it in the appropriate place in the book.

Practical Hints

• on page 6, it is stated," There are several versions of Java, and probably there will be some more due to its continuing development." **Which version should one use**?

You may be surprised to learn that since I wrote this sentence, Sun Microsystems, Inc., re-named **1. 2** version as **Java 2**.

In order to run and view an applet on the Internet, you require a Java-enabled browser. At the time of writing, there are three major versions of the Java language. These are 1.0, 1.1 and 1.2 which is now called **Java 2**. The current versions of Microsoft Internet Explorer and Netscape Navigator do not support Java 2. If you wish to develop applets to reach a wide audience on the Internet, and run these on Internet Explorer and Navigator, then you have to use the Java 1.02 version. This version lacks many of the new developments which are part and parcel of Java 2.

You can view and test your applet with the Java **appletviewer tool**. I have tested all applets in this book with the appletviewer tool. To use this tool, you need to write an HTML document for each applet.

However, in order to make Java 2 applets run on current browsers, Sun Microsystems has been developing a **plug-in program**. This plug-in program works with a Web browser. It can handle data that a browser normally will not handle. You can download the plug-in, at the time of downloading the JDK from the Sun Microsystems. You must install a plug-in for each browser.

 The Plug-in is available for Windows, and Solaries systems. It is possible that by the time you read this book, a plug-in is available for the Apple computer system. There are still some compatibility issues, but Sun might have resolved them by the time you read this chapter.

As this book is primarily designed for students, it is therefore, suggested that you learn the current version of Java, despite the fact that the development of an appropriate browser, which interprets the code, still lags behind Java language developments and its implementation. Even so, for learning how to write applets, you must make the use of the appletviewer tool.

Go forward !

Exercise

- Should you learn the Java language? If your answer is yes, then you must justify your answer in terms of personal development, and language capabilities.

Chapter 2
Java Application Program Development

Your first Java application

This first application is the shortest, but it lays the foundation for much larger applications. The program will be stored as **Learner . java**. Learner is the class name, and java is the file extension. The class name is given by the programmer, and the extension **. java** is also entered by the programmer when storing the program.

==================The Simplest Application ==================

PROGRAM: Learner . java

```
class Learner
  {
              public static void main (String [  ] args)

          {

              System . out . println (" Hello  Java  Learners!" );

          }

  }
```

Diagram 1

Purpose

The purpose of this simple Java application is to illustrate the structure of a Java application program by printing the message **"Hello Java Learners!"**.

Explanation

You can think of Java program as a **class**.

class Learner
          ↓   ↓
        class   class name always begins with a capital letter

Java is **case sensitive**. It is therefore of paramount importance that you appreciate the requirement for the first letter of the class name typed as **capital** letter. It implies that **learner** will not be an acceptable substitute for **Learner**. **Why?** Because in Java, these are two different words, and thus your program will not be compiled successfully.

• Within the outer **{ } pair of braces** is the entire program.

• The first line of code declares the **method** called **method main**. In all Java applications, method **main** is the point where Java interpreter starts the **execution** of the program. It is thus here, where the main part of the program begins. A program must have a main method. It is in your source code for your class. Later on, you will learn that often it is necessary to include several methods to a class and call these methods to perform certain tasks. These methods are called from the main method. You can write method main as method main ( ) or main ( ).

• The general format of the method main declaration is as follows:

public static void main (String [ ] args)

Let's examine each word in this statement:

• **Public** is a keyword in Java. In its simplest term, it can be said that the class to which it refers is accessible to other classes and objects outside of its package once it is loaded. It will become clearer as you progress. In public, the first letter is small p.

Is the keyword public always applicable when creating the main ( ) ?

The main ( ) is always declared as public. Why? This way, it can be accessed by other objects.

• **static** is another keyword. It indicates that method is a class method. It will also become clearer as you learn more. Be patient! The first letter is small s.

. **void** is another keyword. Here, it means that the method main ( ) does not return any value. The first letter v is small.

.

$$\boxed{\textbf{String [ ] args}}$$
$$\downarrow$$

It denotes **string object** of an unspecified number of elements in the string called argument **(args).**

An argument is data that a method accepts in order to carry out its function. Strings in Java are objects. A string is also an array. You will learn about arrays and strings later on. In Java a string is not terminated by a **null** character (but in C++ it is just the opposite).

main (String [ ] args)

$\downarrow$

This declaration sets up an array of string. It has an unspecified number of elements/arguments **Why?** Because there is nothing enclosed within the pair of [ ]. The String starts with the capital letter, but both main and args with small letters.

. The method main has a body (code) which is enclosed within the **inner** set of braces. In the above example, this body consists of only one line of the following code:

$$\underline{\textbf{System . out}} \ \underline{\textbf{.println}} \ (\ \textbf{"Hello Java learners!"} \ ) \ ;$$

$\downarrow$	$\downarrow$	$\downarrow$	$\downarrow$
It is an object	It is a method	an argument or just a message to be displayed on the screen	Semicolon to terminate the statement

Note that System begins with the capital S, and that . are essential in both places as shown above.

What does it do?

Here, the task that is performed by the method main ( ) is to print the message **Hello Java learners!** The **ln** will produce a line feed.

. The **system . out** is an object. In the above statement, **System . out** has been directed to use its **println** method to output on screen or show on screen the message/text, **Hello Java Learners!**

• Having output the message within the " ", the **println method** also terminates this output, and generates a line feed. The **ln** produces a line feed.

Thus, inside ( ), it contains single string (data) that is called **argument**. Multiple values can also be represented by a single string within ( ).

In this simple example, the argument is just a message enclosed within the double quotes. **Why is it enclosed within " " ?** In accordance with Java, the argument (your text) should be placed within double quotes.

• It prints the message or produces the output on the standard output device of your computer system, which may be printer, screen or a special window.

Once the source file has been created, it has to be saved, under the same name as the class name, precisely written, using lower and upper case letters and punctuation as in the class name. The file name ends with the Java file extension. Thus the file will be saved as **Learner. Java**

Running your first Java application Program

So far, I have described the essential requirements for the simplest application in order to introduce Java language. In the previous chapter, I outlined how to download Java Development Kid (JDK), current version 1.2 (called now Java 2) from the Java Web site. We shall use this for running our application programs. I have saved all my examples for this book in a folder called **Examples**.

Step 1. Creating and saving the source file (.java)

Once the source file has been created, it has to be saved, under the same name as the class name, precisely written, using lower and upper case letters and punctuation as in the class name. The file name ends with the Java file extension. Thus the file will be saved as **Learner. Java**

. How do we create a source file ?

• Your Java source file/program is created by a plain text editor. Therefore, you can use any plain text editor, which is available on your computer. My computer is running Windows 95. For creating my source file , I have decided to make use of **WordPad** for this book for the following reasons

- • it can handle several documents at the same time

- • it lists several files under File pull-down menu that have been used before, and any of them can be re-opened again to work with it

- • besides the plain text, it can handle Microsoft Word formats text

. How do I start it?   First open WordPad as shown below.

Click start → **select Programs** → **select Accessories** → **click WordPad.**

This action will open WordPad. This is shown in diagram 3 below.

The **WordPad** has been opened as shown in diagram 4. Just observe the top left hand corner. At present, it reads Document – WordPad. The word Document will be replaced by the name of your source file, once it has been typed in and saved.

. Having opened the WordPad, just type in your program, which is shown in diagram 1. You can also use another text editor available on your computer for creating and storing your source file. I have used WordPad, as I prefer it. See diagram 5.

Diagram 3: WordPad

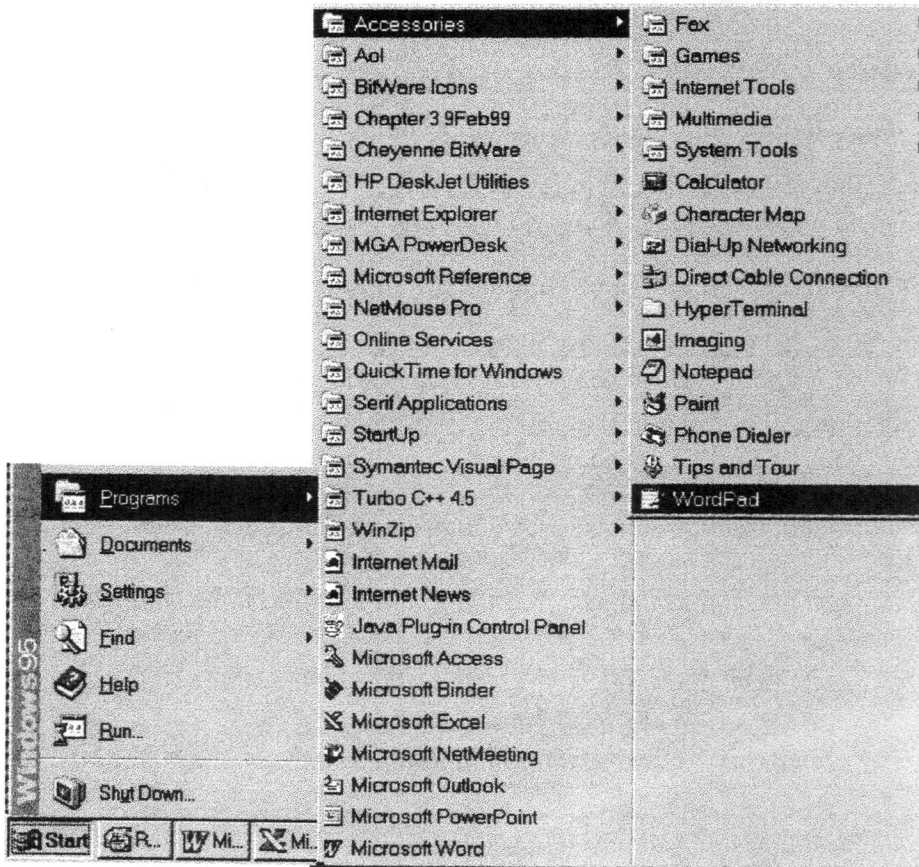

. **Save** this source file under **Learner . java**. How?

.Click **File** on WordPad window → select **Save as.** Enter **Learner.java**.

.Because it is a source file, it has to be saved as plain ASCII file by selecting Text Document. See diagram 6.

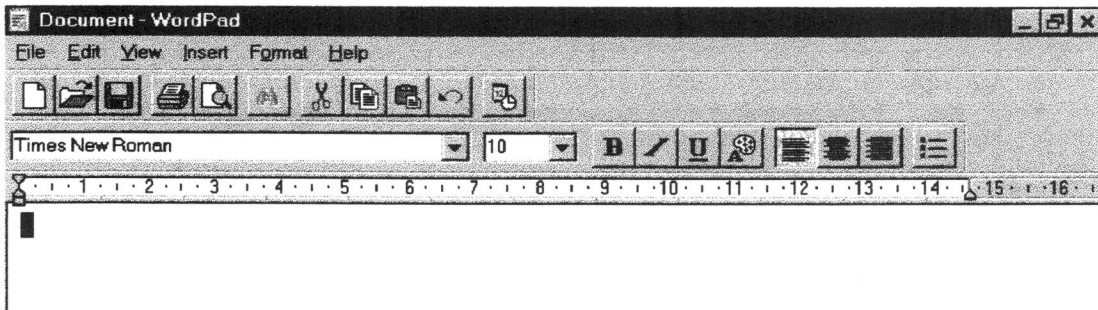

Diagram 4: WordPad is ready for you to enter your source file

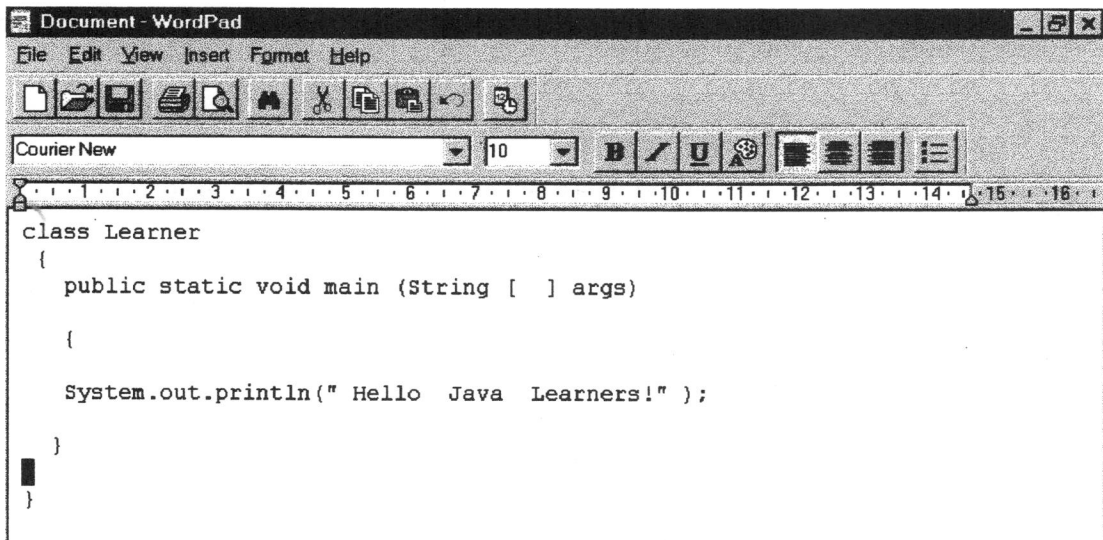

```
class Learner
  {
     public static void main (String [  ] args)

     {

     System.out.println(" Hello   Java   Learners!" );

     }

  }
```

Diagram 5: the first program has been created

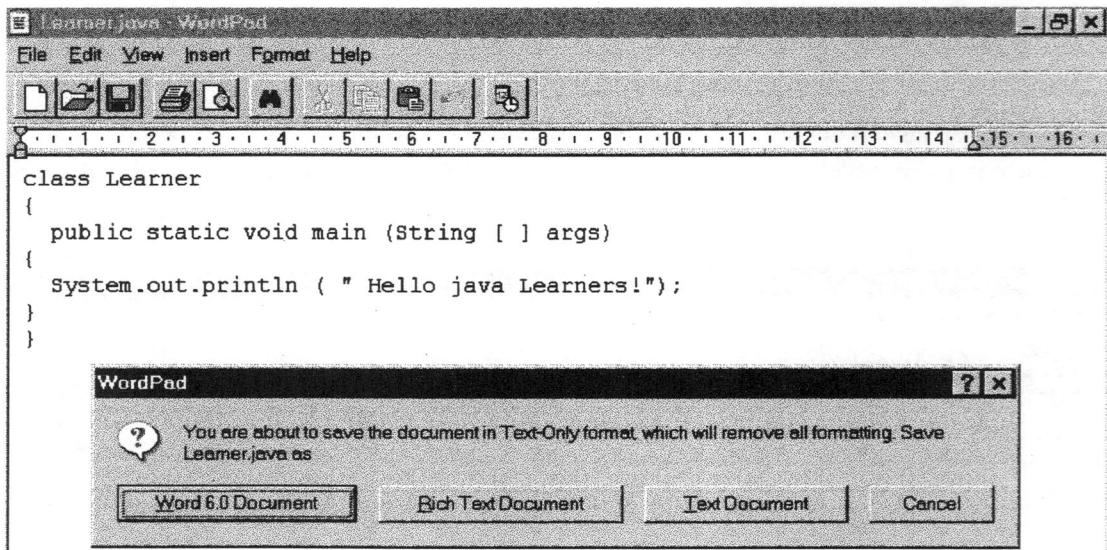

```
class Learner
{
  public static void main (String [ ] args)
{
  System.out.println ( " Hello java Learners!");
}
}
```

WordPad

? You are about to save the document in Text-Only format, which will remove all formatting. Save Learner.java as

[Word 6.0 Document]   [Rich Text Document]   [Text Document]   [Cancel]

Diagram 6

- **What will happen if the file name does not fully match the name of the class it defines?**

In such a case, your program will not be compiled at all. For instance, the file name **Lerner** is not acceptable as here one letter **a** is missing. **Lerner** is not the same word as **Learner**. Thus, you will <u>not</u> be able to compile it. What a pity!

Step 2. Compiling the source file

. under the **Programs menu,** you will find MS-DOS Prompt, which is MS-DOS **shell**. You can start it by using the following sequence of actions

Select start → select Programs → select MS-DOS Prompt

by clicking it to open it.

. The open shell is shown in diagram 7. It is ready for you to type in the required commands to activate Java compiler, **javac.exe**. You can see that I have changed directory, as I wish to save all my examples for this book in my folder called Examples. In order to change directories, I have to use the command:

C:\WINDOWS>CD C:\Examples

Where I have written Examples, you have to write your own folder's name. In reality, you can store your files anywhere on your main drive.

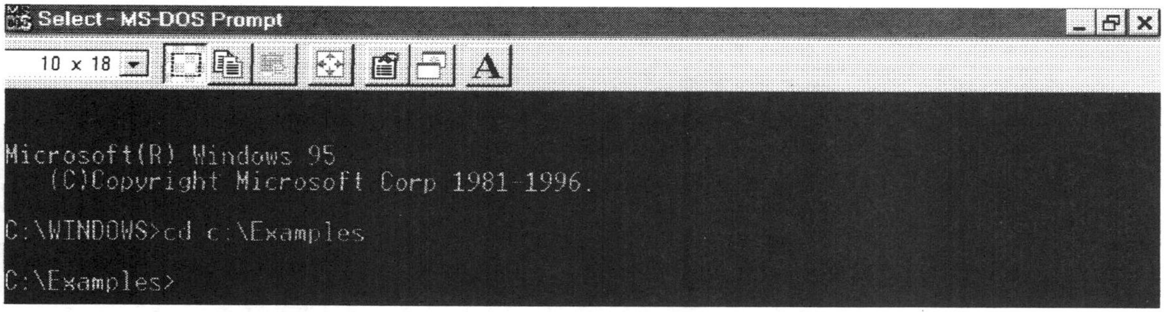

Diagram 7

- Now at the command line, where the cursor is flashing, enter **javac Learner.java**. You can type javac with a small or a capital **j**. Just, wait for a moment for any response from javac. If there are no errors, the cursor moves on to the next command line, and it is still flashing, waiting for the next command from you. As shown below in diagram 8, no error message is generated by the compiler. It means that the program is syntax error-free, and that it has been compiled successfully.

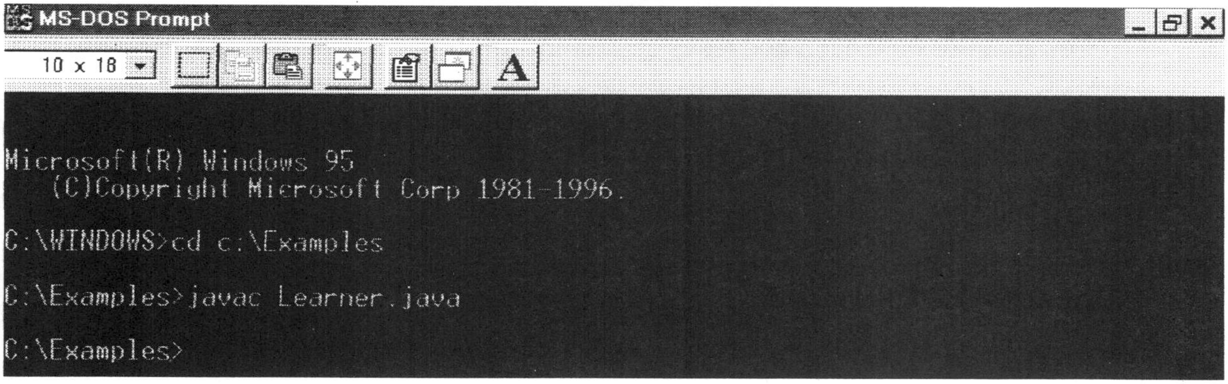

Diagram 8

Step 3 Interpreting the compiled program and running it

- Finally, you have to pass the compiled source file/program to java interpreter. This is achieved by entering in the DOS shell the command **java Learner**. This action is shown in diagram 9 below. The computer found no logic and run time errors in the program. Thus, it was executed successfully.

- The desired program output: **Hello java Learners!** was displayed on the screen.

Diagram 9

.**What will happen if the file name does not fully match the name of the class it defines?**

In such a case, your program will not be compiled at all.

. **How about when the method takes no arguments?** In this case, parentheses are empty ( ).

. **Can we use a carriage return or white space to mark the end of a statement?**

No. In Java, a statement is terminated by a semicolon. It is an important and practical point to bear in mind that without the semicolon, your program will not be compiled successfully. You will get an error message similar to the one which is depicted in diagram 10 below.

An example of Error Message

Workout.java:9: Invalid type expression.
System.out.println ("Add up a, b, c and d together")
                        ^

This is a message generated by the compiler. **Workout** is the name of source file/program. **9** is line number, where an error was found by the compiler. The **error type** is invalid type expression.

Diagram 10

. **Is there any limitation on the length of a statement?**

No. You can make a statement as long as you wish, but be realistic. However, a statement can be written on more than one line. Java compiler will be able to read it. Try not to make statements too long or you will lose sight of them on screen.

Is it similar to a C++ program?

If you are familiar with C++ programming, you will have noticed that this simple application (stand-alone program) is somewhat similar to a C++ program. It is true to say that the format of the output statement differs greatly, but the fact of the matter is that anyone who is familiar with C++ will find it easy to grasp Java and make good progress towards learning it.

Does it need an HTML browser?

No. A Java application does not run in an HTML browser. Furthermore, Java application is not subject to the security restrictions imposed on Java applets.

It has been said that any particular program can be both application and applet. If so, can I run my application as an applet?

Yes, an application can be run as an applet, but first it has to be embedded in an HTML page and then run in an HTML browser or applet viewer.

The major difference between an applet and an application is that an applet has to be incorporated into HTML document for it to be run and displayed inside a Web page. For this reason alone, the development of an applet is more complex than the development of an application.

Statement

I have already used this word several times. **What is it?** Just imagine the English language and think about a sentence. A sentence is constructed in accordance with the rules of English grammar. Similarly, a Java statement is constructed according to Java language. In fact, a program is a sequence of statements. A statement is an instruction that performs a simple task towards the completion of the whole task to be accomplished by the program. The following examples are statements:

a) int a = 5;

b) import java . util .*;

c) System.out.println ("The sum of a, b, and d = " + (a + b +c + d));

d) System.out.println ("_____");

You can have in your program **Compound Statements,** but you have to enclose them within the curly braces **{ }** in order to make a **block**. For instance in the following code, the block is shown in the grey area.

Public static void main (String [ ] args)

```
{                               // beginning of a block
    int a = 12; int b = 12;
    int c= 20;
    int average = ( a+ b + c +)/3;
}                               // end of a block
```

You now know that the grouping of some statements makes a block.

Expressions

Now, it is time to say something about expressions. You might have learnt algebra at some stage in your life so far. If so, you may recall expressions. Expressions involve some arithmetical operations namely, add, subtract, multiply and divide. An expression:

> . can produce a change in the value of something, and
>
> . can compare something with something and generate a result.

Thus, in programming terminology, **an expression is a statement** that can return a value. In Java, expressions are considered to be the simplest type of statements. The following example illustrates how an expression produces or returns a value.

$$\text{int k} = (20 * 23.77)/ 3;$$

is an expression. **Why?**

Because it involves arithmetical operations, and generates or returns a value that produces a change in the initial value of **variable k** of integer type.

• An expression can also use **modulus division**. A **modulus** is represented by **%** which is known as **modulus operator**. It returns an integer reminder of integer type. For example:

47 % 5 = 2   In this example, the reminder is 2.

If you attempt to divide as **38 % 0**, the compiler will produce an error message, as the divisor must not be **zero**.

•I would like to add here, that − **47 % - 5** may give different results on different machines, because of minus values. <u>You will find more relevant information under operators which is a related topic.</u>

Types of Errors

It is likely that when compiling a source file, the compiler finds errors in your program. The compiler searches for **Syntax Errors**. These errors are due to mis-use of grammatical rules of Java language. The compiler reports these detected errors in the form of an error message. The programmer has to eliminate these errors. These errors are fairly easy to remove from the program. Therefore, you have to know well the syntax rules of Java. For instance, in accordance with Java's syntax rules, every **program statement** should end with a semicolon.

Example: **System.out.println;**

If **;** is missing at the end of this statement, your program will not be compiled successfully. Of course, the compiler will report this error. The good thing about the compiler is that it will list this statement with its line number in the error message. Thus, it points out, where the error has occurred, and its nature, if it is syntax error type.

The successful compilation means that the program you have written is syntax error free. At the same time, it does not always mean that the successfully compiled program is now ready to carry out the task for which it is designed. **Why?**

There may still be some more errors other than syntax errors. These can be classified as:

. Logic errors – These errors are usually caused by poor program design. For instance, your program might branch off at the wrong place, giving an incorrect result. Sometimes, the program appears to run alright, but it does not produce the required output. There could be a variety of reasons for these errors, and thus a scrutiny of the program is highly desirable.

. Run time errors – Firstly, I must tell you what run time means. The amount of time, that is used in executing a program is run time. Thus, it is not the same time that is used by the computer to compile a program. Therefore, errors found during the execution of the program (which is also known as running of the program) are run time errors. **What is the nature of such errors?**

These errors occur when certain logical or mathematical rules are not applied properly. For instance, the program is supposed to exit if a certain condition is true. If the condition is false, it will never end, because the loop will repeat over and over again and will go on for ever. It simply means to **think** about the test condition more carefully. A mathematical error will occur, if you divide a number by zero.

Exception Handling

Here is some good news for you. Java has a technique called **Exception** handling. **What is an exception in programming?** An exception is an error that is highlighted by the computer during the execution of a program as an exceptional occurrence that must be dealt with. An exception can make continuation of a program impossible. In Java programming, exceptions are warning messages. These messages are communicated by the program. In other words, in the program, you can have in-built messages to be shown on the screen, when an exception has been met. If you do not include a relevant segment of a code in your program for dealing with exceptions, the computer will close the program safely.

Examples:

. You are trying to divide something by zero, which is not possible.

. You are trying to open a file, but the file is not present.

. You are trying to access an element of an array, but the required element is not part of the array. For instance, an array has only 4 elements in it, and you are trying to access element 5, which is not present. In this case, an array out of bounds message will appear.

. What is the difference between an error and an exception?

In Java, errors refer to faults in a program that are found by the interpreter when the program is being interpreted during the running of a program. On the other hand, exceptions are also errors or faults in a program, but you build a mechanism in your program that will automatically handle the exception when it occurs. In fact, exception handling is a mechanism for remedial action that can either resume the execution of a program , at the point where the exception occurred. Or if desired, exception handling can terminate the program in a controlled manner so that the program is closed safely.

Errors Handling

You already know that there were no errors found by the compiler in the program we have discussed above. In order to illustrate how the compiler reports errors and how you can eliminate these errors, I re-created the same program, but this time, I typed the word **public,** beginning with capital 'P'. You can see it in diagram 10. It was a deliberate typing error. The word **public** should begin with a small letter.

As a result of this mistake, the program was not compiled successfully, and an error message was displayed, which is shown in the lower part of diagram 9. In this diagram, the compiler has also listed some other options and their meanings. You should re-run your application by following the steps outlined below.

correct source file → save it→ compile it → pass the compiled file to the interpreter to run it.

Of course, there could be errors of other types, which I have not yet discussed.

Understanding and eliminating errors

As shown in our diagram 11, the **javac.exe** attempted to compile my program called **Learner . java**, but it did not succeed for the reason it has listed in the error message. You can see that the Javac has listed only one error, which is on line 4. The nature of my deliberate error is reported as **Identifier expected**. What it means is that it could not identify **Public** as keyword **public**, which begins with a small P. On careful study of this error message, you can see that the **javac** has listed:

- Program's name
- the line number on which the error was found

- the nature of the error
- the actual line where the error occurred by using ^ symbol to point it out.

Certainly, this error message demonstrates from a practical point of view that Java is a **case sensitive** language, and great care is needed when entering the source code.

Program 1 re-entered with a deliberate typing mistake

```
class Learner

{
          Public static void main (String [  ] args)        // public should begins with small p
            {

              System.out.println (" Hello  Java  Learners!" );

            }

}
```
=========================== **Error Message** ===========================

```
Microsoft(R) Windows 95
  (C)Copyright Microsoft Corp 1981-1996.

C:\WINDOWS> CD C:\Examples

C:\Examples>javac Learner.java
Learner.java:4: Identifier expected.
          Public static void main (String [  ] args)
              ^

1 error
C:\Examples>
```

Diagram 11

There are occasions when error messages in terms of the nature of errors reported by the **Javac** make no sense at all. On the other hand, often one can identify the nature of an error by carefully reading the message. Sometimes, the **Javac** reports an error and fails to compile the source code due to incorrect installation of **JDK** on your machine. An example of such errors is that the **Javac** fails to read your file. This kind of error can only be eliminated by re-configuring your JDK. Now, it is appropriate to introduce two terms related to errors. These are **bugs** and **debugging**. A bug is simply an error and the process of locating and eliminating an error (s) in a program is known as **debugging**.

Line numbers

You may find line numbers followed by colons shown in programs in some Java books. In this book, I have not done so. Why? The simple reason is that the Java compiler ignores these things. They are not required for Java programming.

Practical Hints

. Java is a case sensitive language, and thus lower and upper case letters are considered as different.
. to avid an error, "**javac: invalid argument**", at the compiling stage, make sure that the file name is exactly the same name as the class name.
. to interpret that is to convert the **bytecode** (complied file) into the binary code and run the application.
. Start the interpreter with the command: **java** followed by your program name, without file extension (**. Java**).
. a Java statement ends with a semicolon (**;**), and it performs the simplest task within the program.
. println ( ) means to display text on the screen; but usually it is termed as printing on the screen.

Exercises

1. Is the following statement correct? If not, correct it.
                                  systemout. Println (" This is my book")
2. Is there any difference between arguments, parameters and data? Write a statement which contains a string as an argument.
3. Make the distinction between Class Book and Book . java
4. When do you use the Javac tool?
5. Complete these two sentences: . HTML stands for --------------- ---------------------. Briefly describe it.
                                   . a logical error is usually caused by -----------------------------------.
6. int a (30* 450) /5 Is this expression a correct Java statement?
7. Javac MyFirstProgram . Java and java MyFirstProgram are two commands. When will you enter these commands, and where?
8. For what purpose is the WordPad used?

Chapter 3

Fundamental Concepts & Applications

The aim of this chapter is to introduce you to some basic concepts of Java programming, and to demonstrate their application by means of simple illustrative programming examples. These programs have been run successfully. You should experiment with these programs. Always remember the motto of this book :

Practice makes perfect!

A Variable

You should think of a computer memory as a row of houses on a street, each house having its own unique number. The occupants of a particular house can be approached by means of its unique number allocated to it. Similarly, a computer memory consists of thousands of cells. We can give unique names to each of these memory locations. In any of these memory locations (cells), we can place a **value or data** and recall it by referring to it by its unique name or symbol. This name or symbol is called a **variable**. The other attribute, which is attached to a variable, is **data type**. In Java, there are eight data types. These are known as primitive data types as shown in Table 1. Their use will become clear through the programming examples, once you have acquired some essential basic knowledge of the Java language.

Using Variables

You must declare a variable before you can use it. How do we declare variables? Let us examine the following variable declaration: **int a ;**

In this variable declaration statement:

• **int** is a variable type. **a** is the name which we have given to a storage location/name of variable, and

• **;** marks the end of our variable declaration statement. You must know by now that a Java statement ends with a semicolon. Once again:

Program - A program is a set of instructions arranged in a sequence for a computer. It tells a computer what to do and how to carry out a task step-by-step.

Another example of a variable declaration: float x = 78 f;
Here,
. **float** is a variable type . **x** variable name . = is assignment operator (operators), which is followed by 78 assigned to variable x. **78** is followed by **f** which is required with float variable type.

Why? In Java, the default type for floating point numbers (real numbers) is **double**. Thus, **f** is added after a numerical value in order to indicate its type.

Primitive Data Type Variable

Type	Description	Size	Range
int	signed integer	32 bits	-2,147,483,648 to +2,147,483,647
short	short signed integer	16 bits	-32,768 to +32768
long	long integer	64 bits	-9,223,372,036,854,775,808 to +9,223,372,036,854,775,807
float	floating point	32 bits	± 1.40239846E - 45 to ± 3.40282347E + 38
double	double floating point	64 bits	± 4.9406564581246544 E -324 ±1.79769313486231570 E +308
boolean	logical true or false	1 bit	
byte	signed integer	8 bits	-128 to 127
Char	unicode character	16 bits	

Table 1

Variable Assignment

If you have not come across the word assignment before, it means giving values to variables. The basic assignment operator is "=". Yes! It is the equals sign. Anyway, it does not mean for instance, **A** equals **B** as in mathematics. In programming, it means giving a value to a variable. There are four different assignment operators that are made by combining the basic = symbol with four arithmetic symbols *, /, + and -. These assignment operators and their meanings are shown in Table 3.

These operators together with arithmetic operators are implemented in program **Calculations. Java**, and their use is explained later through this program. The arithmetic operators are listed in Table 2. At this stage, it is desirable to learn the meaning of an expression, and how to implement arithmetic operators together with the assignment operator. You can make the variable assignment expression as shown below.

. **Example 1 - variable assignment:**   a + b + c = 10;

What does it mean? It simply means that variables a, b and c are assigned the value of 10. You may say the initial value assigned (given) to a, b and c is 10.

. **Example 2 - variable assignment: m = (a + b + c)/2;**

In this case, the values of a, b and c will be first added. The sum is divided by 2, and then its resulting value is assigned to **m**. Thus, the general format is that the right hand side of the assignment operator is first evaluated, and then the resulting value is assigned to the left hand side of the assignment operator.

Operators

. What are operators?

These are special symbols which have a specific meaning. You have already met assignment operator and arithmetic operators above. In Java, these different symbols are almost the same as in C++. There are different types of operators which are used for specific purposes. I will discuss and illustrate these with examples at the appropriate time and place in this book.

Arithmetic Operators

Operator	Meaning
+	addition or
-	subtraction
*	multiplication
/	division
%	reminder of integer division or modulus

Special Characters - escape codes

\n	Newline	\\	Backslash	\b	Backspace
\t	Tab	\"	Double quotation mark	\f	Form feed
\r	Carriage return	\'	Single quotation mark		

Diagram 2

Assignment Operators	

Operator	**What it means**
a += b	a = a + b
a −= b	a = a - b
a *= b	a = a * b
a /= b	a = a/b

Table 3

The order of precedence

It means the order in which an expression will be evaluated. For the arithmetic operators the order of precedence is as follows:

> . starts calculation from innermost brackets ( )
> . then performs multiplication *
> . next performs division /
> . next performs modulus or division calculation %
> . next addition is carried out +
> . lastly carries out subtraction

. What happens when all the operators have the same priority?

In such a case, the order of calculation is from left to right.

. How will you divide an integer by another integer to get a remainder?

You should perform calculations using modulus operator %. By this method the remainder is kept and the result of the division is discarded.

. What sort of result would you get when one operand is integer and the other operand is a floating point?

The answer will be a floating point value.

Workout.java

The program **Workout . java** is designed to demonstrate the application of variables and the assignment operators. It reads values of a, b, c and d, and displays their sum in the required format. The program coding and its output are shown in diagram 1.

Explanation

. Line 1. I have declared **Workout** as a class name. You already know that every class must have a name. You should also remember that a class name must begin with a capital letter. In fact, a Java program may be described as a class. The class name is given by yourself. So, I call it Workout as the main function of this program is to workout the sum of four given numbers.

. Line 2 { - it is an opening curly bracket, one of the two outer curly brackets which enclose the entire code of the program. Without it, your program will not be compiled successfully and the compiler will generate an error message, which is shown in diagram 1 A. This error message was generated by not entering { ; so that I can show you another example of error message and its content. When you read diagram 1 A, you will see the way Java compiler listed the error. You should compare it with the error message shown in diagram 11 on page 35.

. Line 3 - as discussed when dealing with our first program that a program must have **main method**. It is the point in your program where the interpreter commences the execution of your program. The method main has a body which is enclosed within the inner pair of curly brackets. Main method , you can also write it as method main ( ).

. Line 4 - { beginning of the inner pair of curly brackets.

. Line 5 – the body of the method main ( ) begins here. It has four different assignment statements. These statements assigned values to a, b, c and d variables. Thus, I have defined four variables of which two **int** type (whole number) and the other two floating-point type (real numbers/numbers with decimal points) as well as assigned values to these variables. Thus, the method main ( ) has four variables.

. Are variables always declared in this way?

If it is required to assign an initial value to a variable, you can declare it as shown in this program. On the other hand, variables are declared as demonstrated below:
int a:
short b;

are two examples of variable declaration. You can declare these on the same line, as long as each declaration ends with a semicolon (**;**) .

. **Lines 6 – 10** The method System . out . println (   ) – You have met this in program. These statements perform two tasks:

   . to add up the values of four variables, and then

   . print/display on the standard output device (screen) of your computer system, the sum of four variables in the required format.

. **Why have I used + symbol in System.out.println () as shown below?**

System .out .println("The sum of a, b, and d =   " + (a + b +c + d));

In this expression:

 System . out is an object, **println** is a method of System.out, and within the (" ") are parameters/ argument or, in the simplest term, values.

The System . out.println (   ) as a rule accepts a string or a single argument within (   ). The good news is that with the aid of + symbol, you can write in (   ) multiple arguments. <u>Note that it does not mean add.</u>

It is important **not** to omit full stops in **System . out . println** as these are required in order to evoke/call a method. This is Java's syntax. The general format of the method call is given below:

Object . method (parameters or arguments)

. **Lines 11 – 12** } } – without these inner and outer closing curly brackets, your program will not be compiled, and thus it will not proceed to the next stage of interpreting the bytecode and running it successfully. So, do not miss any of these brackets.

<u>Another Example of Error Message generated by the Javac</u>

```
C:\Examples>javac Workout.java
Workout.java:1: '{' expected.
class Workout
            ^
1 error

C:\Examples>
```

Once again, it is demonstrated that care is needed when creating your source file – pay special attention to Java language syntax.

<u>Diagram 1 A</u>

Workout.java

```
class Workout

{   public static void main ( String args [ ] )

    {

      int a = 100; int b = 104; float c = 99.90f; float d = 75.55f;

      System.out.println ("Add up a, b, c and d together");
      System.out.println ("--------------------------------");
      System.out.println ( "The sum of a, b, and d =  " + (a + b +c + d));
      System.out.println ("_____");

    }
}
```

Program Output

C:\Examples>javac Workout.java

C:\Examples>Java Workout

Add up a, b, c and d together

The sum of a, b, and d = 379.45

Diagram 1

Implementing Assignment Operators

Calculations.java

It is designed to demonstrate to you how to use assignment operators which are shown in Table 3 above. The program is listed in diagram 2 and its output is shown in diagram 2A.

The program is in two parts. In part 1, it works out the average of three numbers, and displays it. It is another exercise in using variables, arithmetic operators, and applying the **println method** of:

System . out object.

In part 2, it imagines a number. By manipulating the given number, it arrives back at the same number, in order to illustrate how to manipulate assignment operators. It displays the outcome on the screen. An imaginary number 12 is assigned to variable **num**. To this number another number 20 is added to get 32. The number 32 is doubled to yield 64. The number 64 is divided by 4 to arrive at 16. Finally, 4 is subtracted from 16 to return to the starting point that is the imaginary number 12. Again, **println** method prints on screen outcomes of all 4 operations involved in this example.

Explanation

Part 1 - it is fairly straight forward. The code is identical to the code in the **Work out . Java** program. It gives you another chance to experiment with it on your computer. The more you practise the more you learn!

Part 2 - it begins with the declaration of a variable called **num** of integer (int) type. Of course, you know that a variable is a name of a storage location, where a data or value is stored. It is required to state the type of data, which a variable will hold. In this case, it is of **int** type. **Why?** Because, it will hold only **int** type values. - the whole number.

• The statement **num = 12;** assigned the imaginary number 12 to variable num. The next requirement is to add to this imaginary number 20. This is achieved by the statement: **num += 20;** (12+20 = 32).

• The next arithmetic operation is to double the latest number that is held in variable **num**. This action is performed by the expression (reminder - an expression is a statement) : **num *= 2;** Because of this calculation, the variable **num** holds 64.

• Further arithmetic operation is to divide the latest value held in **variable num** by 4 to get 16. The segment of the code for this operation is **num /= 4;**

• The final requirement is to subtract from the latest number held in variable **num** by 4, in order to arrive back at the imaginary number 12. For this action the statement is **num -= 4;**

• The other statements make apply **println** method of **System . out** object to display the result of each action, as outlined above, on screen. Each statement follows the following structure:

System.out.println ("The number after subtraction = " + num);
              ↓   ↓   ↓
              1   2   3

• Arrows 1-2 point to where spaces (spaces for short) that I wanted to have before and after =.

• Note that if there was no space after = then because of + the value of **num would** have been placed much closer to = , and the output would not have been as clear to read as shown in diagram 2A.

• Arrow 3 - variable **num** holds the latest value calculated by each arithmetic operation using the appropriate assignment operator.

• The program runs well as its output is shown in diagram 2A. Now, it is your turn to enter this program into your computer system to learn more about this technique.

Calculations . java

```
class Calculations          // demonstrate use of some operators

{

public static void main ( String args [ ] )
 {
  int a = 100; int b = 104; float c = 99.90f; float d = 75.55f;

  int num;
  System.out.println("Add up a, b, c and d together");
  System.out.println("----------------------------");
  System.out.println("The sum of a, b, and d = " + (a + b + c + d));
  System.out.println("_____ ");
  System.out.println ( "The average value = " + (a + b + c + d)/5);
  System.out.println (" ----------------------------");
  System.out.println ( );
  System.out.println ("Imagine a number?");
  num = 12;
  System.out.println ("Your imaginary number = " + num);
  System.out.println ("Add 20 to this number");
  num += 20;
  System.out.println ("The number is now = " + num);
  System.out.println ("double this number");
  num*= 2;
  System.out.println ("The double number = " + num);
  System.out.println ("Divide the number by 4");
  num/= 4;
  System.out.println ("The number after division = " + num);
  System.out.println ("subtract 4 from the number");
  num-= 4;
  System.out.println ("The number after subtraction = " + num);
 }
}
```

Diagram 2

Calculations . java Output

C:\Examples>javac Calculations.java

C:\Examples>java Calculations
Add up a, b, c and d together

The sum of a, b, and d = 379.45

_____

The average value = 75.89

Imagine a number?
Your imaginary number = 12
Add 20 to this number
The number is now = 32
double this number
The double number = 64
Divide the number by 4
The number after division = 16
subtract 4 from the number
The number after subtraction = 12

Diagram 2A

Comments

• I have used above // (double slash). **What is it ?**

You can include in your source file any comments for your own sake or for the benefit of other users. The compiler ignores these comments. Use // for a **single line comment**, when you feel there is a need to include a useful comment as a reminder.

• You can also include in your source file a **muli-line comment**. For this purpose, you have to use two symbols, which are / * , and */. You must use these in the order as shown below.

The symbol /* is used at the beginning of the multi-line comment. The symbol */ is placed at the end of the comment.

Example

/* Where were you when the lottery winner was giving away part of his acquired fortune? I do not care about his money. I prefer to work hard for my well earned money to live on." */

Increment & Decrement Operators

. The symbol + +, (double plus sign) is used to increment the value of a variable by 1 only.

. The symbol - - , (double minus sign) is used to decrement the value of a variable by 1 only.

Examples:

. $X = X$ ++ means to increase the value of x by 1. You can also write it as $X = ++X$

. $Z = Z$ - - means to decrease the value of x by 1. You can also write it as $Z = --Z$

For instance, the following code in a program

$$int\ a = 20;$$
$$a++;$$

will increase the value of variable **a** by 1, and thus the value of **a** will change from 20 to 21.

. Is it legal to make a number larger or smaller by using these operators?

No. **10** ++ is not allowed. **Why?** Because these operators are applied to variables only.

. You can write these operators before (prefixed) or after (postfixed) the variable, in accordance with the following two rules:

. Rule 1

If the purpose is merely to change the value of the variable in a given expression, then it does not matter where you place the operator either before or after the variable. Thus

$$X = X++ \ \ \text{is the same as} \ \ ++X.$$

For instance, the following two different codes will generate the same result, that is to change the value of variable **a** .

Code 1	Code 2
---------	---------
int a = 10 ;	int a = 10 ;
a + +;	+ + a ;

Both codes will increase the value of the variable **a** by 1, and thus **a** changes to 11 from 10. Just for changing a value, it does not matter if the operator is a prefix or a postfix.

. Rule 2

Use the postfixed form of the operator when you have to assign the value to another variable in an expression and at the same time incrementing or decrementing the variable in the same expression. Now consider the following two cases:

Case 1 – Postfixed Position

```
int  a = 9 ;
int  b = a++ * 4 ;              // postfix increment
```

This code output : b = 36 and a = 10   **How?**

When the postfixed operator is applied on a variable inside an expression, the value of the variable does not change before the expression has been evaluated. Thus, firstly the variable **b** used the value of the variable **a** which is 9 to get the **answer 36** (4*9), then the variable **a** is incremented (changed) to **10**.

A Word of Warning!

In fact, the value of **a** will be changed, but it will not be assigned to **a** until the whole expression on the right side has been evaluated. Thus, Java changes the value, remembers the incremented value, and assigns it to **a**, after the right side is wholly evaluated. If your work involves complicated expressions, you should consult Java language Specification concerning expression evaluation.

Case 1 – Prefixed Position

```
int  a = 9 ;
int  b =  4 * ++a ;            // Prefix increment
```

This code output : b = 40 and a = 10   **How?**

 Firstly the variable **a** is incremented from 9 to 10, and then 10 is multiplied by 4, giving 40. Thus the prefixed operator changed the value of the variable **a** prior to the evaluation of the expression.

. Can you write a program without being muddled by these operators?

Yes indeed, you do not have to use these operators. You can achieve the same results by using your old faithful friends + and – arithmetic signs/operators.

. Can postfixed operators cause tedious bugs (errors) in your program?

Care must be taken when applying the post fixed operators in side expressions, as they can create tedious errors, which can be both time consuming and difficult to locate and eliminate from the source code.

Computation . java

The program is designed to demonstrate the application of increment and decrement operators. It performs the following tasks:

- to set the initial values of 4 variables called a, b, c, and d,

- to change the values of **d** and **a** variables by applying the prefixed increment operator.

- to change the values of **e** and **b** variables by means of post fixed increment operator, and

- to change the values of **f** and **c** variables by using the post fixed decrement operator.

The program is shown in diagram 3 and its output is listed in diagram 3A.

Explanation

- The first few lines of this program you have met before, and thus it needs no explanation.

- This program has 4 initial values assigned to variables a,b.c and d. These are **int** type.

- **int d = b + (4* ++a);** the expression has to be evaluated in order to find out the value for d variable. This is arrived by evaluating the expression by applying the prefixed increment operator. This expression has generated the changed value of **d = 134**, and the changed value of **a = 26**, as shown in diagram 3A. You should check it manually to confirm the effect of the prefixed increment operator.

- The check is as follows:

According to rule 1 which is stated above, the value of variable **a** was incremented from 25 to 26, prior to multiplying it by 4 within the brackets. Thus, within the brackets the value changed to **26*4 = 104**. This was then added to the value of b, which is 30. Hence, **30 + 104 = 134**. Now, you must see the program output in diagram 3A to confirm the effect of a **prefixed increment operator**.

- **int e = c + (10* b++);** In this statement b++ means **postfixed operator**. The right side of this expression has to be evaluated first to yield the value of variable **e** of int type. In this case, **Rule 2 is** applied. Thus, the e = 40 + (10*3). This gives e = 340. Now, **b** has to be incremented to 30+1 =31. In this case, the value of **a** is incremented after its original value is multiplied by 10 within the brackets. Once again, you must check this calculation to satisfy yourself. See program output in diagram 3A.

- **int f = c + (10* c - -);** Here, **rule 2** is applied. In this case, the effects are to decrease the value of variable **c** after the right side has been evaluated, and the value is assigned to variable **f**. You must now check it against the program output, to confirm that **f = 440**, and the changed value of **c = 39**.

Computation . java

```
class  Computation
 {
  public static void main ( String  args [ ]  )
   {

  System.out.println ( ".");
  System.out.println ( "This program demonstrates the application of prefixed &  postfixed operators");
  System.out.println (" --------------------------------------------------------------------------------");
  System.out.println ( " ");
  System.out.println ("Use of prefixed increment operator");
  System.out.println (" ----------------------------------------");
```

```
// initial values assigned to variables
     int a = 25;
     int b = 30;
     int c = 40;
     int d  = b + ( 4 * ++ a);
                              // use of prefixed increment operator

  System.out.println ( "The variable  d= " + d+ "  and the changed value of a is now =  " +a );
  System.out.println ( "  ");
                              // use of postfixed  increment operator

  System.out.println ( "Use of postfixed increment operator");
  System.out.println (" ---------------------------------------------");
  int e=  c + ( 10 * b ++);
  System.out.println ( "The variable  e= " + e+ " and the changed value of b is now =  " + b);
  System.out.println ( " ");
                              // use postfixed decrement operator

  System.out.println ( " Use of postfixed decrement operator");
  System.out.println ( " -----------------------------------------------");
  int f  =  c + ( 10 * c -- );
  System.out.println ( " The variable f =  " + f + " and the changed value of c is now  =  " + c );
  System.out.println (" -------------------------------------------------------------------------------");
 }
 }
```

Diagram 3

Program output

C:\Examples>javac Computation . java

C:\Examples>java Computation

This program demonstrates the application of prefixed & postfixed operators
----

Use of prefixed increment operator

The variable d = 134 and the changed value of a is now = 26

Use of postfixed increment operator

The variable e = 340 and the changed value of b is now = 31

 Use of postfixed decrement operator

The variable f = 440 and the changed value of c is now = 39

Diagram 3A

Strings

It is not only numbers that a computer system handles, but it also manipulates sequences of characters such as names, addresses, product textual details and the like. For instance the word "**LOVELY**" is a string. It is a perfect example of string, because it is a collection of seven letters from the English alphabet that makes sense, and thus communicates a meaning to those who understand English. This kind of collection of characters is in fact called a string in Java. A string can also have a combination of characters, numbers, punctuation marks, and special characters such as a newline. These special characters are shown in Table 2.

Before I go any further, I must add that a character is a letter, number or any other type of single symbol. For instance \, read it as backslash, is a character that can also be included in a string. Strings are used in C++ and also in other programming languages, because they enable us to store textual data in them. A string is often used to communicate messages to the users, and to pass data between methods.

Creating Strings and Variables

A variable can store string value as shown by the following statement:

- **String   Message = " Learn all about strings in Java";**

  ↓   ↓   ↓

  Keyword   string variable -   This is the string - value
            String's name

Note that double quotation marks are essential to construct a string. These quotation marks are required to enclose the string's text, and thus these are not part of the string's size. An Equals symbol is also required.

In a program, this statement will create a string variable called Message. This string variable will store what is within these double quotation marks, that is the value of the Message.

- **String   empty = " "**   **// see program Empty .java for its use**

Of course, it is a string which contains nothing within the quotation marks. Thus, it is an **empty** string.

. How do you join strings together?

You can use the operator + to join two strings together. Yes, it is the plus sign, but it does not perform the addition function. It creates a new longer string. This technique is often called concatenation. Don't be afraid of this jargon, because you already know what it means. In some books, this technique of joining strings together is also called 'string arithmetic'. Again, you are warned not get bogged down in this jargon. Nevertheless, it has one great practical advantage, that is, if your string is too long and clumsy to see it on a single line on your screen, you can use this operator + to continue entering your text on the next line. When the string is displayed, it will be shown as a single string.

Example:

                String tall = " He is tall and handsome";   // String variable tall created
                String rich = " He is also rich and young.";   // String variable rich created

We can concatenate these two strings together:

    String RichMan = tall + rich ;   // new string variable created by concatenation method

We can print the content of this new string on the screen, which will be:

            " He is tall and handsome. He is also rich and young."

Message . java

The program is designed to demonstrate the application of strings and special characters by coding the above example. It will also print on the screen the content (value) of the new string created by the concatenation method.

Explanation

. The program is shown in diagram 4. The first string variable is called **tall** which holds the string value shown with " ". Your attention is drawn to the special character \" which is placed after the double quotation mark of this string. **Why is it here?**

This special character generates a double quotation mark. I want to print on the screen a new string value within the quotation marks. Thus \"generates the opening double quotation mark for the new string value. You should carefully analyse the following segment of the code in order to familiarise yourself with the positions of the special character and the double quotation mark in this string. Of course, if I do not wish to display the new string within " ", there is no need for this special character \". It is necessary to remind you on that on all occasions you have to insert the string value within the double quotation marks as required by Java.

```
String  tall  =   (  " \" He is tall and handsome. " );
String  rich =   ( " He is also rich and young. \" " );
```

. The second string variable is called **rich**. In this string, the special character is placed within the closing double quotation mark. This closes the new string, when it is displayed on the screen.

. The remainder of the program simply produces the new string called **RichMan**, and displays it as required in the above example. Program output is shown in diagram 4A.

Message . java

```
class Message
{
   public static void  main  ( String [ ] args )

{
                        // to concatenate two strings

     String  tall  =   (  " \" He is tall and handsome. " );
     String  rich =   ( " He is also rich and young. \" " );
     String  RichMan  = ( tall + rich );
     System.out.println ( " ");
     System.out.println (  RichMan  );
}
}
```

Diagram 4

Program Output

C:\Examples>Java Message

" He is tall and handsome. He is also rich and young. "

<u>**Diagram 4A**</u>

Length of a String

You can find out the length of a string in terms of characters by applying the **length method**. How?

Program Length.java

The program in diagram 5 is designed and tested in order to demonstrate the application of **length method ( )**. The string length is also displayed as shown in the required format in this diagram under program output.

Explanation

String city String city = "London is one of the biggest cities in the world";

• In this box, you can see the String city has 10 words, which have 39 characters. This string also has 9 white spaces between words. In total 48 characters as a white space is considered as a character. The **city. length ( ) method** that is shown below counts the number of characters in the string variable called city. Thus, the count is assigned to the **n** integer variable.

---

int n = city.length ( );

• I wanted to have one line space between the command line: `C:\Examples>java Length` and the program output. Therefore, I have made a use of the special character **\n**. In addition, I decided to start printing the program output one **tab** position away from its original setting, and thus, I have included **\t** in the following statement.

System.out.println("\n\t The length of String city is " +n+" characters");

• Now, you should examine both the program and its output to see for yourself that it has achieved its objectives of counting the number of characters in the String city, and printing the output as I planned.

Length . java

```
class Length
{

public static void main ( String [  ] args)

{

String city = "London is one of the biggest cities in the world";
int n = city.length (  );

System.out.println("\n\t The length of String city is " +n+" characters");
}
}
```

===================== **Program Output** =========================

C:\Examples>javac Length.java

C:\Examples>java Length

     The length of String city is 48 characters   // included spaces

Diagram 5

String Class

Java has no built-in string type, but the good news is that the Java library has a **predefined class** called **String**. The String class in Java has more than 50 methods. One of them is **int length ( ) method**, which was used in program Length.java. It returns the length of the string.

In C++, strings are arrays of characters. On the contrary, strings in Java are **instances** of the

       Java . lang . String class   // package name is java.lang

So, in Java, strings are objects, and they have methods. These methods let you manipulate strings in a variety of ways. You have already met one important method:

          main (String [ ] args)

more than once. **What is its function?** This **main method** creates an array of String. This string does not have any number within [ ].

It means that the argument has an unspecified number of characters. **Args** is an abbreviation for argument, which is a variable within square brackets. It has nothing to do with any argument between people. Another word connected with variables is **parameter**. In simplest term parameters are values.

Upper case and lower case letters

. String toLowerCase ( ) method - this method returns a new string that consists of all characters in the original string, with uppercase letters converted to lower case letters.

. String toUpperCase ( ) method - this method returns a new string that contains all characters in the original string, with lowercase letters changed to upper case letters.

These two particular methods are particularly useful when two strings contain the same textual information, but are written in different cases. For instance:

Tony Blair and TONY BLAIR

To the British reader it is the same person as both refer to a man's name, the present British Prime Minister. In Java programming it is not so. In order to handle such things in Java, String toUpperCase and String toLowerCase methods are particularly useful as demonstrated by **Change . java** program.

Change . java

The program shown in diagram 6 is designed to demonstrate how to convert strings as described above. This program has two strings namely Politician and PastMinister.

String politician - it contains lower case letters. Whilst the **String PstMinister** has upper case letters. The aim of this program is to convert the String Politician to upper case letters, so that the new string which is called **Change** should contain all upper case letters. It also converts the String PastMinister to a new string called **Convert**, so that the new string has only lower case letters.

The program is self-explanatory. It works well, as its desired output is shown in diagram 6A.

```
C:\Examples>java Change

 The new string with all upper case letters is printed below

     MR TONY BLAIR IS A BRITISH PRIME MINISTER.

 The new string with all lower case letters is shown below.

 before mr tony blair the prime minister was mr major.
```

Diagram 6A

Change . java

```
class Change

{
 public static void main ( String [   ] args)

{

    String Politician = ("Mr Tony Blair is a British Prime Minister.");
    String Change  = Politician. toUpperCase ( );

 System.out.println("\n The new string with all upper case letters is printed below\n");
 System.out.println ("\t"+ Change );

    String PastMinister = (" BEFORE MR TONY BLAIR THE PRIME MINISTER WAS MR MA-
JOR.");
    String Convert  = PastMinister.toLowerCase ( );
 System.out.println ("\n The new string with all lower case letters is shown below.\n");
 System. out.println (Convert);
}
}
```

Diagram 6

Comparing two strings

This is another useful method that can enable you to compare whether or not two strings are equal. This is achieved by implementing **equals ( ) method**. When strings are equal, this method returns **true**, otherwise **false** is returned.

Equals . java

The program is designed to perform the test of comparing two given strings, and display the outcome in terms of true and false.

Explanation

. In this program, there are two strings namely London and Birmingham. The text is enclosed within

" ". In both strings is the same information, except that two important words London and Birmingham are different. There are an unequal number of characters in these two strings because these two words have different numbers of characters in their spellings.

System . out . println ("\n Is Birmingham a capital city?");

This statement displays on screen, on a new line, the question shown within the " ".

. The equality test compares String London with String Birmingham. This test is carried out by the following statement:

System.out.println("\n It is "+ London.equals (Birmingham)+ ".");

↑

London is compared with Birmingham

This statements incorporates the equals ( ) method. Notice that within " ", I have entered **\n**, the special character in order to begin a new line. The statement ends with **"."** which is for placing a full stop at the end of the value to be returned by this equals method. See the last line of the program output in diagram 7.

. What is the outcome of this equality test?

In accordance with this test, there are only two possibilities. These are true and false. If both variables have the same value (number of characters), then the test returns a **true value**. In this example, the test has returned a false value, because the values in each string are different. It simply means that London and Birmingham have an unequal number of characters, and thus the false value has returned.

. Since the test has proved false, the false value is entered in the above statement by the **println** method of **System . out** object, displaying: **It is false**.

A Word of Warning !

. do not use = = symbol/operator to compare two strings. This will cause bugs which will prove very difficult to trace. You will see the use of = = operator when we discuss conditional testing in the next chapter.

Practical Hints

. An empty string is without any value within the double quotation marks.

. The equals ( ) method returns a true or false value. These are boolean (Boolean) values.

. The + operator joins up two different strings together. For joining integer values of one string to the value of another, there is another technique called **casting.** This will be discussed later on.

. Until now you have seen in action some basic arithmetic operations. Java has a class in the **Java. lang** package, which is called **java . lang . Math**. This class has scores of methods for mathematical work.

Equals . java

```
class Equals          // compares two strings for equality
{

  public static void main ( String args [ ] )

  {

    System.out.println("\nThis program performs equality test");
    System.out.println("---------------------------------\r");
    String London = ("London is a capital city.");
    String Birmingham = ("Birmingham is a capital city.");
    System.out.println ( "\n Is Birmingham a capital city?");
    System.out.println("\n It is "+ London.equals ( Birmingham)+ ".");

  }
}
```

========================= **Program Output** =========================

C:\Examples>javac Equals.java

C:\Examples>java Equals

This program performs equality test

 Is Birmingham a capital city?

 It is false.

Diagram 7

Exercises

1. Write and test a program called **Joint . java**. This program should perform the following tasks. Use the quotations shown below to complete Task A and Task B.

  " I am learning Java." "You are good at it. Please help me to understand it."

Task A: Convert these quotations into two strings namely, String Learn and String Help. From these two strings create a new string called Learning. Print this new string on screen, on a single line, which has these three sentences.

Task B: Find the length of this new String Learning by applying **Length ( ) method**. The number generated by the Length ( ) method should be inserted in the space pointed by the arrow in the following sentence. **The length of string Learning is   characters.**

                                    ↑

                    insert the length (number) in this space.

Print the completed sentence on screen. You must also generate an empty line (space) between the line printed by Task A, and by Task B (Use of a special character).

2. Write and test a program called **MeanValue . java** that will compute the average weekly wages of 10 employees, and display it on screen. Use both whole (integers) and real (decimal) numbers.

3. Write and test a program called **Drink . java**. It should perform the following tasks:

Task A: compare the two strings shown below by applying the equality test, and display the outcome as a sentence, such as **It is true**. Or **it is false**. The following strings are initialised with just one word in each string.

        String early = ("tea") ;   String late = ("Coffee") ;

Raise the following question to generate an answer as the outcome of this equality testing. The question must be displayed on your screen.

            John: Do you always drink tea in mornings and evenings?

Task B: Compare two strings shown below by applying the equality test, and display the outcome as an appropriate sentence: **It is true**. Or **it is false**. The following strings are initialised with two words in each string:

        String morning = ("I drink tea");   String Evening = ("I drink tea");

Use the following question to generate an answer as the outcome of this equality testing. Show this question on the screen: Ann: Do you always drink tea in mornings and evenings?

Chapter 4

Arrays Data Type

In Chapter 3, Primitive data type variables were discussed. In addition, Java also has array type variables. This type of variables are introduced in this chapter.

Arrays

A computer's ability to store and manipulate data is an important aspect of learning programming. You can store a single data value in a variable and then manipulate it. However, often we have to store and manipulate a group of related (similar) data items. These related data items are presented to the computer as a single set. This collection of related data items as a set is an array. This is one method of structuring data. A data item in an array is called an **element**. Each element is identified by its **subscript**, which is also known as **index**.

In Java, arrays are objects. In fact, you have already met **String [ ] args** in the method **main**. This sets up an array of string type of an unspecified number of elements (**args** = **arguments**).

Array Dimensions

The way data is arranged determines the dimension of an array. For instance, if data items are arranged in the form of a list, it is called a one-dimensional array. It is possible to have many dimensions, but from a practical point of view, two dimensional arrays are more meaningful. In a two-dimensional array, the elements are arranged in the form of a table (or matrix). The number of elements in both rows and columns are fixed. **How can you make a distinction between elements in a two-dimensional array?** The position of each element in a two-dimensional array is given by the relevant pair of indexes.

one-dimensional array

An array can be a **one-dimensional array**, which is in fact, a single list which consists of some individual similar data items. Now consider the following two illustrations:

Illustration 1			**Illustration 2**
Jane	Student [0]	→	Student [Jane]
James	Student [1]	→	Student [James]
Bill	Student [2]	→	Student [Bill]
Robin	Student [3]	→	Student [Robin]
Chris	Student [4]	→	Student [Chris]

This array has **5 elements**, which are data items (values or elements). These elements are the actual names of 5 students namely, Jane, James, Bill, Robin, and Chris. In illustration 1, each pair of [ ] has a subscript or index, which is replaced by the respective actual element in illustration 2 . Let's analyse it further below.

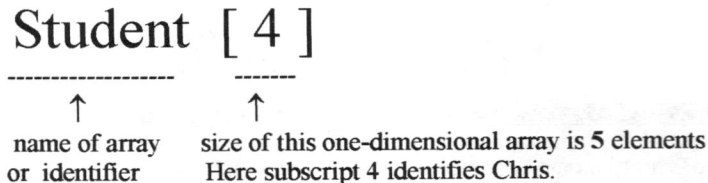

Student [4]

name of array   size of this one-dimensional array is **5** elements
or identifier   Here subscript 4 identifies Chris.

In this example, **Student [0] is Jan.** You might have noticed by now that subscripts began with **0** and ended with 4 in [ ]. **Why?**

It is because of the application of the **Zero-based indexing method**. In accordance with this method, subscripts are from 0 to **(size of array −1)**. In other words, the general rule is that if the array has **n** elements, their subscripted values are **$n-1$**. The first subscript always begins with **0**.

. What is the value (data) of Student [3]?

Its value or data is **Robin**. Its position is determined by applying the Zero-based indexing method.

. What is a subscripted variable?

It is an individual element of an array. In the above example **student [2]** is a subscripted variable.

. How do you declare array variables?

The first thing you must think is how to hold the array. You know well by now that to hold data in the computer memory, you must declare the required variables of the correct type. The following two declarations exemplify array declaration :

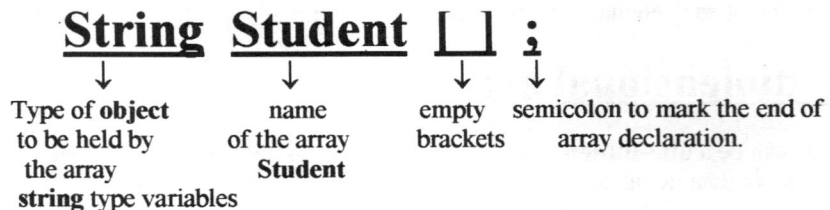

+ ## String Student [] ;

Type of **object**   name   empty   semicolon to mark the end of
to be held by   of the array   brackets   array declaration.
the array   **Student**
string type variables

+ Another example of array declaration: ## int Grades [ ];

Indeed, it follows the same pattern. The difference lies in the type of object the array will hold. In this example, the type is integer variables.

. How do you create an array object?

The above two array variables illustrate how to create arrays, but if you insert these in two programs, they will not store any values initially. In order to store data in the array, you must first create an array object. How do you achieve it? You can create an array object by using any of the two techniques:

a) You can implement a **new** statement. It is called the constructor method, which creates an object.

b) if you wish, you can also initialise data within a pair of { }. Each element within { } must be separated by a comma.

Both techniques are demonstrated by programming examples that are shown in diagrams 1 and 1A.

. How do we access an element of an array?

In order to access an element in an array, you have to apply the zero-indexing method, which means refer to the index of the element to be accessed. **For instance:**

System.out.println (Student [2]) ;

This print statement will print **Bill Clinton** on your screen. You should check this answer for your satisfaction. See diagrams 1 and 1A.

Student . java

The program is designed and tested to demonstrate how to **create** a one-dimensional array, and **print** data stored in the one-dimensional array called **Student**. It also puts into practice the **zero-based** indexing method. The program is listed in diagram 1. The output is also shown in the same diagram.

Explanation

. In this program, the class is called **Student**. It has one instance called **Student** (object) variable that holds arrays of String type variables (objects). Let me make it simple. It means that the class student has an instance called student, which will store names of 5 students.

. When writing a program that deals with arrays, one must think first about:

> . the type of data it will hold
> . the size of the array in terms of the number of elements in it
> . how to create an array object and assign it to the array variable

For this example, the data type is string variable, because we want to store the names of some students.

There are only 5 students whose names have to be stored and displayed. Thus, the size of the array is 5 These 5 names have to be stored and displayed in the order ranges from 0 to 4.

. In program **Student . java**, I have used the **new constructor** to create a new **instance** of an array (object). The code for it is shown below.

```
String [  ] Student  =  new String [ 5 ];
```

• You can see that the number of elements, which is 5, is enclosed within [ ] in the array object. This will allocate memory cells for 5 strings (5 names of 5 students). It does not actually place these elements in these 5 memory cells.

In other words, it has initialised as many memory spaces as shown within [ ].

• How many string objects are there altogether in this example?

There are 5 string objects in this example.

• How do you assign the actual objects (values, data, or elements) to these 5 cells?

The following segment of the code initialised the actual objects to be placed in the 5 allocated memory spaces. Note that each assignment statement has included the correct subscript in the same order as I wanted to display.

```
Student [ 0 ]  =  "Jane    Smith" ;
Student [ 1 ]  =  "James   Taylor" ;
Student [ 2 ]  =  "Bill    Clinton" ;
Student [ 3 ] =  "Robin   Robson ";
Student [ 4 ]  =  "Chris   McDonald" ;
```

• Would it matter, say for instance, if the last two statements changed places?

No, except that **Chris McDonald** would be displayed in the place of **Robin Robson**, and **Robin Robson** would be shown in the place of **Chris McDonald**.

In all circumstances, you must not write within [ ] a subscript that exceeds the required number. In this example the highest required subscript is **4**, in accordance with the zero-based indexing method.

• The rest of the program is aimed at displaying as a list the names of 5 students. These print statements have included special characters \t and \n to display the list in the format as shown in **Program output**. The program ran successfully. See the output which proves it.

<u>Student . java</u>

```
class Student

{
 public static void main ( String [  ] args)

 {

    String [  ] Student  =  new String [ 5 ];

        Student  [ 0 ]  =  "Jane    Smith" ;
        Student  [ 1 ]  =  "James  Taylor" ;
        Student  [ 2 ]  =  "Bill    Clinton" ;
        Student  [ 3 ] =   "Robin  Robson ";
        Student  [ 4 ]  =  "Chris  McDonald" ;

System.out.println ( "\n\t"+ "List of Java Programming Evening Students");
System.out.println ( "\t"  + "-------------------------------------------------\n");
System.out.println ("\t\t\t" + Student [ 0] );
System.out.println ("\t\t\t" + Student [ 1] );
System.out.println ("\t\t\t" + Student [ 2] );
System.out.println ("\t\t\t" + Student [ 3] );
System.out.println ("\t\t\t" + Student [ 4] );
System.out.println ( "\t"  + "-------------------------------------------------\n");

 }
}
```

<u>Program Output</u>

```
C:\Examples>javac Student.java

C:\Examples>java Student

    List of Java Programming Evening Students
    ---------------------------------------------

        Jane     Smith
        James   Taylor
        Bill      Clinton
        Robin   Robson
        Chris   McDonald

    ---------------------------------------------
```

<u>Diagram 1</u>

Student.java   (second method)

```
 class Student

{
   public static void main ( String [ ] args)

{
String [ ]
Student = { "Jane    Smith" , "James  Taylor" ,  "Bill   Clinton", "Robin  Robson " , "Chris
          McDonald"};
                              // directly initialising the contents of the array

System.out.println ( "\n\t"+ "List of Java Programming Evening Students" );
System.out.println ( "\t"  + "-------------------------------------------------------\n" );
System.out.println ( "\t\t\t" + Student [ 0 ] );
System.out.println ( "\t\t\t" + Student [ 1 ] );
System.out.println ( "\t\t\t" + Student [ 2 ] );
System.out.println ( "\t\t\t" + Student [ 3 ] );
System.out.println ( "\t\t\t" + Student [ 4 ] );
System.out.println ( "\t"  + "-------------------------------------------------------\n" );

}
}
```

Program Output

```
C:\Examples>javac Student.java

C:\Examples>java Student

    List of Java Programming Evening Students
    ---------------------------------------------------

            Jane    Smith
            James   Taylor
            Bill    Clinton
            Robin   Robson
            Chris   McDonald

    ---------------------------------------------------
```

Diagram 1A

Direct Initialisation

• The **second method** of creating an array object is to directly initialise the contents of the array. This is achieved by the following assignment statement.

```
String [  ]

    Student = { "Jane   Smith" , "James   Taylor" , "Bill   Clinton", "Robin   Robson " , "Chris
                McDonald"};
```

• Validation of second method – see **diagram 1A**, which has both the program and its output. The above statement has also generated the same desired output which was produced by using the **new** constructor method. Test these programs on your own system in order to compare these two programs and their outputs, and above all learn by doing.

• What is the difference between these two methods ?

The new constructor method allows you to allocate memory cells to the number of elements to be stored later on. The direct initialisation method lets you create an array, and at the same time to initialise its contents, by enclosing the array elements inside the pair of { }, separated by commas.

EnrolNumbers.java

The program is designed and tested to show you another solved programming example. It provides you with further opportunity to put your knowledge into practice. Like the last program, this program performs the task of creating an instance called **enrol**, stores in a one dimensional array, the data of 10 students, and prints these in the desired format as shown in the program output in diagram 2A. The program is listed in diagram 2.

Explanation

A comparison between the following two programs:

Student . java	EnrolNumbers . java
• class Student	• class EnrolNumbers
• array type string	• array type integer
• instance created enrol	• instance created Student
• 5 elements/data to be stored in the array called Student	• 10 elements/data to be stored in the array called enrol

EnrolNumbers . java

```
class EnrolNumbers

{
 public static void main ( String [ ] args )

 {
   int [  ] enrol = new int [10 ];

   enrol [ 0 ] = 1079;
   enrol [ 1 ] = 1081;
   enrol [ 2 ] = 1082;
   enrol [ 3 ] = 1083;
   enrol [ 4 ] = 2100;
   enrol [ 5 ] = 3156;
   enrol [ 6 ] = 1087;
   enrol [ 7 ] = 1118;
   enrol [ 8 ] = 1158;
   enrol [ 9 ] = 1068;

   System.out.println ( "\nList of Java Programming Group Enrol Numbers\n" );
   System.out.println ( " -----------------------------------------------------------\n" );
   System.out.println (  "\t\t\t" + enrol [ 0 ] );
   System.out.println ( "\t\t\t"  + enrol [ 1 ] );
   System.out.println ( "\t\t\t"  + enrol [ 2 ] );
   System.out.println ( "\t\t\t"  + enrol [ 3 ] );
   System.out.println  ( "\t\t\t" + enrol [ 4 ] );
   System.out.println ( "\t\t\t"  + enrol [ 5 ] );
   System.out.println ( "\t\t\t"  + enrol [ 6 ] );
   System.out.println ( "\t\t\t"  + enrol [ 7 ] );
   System.out.println ( "\t\t\t"  + enrol [ 8 ] );
   System.out.println ( "\t\t\t"  + enrol [ 9 ] );
   System.out.println ("----------------------------------------------------------");
 }
}
```

Diagram 2

The program **EnrolNumbers . java** follows the same pattern as program **Student . java**. The Program **EnrolNumbers . java** has worked well to generate the desired output as shown in diagram 2A.

EnrolNumbers . java Output

C:\Examples>javac EnrolNumbers.java

C:\Examples>java EnrolNumbers

List of Java Programming Group Enrol Numbers

```
                    1079
                    1081
                    1082
                    1083
                    2100
                    3156
                    1087
                    1118
                    1158
                    1068
```

Diagram 2A

. What should you do now?

Re- write program **EnrolNumbers** .java. In your program, you should **directly** initialise the contents of the array. Compile and run the program to generate the same output as shown in diagram 2A. Compare your program and its required output with this program. Remember that you can learn more by practising with these programs.

Using Arrays

By now, you have sufficient knowledge of one-dimensional arrays. You can use arrays in a program, as you would use any primitive type variable. What you have to bear in mind is that the structures of both print and assignment statements involving arrays, have to enclose within the pair of square brackets [ ], the subscript of the element. E.g. **Grade [0] ;** In this statement, **Grade** is the array's name, **0** is the subscript of the element or the value, which is to be stored in this location.

Grades . java

The program is written in order to achieve the following tasks:

1) to set up an array called **grade** in order to store integer type 6 values. These values are percentage grades gained by 6 students in a Java practical examination. Display all percentage grades, as a long list, under an appropriate heading, which should be underlined.

2) work out the average percentage grades gained by the Java class, and display it.

3) access from array grade the percentage grade for the element whose subscript is 4, and display it

Explanation

. The program follows the pattern of the previous programs. In addition, it shows you how to manipulate array variables. The class that I have created for this program is called Grades. Like the previous program, it has only one **instance variable** that holds arrays of **int objects** (data).

. In addition to creating an array object **int [ ] grade = new int [6];** you have to declare **int subsc;** This declaration is needed for the completion of task 3.

. **Task 1**- the segment of the code for this task hardly differs from the code of **EnrolNumbers . java**. Thus, you should be able to follow it.

.**Task 2** – the following code calculates the average percentage grade, and displays it on the screen. If a line is too long , you can write it on more than one line as shown below.

```
System . out . println
("The average group grade =   "
            + ( grade [0] + grade [1] + grade [2] + grade [3] + grade [4] + grade [5] )/6 + "%");
```

. **Task 3** – **int subsc;** Here, subsc is declared **as int** type, because, you are asked to find the grade of the element whose subscript is 4, which is int. You can call your variable by any name, which you think is sensible

---

Note

The use of a pair of ( ) in this code. Without these brackets, your program would be compiled successfully, but the average group grade would be computed incorrectly. In this case, the answer would be "The average group grade = 795567757910%". This is incorrect.

Without enclosing grade [0] ......grade [5] within ( ), the interpreter the printed the first 5 percentage grades as given, and also divided the last percentage grade 65 by 6 to get 10. This 10 is also printed as the last number. This is why it is 795567757910%. The computer also printed % sign as required. This is all wrong. Now, you can check it manually to satisfy your curiosity. Why is it so?

The reason why these were printed as such, is because of the symbol +. In this code, it means on the same line, when it is outside the ( ). On the other hand, it means the plus sign, when it is within ( ).

. Also note that a space is essential between =   " in this statement, so that both the computed figure and % sign can be inserted as shown in the program output.

. **subsc = 4;** This statement assigns 4 to **subsc**. In fact, you can declare just one statement:

int subsc = 4;

. **grade [subsc]** – it is in the print statement. **Subsuc** is enclosed within **[ ]** not 4, because 4 is already assigned to **subsc**.

. The program compiled and ran successfully. See the program output in diagram 3A in order to match its output with the code so that you can appreciate the whole code and explanation.

Grades.java

```
class Grades
 {
  public static void main (String [ ] args)
  {
   int [ ] grade = new int [ 6 ];
   int subsc;
   grade [ 0 ]  = 79;
   grade [ 1 ]  = 55;
   grade [ 2 ]  = 67;
   grade [ 3 ]  = 75;
   grade [ 4 ]  = 79;
   grade [ 5 ]  = 65;
   System.out.println ( "\n\t"+" List of Percentage Marks gained by Java Class" );
   System.out.println ( "\t" + "...................................................\n" );
   System.out.println ( "\t\t\t" + grade [ 0 ] );
   System.out.println ( "\t\t\t" + grade [ 1 ] );
   System.out.println ("\t\t\t" + grade  [ 2 ] );
   System.out.println ("\t\t\t" + grade  [ 3 ] );
   System.out.println ("\t\t\t" + grade  [ 4 ] );
   System.out.println ("\t\t\t" + grade  [ 5 ] );
   System.out.println ("\t\t\t" + "......\n");

   System.out.println
   ("The average group grade = "
            + ( grade [0] + grade [1] + grade [2] + grade [3] + grade [4] + grade[5] )/6  +  "%");
   System.out.println ("...........................\n");
   subsc = 4;
   System.out.println
     ( "The grade for the element whose subscript is 4  =  " + grade [subsc] + "%" );
   System.out.println
   (".......................................................");
 }
 }
```

Diagram 3

Grades . java Output

C:\Examples>javac Grades.java

C:\Examples>java Grades

    List of Percentage Marks gained by Java Class
    ....

             79
             55
             67
             75
             79
             65
             ......

The average group grade = 70%
....

The grade for the element whose subscript is 4 = 79%
....

Diagram 3 A

Two-dimensional Arrays

A two-dimensional array is a table which consists of a number of **rows** and **columns**. Java does not have two-dimensional arrays, and thus, two-dimensional arrays are arrays of arrays.

Table 2: KBL PLC sales data for the period 1997 - 1999

Year	UK	EU	USA
1997	1,200,590	1,700,000	2,190,790
1998	1,690,587	2, 567,879	2,800, 543
1999	1,900,000	2, 900, 854	3, 000, 600

Table2 has 3 rows and 3 columns. The **array [3] [3]** is thus a two-dimensional array. From this table, if you want to know sales data for any of the three trading areas for any year, you have to find it by referring to the intersection of a relevant row and column.

For example, the sales data for **EU** trading area for the year 1998 is obtained by referring to:

array [2] [2]

It is where sales data for EU is stored in the computer memory. It is the intersection of the **2nd row** of the **2nd column**.

. Location map of elements in the above table(or matrix)

The following table 3 illustrates the ordering of elements in the above two-dimensional array, and how to refer to each element in order to refer these in a program.

Table 3: KBL PLC sales data for the period 1997 - 1999

Year	UK	EU	USA
1997	[0] [0]	[0] [1]	[0] [2]
1998	[1] [0]	[1] [1]	[1] [2]
1999	[2] [0]	[2] [1]	[2] [2]

For instance, at the intersection of **[1] [2]** , figure **2 800 543** will be stored. The first index in a pair of brackets gives the row, and the second index in the same pair of brackets refers to the column of the array in which the element is located. In a program, you have to refer to data in any two-dimensional table by means of the relevant intersection.

If you do not write the correct numbers within brackets, your program will be compiled and run, but the output will be incorrect due to a logic error caused by the programmer's poor thinking.

Again here is the theory put into practice in the following two programs for your benefit.

Sales . java

The program has the following two versions:

. Version 1 – Diagram 4 contains the code and its output as shown in diagram 4A. The purpose of this program is to demonstrate how to handle two-dimensional arrays by using sales data from table 2 above. It sets up a matrix, stores, and displays its contents on the screen as a long list, instead of a matrix.

. Version 2

The program and its output are shown in diagram 5. It uses the same set of data, stores and displays sales data in the form of a matrix, with trading years (rows) and trading areas (columns).

Explanation

. Like one-dimensional arrays, a two-dimensional array (matrix) also has a name. The above array is called sales. Both programs are called **sales . java**.

. Since it has a name, I can **declare** it as: **int [ ] [ ] sales;**
without any subscripts within brackets. It has to be declared as int type because sales data are whole numbers.

. Strictly speaking, Java does not support multi-dimensional arrays, as C++, and some other programming languages do. In Java, multi-dimensional arrays are arrays of arrays. Thus, **sales array** is an array, which has three elements, each of which is also an array of three integer type numbers.

. You have already learnt that before an array can be used, it must be first initialised. You have also seen the role played by the operator (constructor) **new** in initialising an array. Here, **new** can be used to initialise this array as shown below:

sales = new int [3] [3] ;

Note that here you must write within brackets the <u>actual</u> numbers of subscripts for both rows and columns.

. Once you have initialised the array, its elements can be accessed as desired.

. The rest of the code in diagram 4 is similar to the code of previous programs.

. The program has worked well as it has generated the required output in the desired format. Test it!

. Diagrams 5 & 5A

It contains version 2 of **Program Sales . java**. The program in this diagram differs from the code shown in diagram 4 in respect of **System . out . println** objects and their **println** methods only. These statements are carefully designed with the aid of table 3 above to display data in the required format as shown in the program output section in diagram 5A.

. The position of each element must be correctly stated in the print statement, so that each element is displayed in its rightful place in the matrix.

. The program ran successfully, as the desired table was displayed on the screen. See its output.

Sales.java

```
class Sales

{

  public static void main ( String [ ] args )

   {

   int [ ] [ ] sales;
   sales =  new  int [3] [ 3];
   sales [ 0 ] [ 0 ]  =  1200590;
   sales [ 0 ] [ 1 ]  =  1700000;
   sales [ 0 ] [ 2 ]  =  2190790;
   sales [ 1 ] [ 0 ]  =  1690587;
   sales [ 1 ] [ 1 ]  =  2567879;
   sales [ 1 ] [ 2 ]  =  2800543;
   sales [ 2 ] [ 0 ]  =  1900000;
   sales [ 2 ] [ 1 ]  =  2900854;
   sales [ 2 ] [ 2 ]  =  3000600;

   System.out.println ( );
   System.out.println ( "KBL PLC sales data for the period 1997-1999" );
   System.out.println ( "-------------------------------------------------------\n" );
   System.out.println ( "\t\t" + sales [ 0 ] [ 0 ] );
   System.out.println ( "\t\t" + sales [ 0 ] [ 1 ] );
   System.out.println ( "\t\t" + sales [ 0] [ 2 ] );
   System.out.println ( "\t\t" + sales [ 1] [ 0 ] );
   System.out.println ( "\t\t" + sales [ 1] [ 1 ] );
   System.out.println ( "\t\t" + sales [ 1] [ 2 ] );
   System.out.println ( "\t\t" + sales [2 ] [ 0 ] );
   System.out.println ( "\t\t" + sales [2 ] [ 1 ] );
   System.out.println ( "\t\t" + sales [2 ] [ 2 ] );
   System.out.println ( "------------------------------------------");

}
}
```

Diagram 4

Program Output

```
C:\Examples>javac Sales.java

C:\Examples>java Sales

KBL PLC sales data for the period 1997-1999
---------------------------------------------------------
                1200590
                1700000
                2190790
                1690587
                2567879
                2800543
                1900000
                2900854
                3000600
---------------------------------------------------------
```

Diagram 4A

Program Output

```
C:\Examples>javac Sales.java

C:\Examples>java Sales

    KBL PLC sales data for the period 1997-1999
-----------------------------------------------------------------

Year        UK          EU          USA
.....       ....        .....       ......

1997        1200590     1700000     2190790
1998        1690587     2567879     2800543
1999        1900000     2900854     3000600
-----------------------------------------------------------------
```

Diagram 5A

Sales . java

```
class Sales
 {
  public static void main ( String [ ] args )
   {
    int [ ] [ ]sales;
    sales =  new int [ 3 ] [  3 ];

    sales [ 0 ] [ 0 ] = 1200590;
    sales [ 0 ] [ 1 ] = 1700000 ;
    sales [ 0 ] [ 2 ] = 2190790;
    sales [ 1 ] [ 0 ] = 1690587;
    sales [ 1 ] [ 1 ] = 2567879;
    sales [ 1 ] [ 2 ] = 2800543;
    sales [ 2 ] [ 0 ] = 1900000;
    sales [ 2 ] [ 1 ] = 2900854;
    sales [ 2 ] [ 2 ] = 3000600;

    System.out.println ( );
    System.out.println ("       KBL PLC sales data for the period 1997-1999" );
    System.out.println ("------------------------------------------------------------------\n" );
    System.out.println ("Year" + "\t\t" + "UK" + "\t\t" + "EU" + "\t\t" + "USA" );
    System.out.println ("......" +"\t\t" + "...." + "\t\t" +" ...." + "\t\t" +".......\n" );
    System.out.println ("1997" + "\t\t" + sales [0] [0] + "\t\t" + sales [0] [1] + "\t\t" + sales [0][2] );
    System.out.println ("1998" +"\t\t"  + sales [1] [0]  + "\t\t" + sales[1] [1] + "\t\t" + sales [1][2]);
    System.out.println ("1999" +"\t\t"  + sales [2] [0]  + "\t\t" + sales[2] [1] + "\t\t"+ sales [2][2]);
    System.out.println ("------------------------------------------------------------------\n");
 }
 }
```

Diagram 5

Exercise

The aim of this programming exercise is to enable you to gain further experience of arrays. You have to use the table shown below, and manipulate the data stored in this matrix in the following ways:
. Create a two-dimensional array to **store** commission data paid to sales representatives, working for Friendly Insurance PLC, in Asia, Europe and USA, during the period 1997-1999. Your program should create a matrix and store all information shown below.

Friendly Insurance PLC Commission paid 1997-1999
....

Year	Asia	Europe	USA
......	......	....	......
1997	45000	42580	35060
1998	44000	25678	28005
1999	39000	29008	34006

....

. Work out the total (sum) for each trading area separately, and display each sum in the appropriate column below the dotted line as shown above.

. Calculate the average commission value for Asia, Europe and the USA separately.

. Display the average value for each trading area, just below the sum figures for each area.

. Draw a dotted line to complete the new matrix with sum and average values added to it.

. Create a new heading as shown below:

　　　　　Friendly Insurance PLC
　　　　　...............................

. Create a white line underneath it.

. Work out the average commission for all trading areas as one figure, and display it in the following format, under the white line created above:

　Commission paid to sales representatives 1997-1999

　Average Commission =

The required figure should be computed by your program, and place it next to = to make it an equation. Also create an empty line (white line), so that underneath, you can display:

　　Commission earned by American sales representatives in 1998 =

　　Place the correct figure, just after = in the above to make it an equation.

Note – Design display format to include all above requirements. This will enable you to build up your overall skills, and increase your confidence.

Chapter 5

Conditions Testing

Computers' strength lies in their ability to repeat groups of instructions at electronic speeds within a program, and to choose which instructions to execute first.

Some programming techniques have been developed to exploit a computer's ability and power, which enable programmers to control the flow of execution. Therefore, programmers can include different means by which a group of instructions can be repeated, and executed accordingly. You can design a program which has a mechanism for controlling how many times an instruction or group of instructions is to be obeyed by the computer. You can direct your program to execute another part of the program. You can tell the computer to do something a fixed number of times and so on. You have to build a **control structure** in your program by means of loops and conditional statements as demonstrated in this chapter.

Until now, the programs you have met were simple in the context of carrying out instructions according to a sequence, without any branches and loops, and without testing any conditions whatsoever. Such programs have limited practical application, but they lay the foundation for building more useful programs, involving **loops** which can repeat an instruction or set of instructions until a pre-set condition is met, or an instruction is repeated a fixed number of times.

Control Structures Statements

Statement Type	Action to follow
. if	Allows conditional execution of a statement/s
. if ..... else	Allows selection from two alternatives
. for loop	Allows fixed number of times repetition
. while loop	Evaluate the condition first. If it is true then the statement is executed. Repeated the test until the condition is evaluated to false (zero value)
. do .... While loop	Executes the statement first, and then evaluates test condition. Repeat the test until it is false
. nested loop	Allows inside loop to be executed unknown number of times for each execution of the outer loop
. case, switch	Allows multiple selection
. break	Allows early exit from the loop –jump statement
. continue	Returns control to the start of a loop's block

Table 1

You can incorporate branch instructions in your program, which can enable you to re-direct the flow of your program to another part of the program. I have summarised control structure statements in Table 1 above. To those who are familiar with C ++, you will have noticed that the content of the table 1 has been derived from C++.

Relational & Boolean Operators

Relational operators are used when testing the relationship between values, under some given conditions. In general terms, these are used to compare things with each other.

The **boolean** type variables **true** and **false** can be used in a test to describe the result of the test. The **boolean** values are not integers. You cannot treat them as integers or cast to or from other type. The true and false are also keywords, which you can use in your code. The relational operators are given in table 2 below.

Relational Operators

Relational Operator	Test Condition
==	equal to
!=	not equal to
<	less than
<=	less than or equal to
>	greater than
>=	greater than or equal to

Table 2

Consider the following two examples:

Example 1

A > B - that is A is greater than B

- When it is written as a conditional statement, then this will perform a magnitude test. When it is evaluated as **true** then a specific line of action is followed.

- When the condition is evaluated as **false**, an alternative action is taken. Like C++, Java has the above relational operators, which enable you to test given conditions.

It is worth knowing that through this condition, we are testing the magnitude of two variables namely, **A** and **B**, and then it returns a **boolean value** (true or false).

Example 2

> **. a ! = 10 - read it as a is not equal to 10**

• When it is written as a conditional statement, it will perform an inequality test, and thus it will return a value in terms of equality rather than magnitude. If it is evaluated as **true** then a specific line of action is followed. On the other hand, if the condition is evaluated as **false**, the opposite action is followed.

• For equality testing use = = (double equal sign). For instance (9 = = 10) will test equality. In this case, the test will return 0 value as it is **false.**

(Recall: do not use = = to compare two strings. A Word of warning!)

Logical Operators

Until now, you have used simple conditions. Relational operators can be used to create compound conditions, combined with logical operators.

Logical Operators

Logical Operator	How to read it	Definition
&&	AND	a **&&** b must evaluate to 1, that is return nonzero value when both **a** and **b** evaluate to 1 →logical truth
||	OR	a || b must evaluate to 1, when **a** and b evaluate to 1→ logical truth **Also** a || b must evaluate to 1, when either **a** or **b** evaluate to1 →logical truth
!	NOT	! a must evaluate to1 when either **a** evaluate to **0**

! stands for negation operator

Table 3

We can draw the same conclusions from our Truth Tables shown in table 4 . These tables may help you to implement these rules, when testing compound conditions. These tables are from Boolean Algebra. In Boolean Algebra. Truth values are manipulated in accordance with these rules. The value of **1** for **true**, and the value of **0** for **false**.

Truth Table

AND Truth Table			OR Truth Table			NOT Truth Table	
a	**b**	**a && b**	**a**	**b**	**a || b**	**a**	**! a**
1	1	1	1	1	1	1	0
1	0	0	1	0	1	0	1
0	1	0	0	1	1		
0	0	0	0	0	0		

1 = logical truth   0 = logical false

Table 4

The if statement

It allows conditional execution of a statement and a block of statements, as the case may be. Of course, the keyword **if** is required in the construction of the **if** conditional statement. To execute an **if** statement, the test condition must evaluate to **TRUE** or **FALSE**. The syntax for a simple **if** statement is shown below:

```
if ( test condition )          // if  keyword
   {
      statement  ;
      do this task ;
   }
```

SalesAccount.java

The program is aimed at demonstrating how to implement a simple **if** statement. The program generates a random number. If the number is greater than 1000,. then it is displayed as: **New Sales Account Number** = **?** (random number is to be printed where **?** is shown).

Explanation

- The variable declaration is **int account**, because it is desired to generate an integer value.

- In order to generate the desired random number, the use of method called **random ( )** is made. This method is from the **java . lang . Math class**.

- The random ( ) method generates, in the first place, numbers in the range **0. 0 to 1. 0**. This means that if you do not convert it into an **int type**, it will produce only a number less than 1, which is not required here.

- Since the required number has to be greater than 1000 and **int type**, you have to place **(int)** before this random ( ) method.

- It is also required that the number must be greater than 1000. For this reason, you have to multiply it with a number that will generate a large number.

- I have multiplied it with 5000 and also added 10. **Why ?** There is no other reason, except to show you that you do not only have to multiply it, but you can also carry out such a manipulation. The whole idea is to generate a number, which is a whole number and greater than 1000. You may arrive at another random number by another arithmetic manipulation of random ( ) method.

- The code for our requirement is shown below:

  account = (int) (java.lang.Math.random ( ) *5000 + 10 ;

- The **if** test begins with the keyword **if** which is followed by the condition within the ( ), that is **(account > 1000)**, without the " **;** " as it is not yet the end of the conditional statement. **Why?** Because, the conditional statement is not yet fully stated. The second part of this conditional statement is to display/ print the randomly generated required number. The code for it:

  System.out.println ("\nNew Sales Account Number = " + account);

This ends with the **;** as it completes the whole conditional statement.

- Now you should examine the program in diagram 1. The diagram 1A shows you the program output, so that you can compare the code with its desired output.

Program Output

C:\Examples>javac SalesAccount.java

C:\Examples>java SalesAccount

New Sales Account Number = 1373   **// Outcome of test is highlighted - true**

Diagram 1A

SalesAccount.java

```
class SalesAccount
{
  public static void main (String[ ]args)

{
  int account;
  account = ( int ) ( java.lang.Math.random ( ) * 5000 +10 );
   if

    (account > 1000)                                      // greater than 1000
     System.out.println (  "\nNew Sales Account Number =  " + account );
}
}
```

Diagram 1

. What happens when a test condition is false?

The above program is not designed to evaluate TRUE and FALSE . It evaluates only nonzero value, that is logical TRUE. To take any of the two separate actions, on the basis of TRUE or FALSE, you have to construct **bi-conditional if---- else** statements. The syntax for if ---- else is as follows:

The if ---- else test general format

```
    if                              // Keyword
        ( test condition  )          // no semicolon needed
      {
        perform  task 1;
      }
    else                             // keyword

      perform  task 2;
      .
      .
```

I will explain it now:

. **task 1** will be completed, when the test condition is evaluated to a logical true, which is a nonzero value. It means that the code for task 1 will be executed.

- **task 2** will be completed, when the test condition is evaluated to a logical false, which is a zero value. In this case, the code for task 2 will be executed.

SalesAcc . java

The purpose of this program is to demonstrate the application of if ---else statement. The program makes use of **java . lang . Math . random ( )** method as discussed above to generate a number, which is less than 1000. When the required number is encountered, it is printed as New Sales Account Number = ; otherwise, the program generates the message: " Wrong Number! Run it again ! "

Explanation

- **account = (int) (java.lang.Math.random ( )* 50+10);**

The above statement generates the required random number. You have already met this method. The number generated is then tested against the condition: **If   (account < = 1000)**. The test condition has two parts.

- The task 1: System . out . println ("\nNew Sales Account Number = " + account);
  This statement is executed, only when the test condition is evaluated to a logical **true,** which is a **nonzero** value. It means that **"New Sales Account Number =   "** will be displayed. The execution of the program will cease.

- The task 2: If the generated random number is not the required number then the test condition is evaluated to a logical false, which is a zero value. The code which follows the keyword **else** is then executed. In this case, it is the following statement that will be executed.

- **System . out . println ("\n Wrong Number! Run it again !");**

and the message, " Wrong Number! Run it again ! " will be displayed.

- The program in diagram 2 was 'run' twice to test its working. During the **Run 1**, the test condition was evaluated to logical false. On the other hand, the **Run 2**, generated a random number that was within the required limits, and that the test condition evaluated to logical true. The outcomes of both tests are shown in diagram 2 A, so that you can study these and relate these to the code in diagram 2.

The iteration

Iteration is the process of repetition of a statement or a block of statements in a program. In involves a **loop**, which is repeated or iterated until a specified condition is met. There are three types of loops. These are **for loop, while loop and do .... While loop.**

SalesAcc . java

```
class SalesAcc
{
  public static void main (String[ ]args)

{
  int account;
  account =  (int) (java.lang.Math.random ( )* 50+10);
   if

    (account <= 1000)                          // Less than or equal to 1000

      System.out.println( "\nNew Sales Account Number = " + account);

      else

          System.out.println ("\n Wrong Number! Run it again !");
      }
}
```

Diagram 2

Program Output

                                              // Run 1

C:\Examples>javac SalesAcc.java

C:\Examples>java SalesAcc

Wrong Number! Run it again !   // Outcome of test highlighted - Flase
....
                                              // Run 2

C:\Examples>javac SalesAcc.java

C:\Examples>java SalesAcc

New Sales Account Number = 41   // Outcome of test highlighted - True

Diagram 2A

The for Loop

It allows fixed number of times repetition, until a condition is satisfied. Its general format is as follows:

```
for ( initialisation value ; condition for the repetition of the loop ; counter to update the loop)

                                                            // for keyword
     {
          statement or a block of statements;
     }
```

Program AccNum.java

The program is designed and tested to illustrate how to implement a **for loop**. It generates a series of numbers between 1000 and 1010. These numbers are displayed as a long list, under the heading: **New Sales Account Numbers Today**. The heading has to be underlined. The whole output has to be displayed three columns away from the left of the screen (Paper). The program is listed in diagram 3 with its output.

Explanation

• **int account** – the numbers to be generated and stored in the variable account. It is of **int type** as the required numbers have to be whole numbers.

• The **for loop** begins with the keyword for. The for loop is controlled by the following condition:

```
for    ( account  = 1000 ;  account  <=  1010 ; account++ )
         ---------   ------   ------------------  -----------
             ↓          ↓            ↓                  ↓
         variable   initial value    condition         counter to update loop
                    given to variable  for the repetition   initial value 1000 of account
                    account           of loop up-to        is up-dated by 1 each time
                                      11 times             loop is repeated unit the
                                                           account holds 1010
```

• This is followed by two statements designed to display, in the required format, the output of this program.

• It is suggested that now you examine both the program and its output to understand the mechanics of the for loop.

AccNum.java

```
class AccNum
{
  public static void main (String[ ]args)

  {
    int account;

    System.out.println ( "\n\tNew Sales Account Numbers Today");
    System.out.println (     "\t-------------------------------------------\n");
    for (account =1000; account <= 1010; account++)              // for loop
     System.out.println ( "\t\t\t" + account);
     System.out.println ( "\t-------------------------------------------");
  }
}
```

Program Output

C:\Examples>javac AccNum.java

C:\Examples>java AccNum

New Sales Account Numbers Today

                    1000
                    1001
                    1002
                    1003
                    1004
                    1005
                    1006
                    1007
                    1008
                    1009
                    1010

Diagram 3

The while loop

It is executed continuously **while** some condition is **true**. It only ends when a condition becomes **false**. It is very useful where the number of repetitions is unknown. It is therefore, worth using for conditions where no action is required.

The while loop involves a two-step process:

• first the test evaluates the condition. If it evaluates to nonzero value, the statement is executed, and

• the test is repeated again.

This two- step process continues, until the test condition evaluates to zero value.

WhileRepeat.java

The program in diagram 4 illustrates the application of a **while** loop. It generates a series of 5 different whole numbers, starting from 10. These numbers are displayed/printed as a long list, under the heading: **Numbers Generated**. The heading has to be underlined. The whole output has to be displayed two columns away from the left of the screen (paper).

Explanation

• **int Repeat = 10 ;** - this statement sets the initial value to 10, where Repeat is a variable of **int** type. This holds the numbers to be generated.

• In accordance with the test condition: **while (Repeat < 15)**, the program begins to execute the loop.

• Since the initial value is less than 15, the test condition is evaluated as nonzero, that is **true**.

• Because of this truth, the control is passed on to the next statement within this **while** loop. This statement is: **Repeat ++ ;**. Its execution means to increase the initial value of Repeat from 10 t0 11.

• Next the control is passed on to statement: **System.out. println ("\t\t\t" + Repeat);** The purpose of this statement is to display or print the current value stored in variable Repeat. At this stage, it is 11. This value is displayed under the heading as required. Note that in this example, headings are outside The **while** loop. **What happens next ?**

• Since the condition is evaluated true, the loop is repeated again. The whole process is repeated four times, at each iteration, incrementing the current value stored in Repeat, and displaying it as it happens.

• When the current value is 16, the condition is evaluated to zero, that is **false**. At this stage, the loop is ended, and program execution is terminated.

WhileRepeat.java

```
class WhileRepeat                                    // while loop application
{
  public static void main (String[ ]args)
 {
  System.out.println ("\n\tA demonstration of While loop working\n");
  System.out.println ("\t ........................…………………….\n");
  System. out.println("\t\t Numbers Generated\n");
  System.out.println ("\t\t …………………….\n");
  int Repeat = 10;
  while ( Repeat < 15)
  {
   Repeat ++;
  System.out. println ("\t\t\t" + Repeat);
  }
  System.out.println ("\t\t ……………..\n");
}
}
```

Program Output

```
C:\Examples>javac WhileRepeat.java

C:\Examples>java WhileRepeat

    A demonstration of While loop working
    ……………………………………………

        Numbers Generated
        …………………….
             .
            11
            12
            13
            14
            15
        …………………….
```

Diagram 4

Now you should match the program and its output in diagram 4 above.

. The initial value is 10. Why did the system not display it as first value?

The answer is simple. When the loop began, it started with 10, and found it true (less than 10), and passed on the control to the next statement. When this statement was executed, the current value was incremented from 10 to 11. Thus, the initial value was incremented after the test. It should also be noted that the displaying of value is also done at the end of the test at each repeat.

. **What will happen if the initial value is 10, and the for loop is repeated 5 times?**

In this case, as the initial value is evaluated to nonzero, the value is displayed. The initial value is increment after the print statement, and the loop is repeated till the condition is evaluated to zero.

The following code illustrates this answer. Now analyse it for yourself.

```
for ( Repeat = 10 ; Repeat < 15 ; Repeat ++ )
{
   System.out. println ("\t\t\t" + Repeat);
}

      This will display values 10,11,12,13,14
```

Comparison between for and while loops

. The **for** loop repeats a set of instructions for a specified number of times. At each repetition, the control is given back to the **for** statement, and the whole process is repeated for a given number of times.

. The **while** loop evaluates the condition first. The **while** statement is not executed, if the condition is evaluated as **false** (zero). It performs the test for n number of times as long as the test condition is evaluated as **true** (nonzero).

The do --- while loop

The While loop executes the statement first, and then evaluates the test condition. It repeats the test until it is false.

. The following is the distinction between while and do --- while loop

The **do --- while** loop executes the statement at least once, whilst the **while** loop does not do so, be cause the condition has to be evaluated before the statement is executed. The **do --- while** loop iterates at least once, regardless of whether the condition is evaluated as true or false.

The general format of the do --- while loop is shown below.

```
                    do
                    {
                      statement a ;
                      statement b ;
                        :
                        :
                      statement  z;
                    }
                       while ( condition ) ;
              test condition ⌐
```

Program RepeatDo.java

The program demonstrates the technique of implementing the **do --- while** loop, by way of creating and displaying a series of whole numbers between 10–20 (inclusive). The program also generates square and cube values of each number within this series. It displays these in the desired format as a table consists of three columns, equally separated from each other. See diagram 5.

Explanation

- The variable **int x** is initialised to 10 outside the loop. Outside the loop are also 4 statements to print the required headings, so that the generated numbers and their computed values can be printed under the appropriate columns.

- When the program reaches the keyword **do**, the loop begins. A block of two statements within the { } are executed as the first iteration.

- At the end of the first iteration, the **while condition** is evaluated. The condition is evaluated as **true**.

- Thus, the loop entered the block of statements again, and repeated the execution of the block, until the while condition is **false**. The loop is terminated and the last statement of this program:

    System.out.println ("\t--");

is executed and the program execution finished.

- It is suggested that now you compare this program and its output to the last program and its output. This will help you further to understand the working of these two loops.

Program RepeatDo.java

```
class RepeatDo                                    // do — while loop application
{
   public static void main (String[ ]args)
    {
   int x = 10;
   System.out.println ("\n\t Number, Square and Cube Generation");
   System.out.println (  "\t-------------------------------------------\n");
   System.out.println ("\tNumber" + "\t\tSquare" + "\t\tCube\n");
   System.out.println ("\t------" + "\t\t------" + "\t\t----\n");

    do

      {
      System.out.println ("\t" + x + "\t\t" + (x*x)+ "\t\t" + ( x*x*x));
      x++;

      }
      while (x <= 20);
      System.out.println ( "\t-------------------------------------------");
}
}
```

Program Output

C:\Examples>java RepeatDo

    Number, Square and Cube Generation

Number	Square	Cube
-------	-------	------
10	100	1000
11	121	1331
12	144	1728
13	169	2197
14	196	2744
15	225	3375
16	256	4096
17	289	4913
18	324	5832
19	361	6859
20	400	8000

Diagram 5

NestedLoop . java

```
class NestedLoop
{
  public static void main (String[ ]args)

{
  int x = 169;
  int y = 309;
  int z = 240;
  int max;

    if ( x > y )
     if ( x > z ) max = y ;                    // x > y and x > z

      else max = z;                            // z >= x > y
       else
        if ( y > z ) max = y ;                 // y >= x and y > z

          else max = z ;                       // z >= y >= x

    System.out.println ("\n The largest number = " + max ) ;

}
}
```

Program Output

C:\Examples>javac NestedLoop.java

C:\Examples>java NestedLoop

 The largest number = 309

Diagram 6

Nested Loops

Nested loops mean loops inside each other. Thus, you can have a particular loop within the compound statement of another loop. A nested loop occurs when a conditional statement of a particular loop is used within the conditional statement of another loop. There is no limit to how many loops you can nest in a program. If you use too many loops, it can be very complex to sort them out. It is advisable to keep the program simple. The mechanics of nesting loops is that the inside loop is executed *n* times for each execution of the outer loop.

NestedLoop.java

The program in diagram 6 is designed and tested to exemplify the application of nested loops. In this program three variables are given their initial values. The task is to pick up the largest number, and display this number as : **The largest number =** . Note the blank space for the number to be entered by the system.

Explanation

- There are three variables **x**, **y**, and **z** of **int** type with their initial values. The fourth variable **max** is to hold the largest number.

- In a nested loop, in order to parse the statement, each **else** is matched with the unmatched **if**. This way, the system easily deciphers the code.

- The nested loop starts by testing the first condition (x > y). The test fails.

- The second **else** matches (y > z) . Once again, the test fails.

- The control passes on to the third else which assigns **z** to **max**.

Diagram 6 also provides useful information (see //) , so that you can analyse how conditions are evaluated in this nested loop. The program output is in the same diagram 6.

Switch-case statement with break

You can use switch-case statement with break, when the **if** --- **else** nesting may be difficult to follow and implement. A switch statement can enable you to easily code a program which involves multiple choices.

. How does it operate?

- The switch statement starts by evaluating the switch variable. It searches for its value amongst the cases listed. If a match is made with the variable in **case 1**, then statement(s) in case 1 will be executed.

- If a match is not made, it will look for a match until the variable value amongst the cases is found.

- When a match is made, then a statement (s) , in that particular case will be executed. If no match is found, then the **default** statement will be executed until the **break** statement. If there is no default statement, then the program finds its exit through the } .

Reason for break statement

• When a match is made in a particular case and statement (s) is/ are executed, it is the break statement that causes the remaining switch-case to be skipped. Without the break statement, all other statements from the next case will be executed.

• If the next case does not include a break statement, then all statements from this case, which follow it will also be executed. It is therefore important to include a break statement at the end of each case to avoid disorder.

• The general format of switch-case and break statements is as follows:

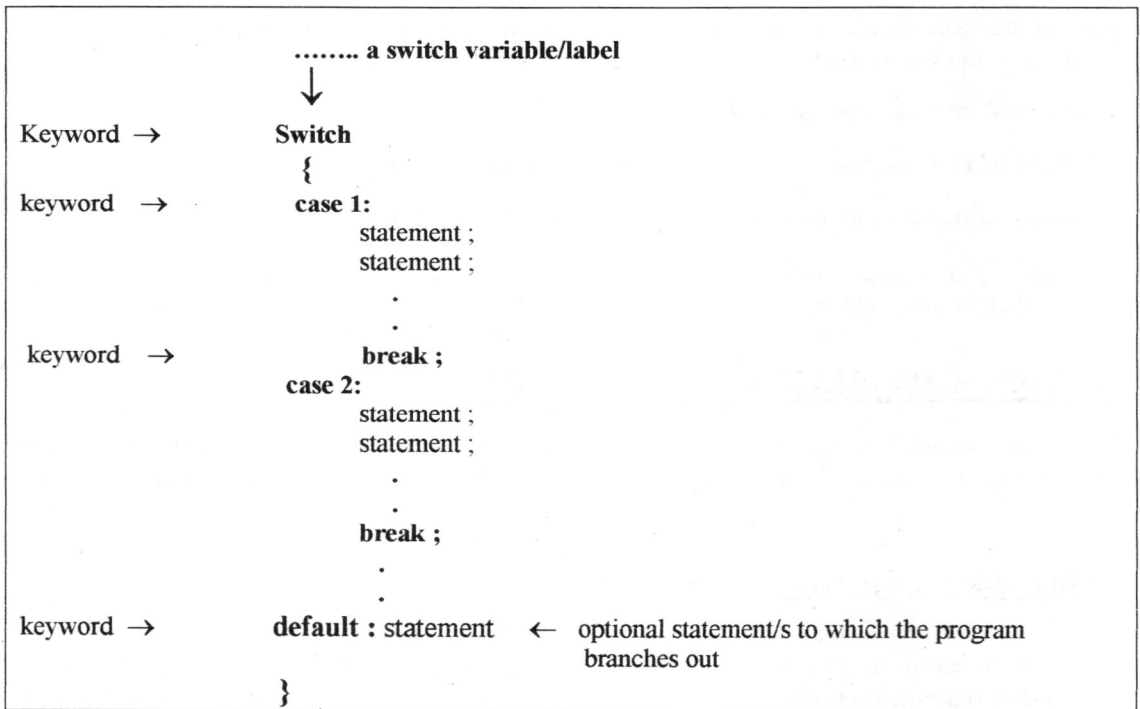

```
                ........ a switch variable/label
                        ↓
Keyword →        Switch
                {
keyword →           case 1:
                        statement ;
                        statement ;
                            .
                            .
keyword →               break ;
                    case 2:
                        statement ;
                        statement ;
                            .
                            .
                        break ;
                            .
                            .
keyword →        default : statement    ←   optional statement/s to which the program
                                             branches out
                }
```

Figure 1: Switch-case-break statements relationship

TestSwitch . java

The program shown in diagram 7 is designed to demonstrate the use of switch structure. The program handles three cases, which involve three different calculations and displays the outcomes as required.

Explanation

• Outside the switch, initial values are assigned to variables. The formulae which will be applied to calculate values are also given. A **for** statement is set outside the switch. The **int i** in this **for** statement generates variable values which are inserted in the **switch (   )**. The **i** is the switch variable or label, which handles the switch statement.

• The **switch (i)** specifies the variable that is to be tested. Here, it is **i.** This switch statement is followed by {, which is followed by a number of statements that are followed by }. Within these two curly brackets is the block of statements.

• Within this block of statements, are cases. These cases or choices, namely **case 1:**, **case 2:** , and **case 3:**

• When **i =1** matches with the **case 1:** , the following statement is executed.

System.out.println ("\nAverage Value = " + average);

This statement will result in displaying on a new line Average Value = 7. 0. You can see this in the program output in diagram 7A. The average value is calculated outside the switch statement, but it is displayed when switch variable (i) is matched with case 1:

• When the computer has finished the execution of the above statement, the control is passed on to the next statement which is a **break;**

• This process is repeated until the last break statement is encountered and there are no more cases to match.

• The structure of statements within the program is similar to the statements you have learnt about in this chapter.

Keyboard Input

If you are familiar with C++, you know that it is not an issue how to input data from the keyboard. In Java, data input from the keyboard is a serious drawback. For instance, entering a response to a question, using the keyboard, prompted by the program is a nightmare, whilst in C++ or BASIC or any other High Level language it is ever so easy. **What is the reason for it ?**

Java programming is graphical oriented. Java programs have facilities for user input from a dialogue box. There are easy methods of data input into Java programs running on the Internet thus, in this case, it is not an issue. In real the world Java programmers hardly ever encounter key input. On the other hand, If you were learning switch statement or condition testing, in C++, it would have been much easier and quicker to introduce you to condition testing by direct input from the keyboard.

TestSwitch . java

```
public class TestSwitch
{
 public static void main (String [ ] args)
{
  int a = 6, b= 5, c = 10;
  double  average = ( a + b + c )/3;
  double x = (( a*a ) + ( average ))/5;

 for ( int i =0;i <4; i++ )
{
 switch ( i )
{
   case 1:
          System.out.println ( "\nAverage Value = " + average );
    break;
   case 2:
           System . out. println ( "\nThe calculated value = " + x );
    break;
    case 3:
            System .out. println  ( "\n\tNumber" + "\t\tCube" );
            System .out .println  ( "\t...............………..." );
   do
   {
           System . out. println ( "\t"+ a+ "\t\t"+( a*a ));
           a++;
   } while ( a<= 10 );
           System .out .println ("\t...............…………...");
}
}
}
}
```

Diagram 7

Program output

Average Value = 7. 0

The calculated value = 8. 6

Number	Cube
6	36
7	49
8	64
9	81
10	100

Diagram 7A

Exercise

1. Write and test a program in order to demonstrate how to use:

    • a while loop. The initial value is **int 11**. Use this loop to generate numbers 12,13,14, 15 and 16. For each number 11 to 16, work out values by applying (number *3/2). The work out values are whole numbers - integer type.

    • display the program output in the following format;

How to exit a loop

Number	(Repeat*3/2)
11	?
12	.
13	.
14	.
15	.
16	.

The Required end has reached which is

You must make use of special characters (\n and \t) in order to design the format as shown above.

Chapter 6

Working with Objects and Classes

Since the beginning of computing, program definitions have been emphasising that a program is a set of instructions that tell a computer what to do. On the other hand, the OOP approach emphasises the importance of objects in programs. These objects work together in order to perform the task for which the program is written. In this chapter, some basic OOP tools are discussed.

In chapter 1, you were introduced to the basic ideas of class, object, instances of classes, data, methods, attributes and inheritance. These concepts form the basis of our practical work in this chapter and elsewhere in this book. However, to be able to work with objects, you should recognise the importance of three major characteristics of objects. These are identity, state and behaviour of objects.

Identity, state and behaviour

Attributes are specific characteristics that belong to a particular object. The specific traits of an object enable us to differentiate one object from another object. For example, consider a bookshop, where a computer system is at the heart of its stock control system. The stock control system uses OOP techniques, and has the following structure of stock control file.

Superclass: stock

Subclasses: computer book, business book, science book, maths book, languages.

Objects   :   many different titles under each sub class.

Attributes :   title, author, publisher, ISBN, cover, price, minimum level, maximum level,
             current stock, quantity order, date order, date received.
In order to work with OOP, it is essential to establish three key attributes of an object. These key

attributes are known as: • **object's identity**   • **object's state**   • **object's behaviour (methods)**

.Object's identity

All individual objects are instances of a class. In practical terms, in this example, **ISBN** is a unique number for each book. Thus, an object's identity is easy to determine. Since all individual objects in the stock control system are instances of a stock class, they all have different identities. ISBN 190 1197 000X and ISBN 190 1197 999 are two different identities for two different books.

.Object's state

A book's attributes namely, title, author, publisher, ISBN, cover, and price are given before the publication of any book. Once the book is published, these attributes are permanent in its current format. In this stock control system, there are other attributes attached to each book in order to manage stock efficiently. These are:

minimum level, maximum level, current stock, quantity order, order date, received date.

These values can be changed when necessary. In this stock control system, each object (book) stores information on its attributes, and this information gives its current **state.** Usually, the stock changes over time, and so does the current state of the object.

. Object's behaviour (methods)

The word behaviour does not have the same meaning in this context as it is generally understood. It is rather confusing jargon. A class is created for the accomplishment of a particular task. It cannot do so, without creating behaviour. In a Java program, behaviour gives information on different components of a class. Each component of a class is in fact a method, which performs a specific task towards the completion of the whole task for which the program is designed. (a Java program is a class)

. How does a specific change occur in an object's current state in a stock control or any other real world system? It is a result of a message sent to the object (Jargon). It sounds complicated, but it is not. I explain it below.

In chapter 1, in the definition of a class, it is stated:

. **A class contains both objects and methods. These methods operate on objects.**

In its simplest term, a method performs a certain task. It is inside the class. A class can have several objects, and several methods. If you work with objects, you must use methods.

. Now, assume that the current quantity order level is set to 4, and you wish to change it to 6. This can be achieved by the method called **orderQt ( )**. This may take the form:

$$\text{ISBN . orderQt (6);}$$

$$\downarrow \qquad \downarrow \qquad \downarrow$$

object   method   parameter/value

. In this case, this statement is a method, which handles the task of altering the value of quantity order level. A behaviour can have more than one statement in order to handle a specific task within the object. It can have several methods. Behaviour is needed for a class to accomplish task for which it was created in the first place.

Note that it has to be a specific ISBN. This will change the current quantity order level 4 to 6 books. This what it means that a method operates on the object.

. Once again in the jargon, the programmer sends a message to the orderQt ( ) method, which operates on a specific object, with the value/ parameter 6. The change in the state of the object is a consequence of this message sent to the object. It only means that the quantity order level has changed from 4 to 6 by this method.

Figure 1: Stock inheritance hierarchy

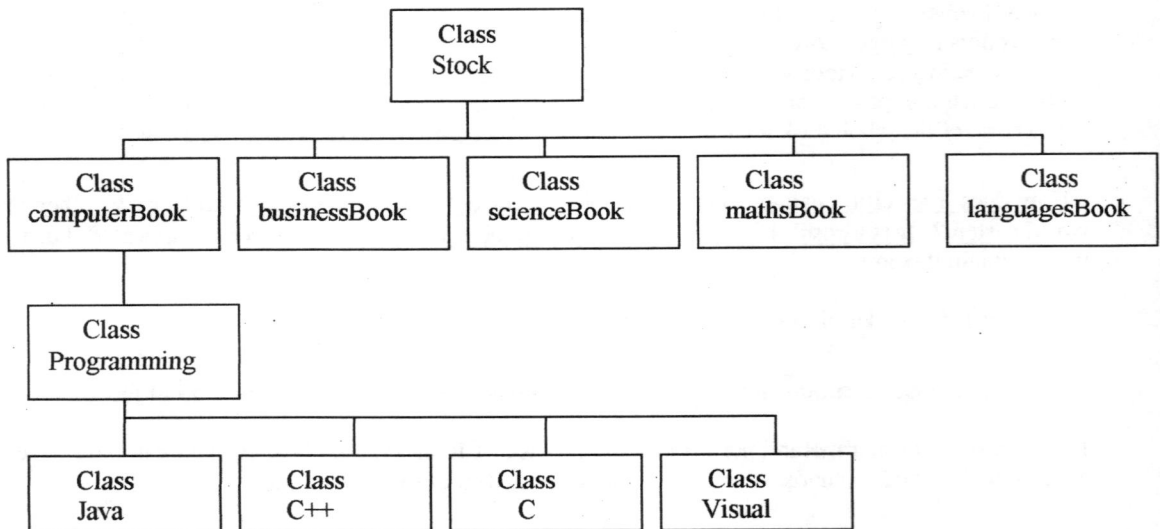

Inheritance hierarchy depicted in diagram 1 above. It is a **collection** of all sub classes derived from the parent or superclass **Stock**.

At the top of the pyramid is the superclass of all classes below it. The path from a particular class, say from **Class Java** to its all ancestors can be traced by **inheritance chain** as shown below.

Class Java → **Class Programming** →**Class computerBook** →**Class Stock**

Inheritance chain is a path from any particular class to all its ancestors.

. Inheritance chain for Staff inheritance hierarchy is shown in Figure 2 below.

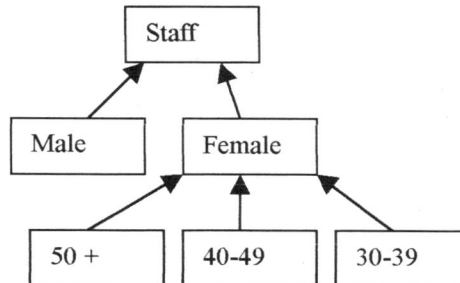

Figure 2

30 - 39, 40 – 49 and 50 –59 years are age groups.

.Creating Objects from a Class of Objects

The following explanation leads to the creation of objects and shows how to use them in programs.

Class of Objects definition

```
public class Stock        // Stock is a class of objects.
                          // public implies that class Stock can be used by any program for making
                             use of Stock objects
{
                 // it has no attributes
                 //  it has no methods
}
```

Diagram 1

.What can it do in its current format?

It cannot perform any programming task, except to show you that it is a class of Stock objects (**class of objects**). How? You must know by now that a class is a template for a set of objects which, of course, share some common features. For instance, all objects in this class are books.

. You also know that an object must have an identity, some attribute(s), and behaviour (method/s). Therefore, it requires more information to be useful. The diagram 2 includes further requirements.

. In this diagram, **String variable** called title has been declared. The **title** is indeed, an attribute that is attached to the object. Each book has its title. A number of books can have the same title, but there are other attributes of an object that make it a different object. For instance, each book has an unique ISBN. It is one attribute out of 12 attributes listed above.

. public void addISBN is included. It is the behaviour/method, which has only one statement, whose purpose is to display ISBN on screen. **Void** means that this method returns **no** value.

. Do you think that the code in diagram 2 is ready to be compiled and run?

No. If you attempt to compile it, you will get the following error message: It speaks for itself – there is no method **main**. Every Java program must have method main.

```
C:\Examples>java Stock
Exception in thread "main" java .lang. No Such Method Error: main
```

Class of objects definition with one attribute and behaviour (method)

```
public class Stock          // Stock is a class of objects.
                            // public implies that class Stock can be used by any program for making
                                use of Stock objects
{

String title;               // Attribute- instance variable called title. It can store String object  title


public void  addTitle ( );  //  Behaviour (method) – this will allow you to enter title

{
    System.out.println ( "Java Simplified");

}
}
```

Diagram 2

So far so good, but;

. How do we create an object from a class of objects?

In order to create a **Stock object called computerBook**, you have to make use of the keyword called **new**. Some people call it, a special method or new operator. The **new** operator creates an instance of the class, that is an object. At the time of object creation, Java allocates memory for the object. When the object is not required, the memory is de-allocated automatically. Thus, the memory management is dynamic and automatic.

- The object is created as follows, and it can be used in a program:

$$\text{Stock computerBook } = \text{ new Stock ( );}$$

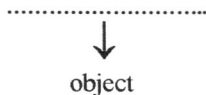

object

- Having created the object, you must give it its attribute, that is its title. This is achieved by the following statement:

$$\text{computerBook . title } = \text{``Java Simplified'';}$$

object   object's attribute   attribute's value

- the **dot .** – It is essential when you have to refer to an instance variable.

- The object must also have its behaviour or method, to display its title. The code for it:

$$\text{computerBook . addTitle ( ) ;}$$

Note again the use of **dot**. The following is another example of working with objects.

Creating an Object from a Class

```
public class Employee {          // Employee is a template for all objects ( employees in this class)

  Employee director1;            // director1 is an instance variable which refers to an employee
                                    Object. Director1 is of Employee type

Employee director1 = new Employee ( );

                  // creates an instance of Employee class called director1 – an employee object
}
```

Diagram 3

This **class Employee** is an abstract or super class, which cannot be instantiated itself. It is therefore necessary to create an instance of a particular employee to work with it. The **instance** of class Employee:

Employee director1 = new Employee ( );

This has created an instance of the class Employee, and stores this instance in a variable called **director1** of Employee type. Here, **director1** is an instance of Employee class. Thus, it is an employee object. It is assigned to the variable of type Employee.

. You may have to create several instances of a single class. In addition, you may have to specify their initial values, as shown in the example below:

$$\text{director1 . name} = \text{``John Baker''} ;$$

↓	↓	↓	↓	↓	↓
object	dot notation	variable	assignment operator	value for the variable name	to end statement

. To work with an object, you must also call a **method.** For example to pay this director, you have to call a method: **director1. pay ( );** Note again the use of **dot** in this statement.

The use of keyword *new* (also called **new** method) results in three things:

. an **object** is created,

. **memory** is allocated for the created object, and

. a **constructor method** is called automatically. It is of the same class to which the object itself belongs. It handles the work that is needed to create an object.

Constructor Methods

. Constructor methods are special methods. They are not like other methods you have met so far.

. These methods do not return a value, but other methods do so.

. A constructor method can have no, one or more parameters.

. A class can have more than one constructor method.

. A constructor method (or just constructor) always has the same name as the class name.

. A constructor method initialises new objects when they are created.

The statement: **Employee director1 = new Employee ( );** creates a new Employee object called **director1**.

A constructor method (or just a constructor) initialises any variables for the object created. If you do not define any constructor methods for a class in your program, the class will inherit at least one constructor method from the super class. This inherited constructor method will not inherit any arguments from its super class. You can have several constructor methods in a class.

. How to define a constructor method?

The constructor definition is exemplified by the following two examples. **Example 1**:

```
public  Stock  ( String t , int min )
    {
        title  = t;                    // instance variable giving an initial state
        MinimLevel = min;              // instance variable  giving an initial state
    }
```

It can be used to initialise objects of Stock class. The instance variables are given their initial state. This constructor method could be called, if a string and integer were sent as arguments with the **new** statement, such as:

Stock computerBook = new Stock ("C++ Simplified", 4) ;

Example 2:

```
public CricketScore (   )
    {
        player  =  " John ";
        highestScore  = 101;
    }
```

This constructor would be called when a statement as shown below is met. It contains no arguments within (   ).

CricketScore Highest = new CricketScore ( );

Class methods

. Class methods are available to all instances of the class. These can also be made available to other classes. When is it best to use a class method?

. It is best to use a class method, when it cannot affect an instance of the class. How to make a method into a class method? The class method general format is shown below:

static	type	variable	(argument) ;	// keyword is essential here
↑	↑	↑	↑	
keyword	variable type	name of variable	list of values	

Example of creating a class method

```
static int average ( int a, int b, int c, int d  )

    {

            system . out . print (  " The average value  =   " +   a  + b + c + d )/4;

    }
```

• The application of class methods is also demonstrated under converting variables to objects and vice versa, later on in this chapter.

A meaning of inheritance

This topic was introduced in chapter 1 initially. It is now the right time to explore it. In chapter 1, I have given two examples of inheritance hierarchy. In one example, the superclass is train. From this superclass, goods and passenger subclasses are derived. From the subclass passenger, two further subclasses namely main and local are derived. The example is simple, and it clearly demonstrates the core relationship between all kinds of trains – they are all trains. I can say, all trains belong to the same family called train. This relationship is the distinctive feature of inheritance. I can call a train an object. I can also add that all train objects are somehow like other train objects. Thus, the idea of inheritance helps to develop a number of related classes, as inheritance can be passed down from the class to another class and so on.

In case, it is not yet clear to you what is meant by a superclass and a subclass. It can be emphasised that a class that is derived from another class is called the subclass. A class from which a subclass is derived is called the superclass. You can imagine the concept in terms of **granfather** → **father** → **son**. Here, grandfather is the superclass. The **parent** → **child** analogy is also used to describe the relationship between superclass (it is also called the **base class)** in the inheritance hierarchy.

Inheritance & classes

From a practical point of view, it is important to have some basic understanding of inheritance hierarchy in Java. In Java, the class hierarchy is very complicated, and there is a limited space in this book for this topic. The basic knowledge of inheritance will certainly enable you to make use of most of the classes, which come with the Java language. However, It should be born in mind:

• a class has its own attributes and behaviour (methods). In addition, it inherits both attributes and behaviour (methods) of its superclasses, that is to say all classes that are above it in the inheritance hierarchy.

The concept of inheritance hierarchy can help you to develop related classes as shown in Figure 3. In this inheritance hierarchy structure:

• the Members of Parliament is the **superclass** of Labour Members. The Labour Members is thus a subclass of Members of Parliament.

• Central Government is a subclass of Labour Members. Thus, the Central Government subclass would inherit from both the Labour Members and Members of Parliament classes. In general, that is to say, from all classes above it in this hierarchy.

• Ministers is a subclass of Central Government. It would therefore, inherit from not only Ministers class, but also all classes above Ministers class.

• The superclass also has a Conservative subclass. It is true that it is the subclass of Members of Parliament, but it has attributes and behaviour, which differ very much from the attributes and behaviour of Labour Members. Thus, these are two different classes.

• This way, inheritance hierarchy can help to create new classes of objects by defining how one class differs from the other class. The Labour Members of Parliament have very different attributes, and act differently (behaviour).

Inheritance Hierarchy

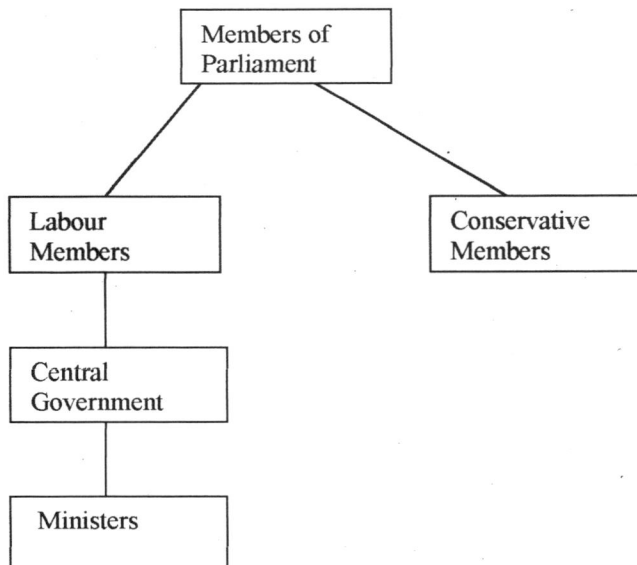

Figure 3

. The extends Keyword – When it is used in the header of a class, it means that you want to make a new class, which is derived from an **existing class** (base or the superclass). It will create a new class of objects, as demonstrated below by two examples. With extends, you can create many new classes.

Example 1

```
class LabourMembers extends membersOfParliament          // the header of a class
{
    your  code – attributes and behaviour
}
```
• This way you can create a class as the subclass of another class.

Example 2

```
class ComputerBook extends stock          // the header of a class

    {
        your code – attributes and behaviour

    }
```

. The super statement – super is a keyword. In a' statement, it refers to the immediate superclass of an object. It is the first statement of a subclass. Its use is exemplified by the following examples:

Example1

```
public ComputerBook extends Stock
  {

public ComputerBook ( String t, int y, double p )

{
   super ( t, y, p );                 // to call a constructor with comparable arguments in the
                                       superclass  Stock
}

 code ....

}
```

• As shown in this example, the **super** keyword is in the subclass called ComputerBook. **Why?**

• It is because of the fact that a subclass inherits both the attributes and behaviour of its superclass. It is therefore, necessary to link each constructor method of a subclass with each constructor method of its superclass. **What will happen, if you do not do so?**

• If you do not create an association as described above, then it is highly likely that some attributes and behaviour are wrongly set up and because of it the subclass may malfunction, and your program might not be compiled and run successfully.

• It is worth knowing that when a subclass begins without calling a superclass constructor, Java itself calls a constructor of a superclass, which has no arguments within ( ). When such a constructor is not included in the superclass, then you will get from the Java compiler an error message. The constructor without arguments is called the **default** constructor.

• **What is the best advice?**

You must include in your subclass a constructor. This will be the first statement (the call) in your subclass, calling the data fields of the superclass. It is required by the Java compiler.

Example 2

```
super . price = 14.99 ;
```

In the above example, the **super** is used with the dot in order to refer to a variable called price that is in the superclass.

Example 3

```
super .  totalValue ( ) ;
```

In this example, the **super** statement refers to a method called totalValue of the superclass.

Abstract class

• An important feature of class hierarchy is the fact that as you move up the class hierarchy, classes contain less and less information. Because of this feature, at the top of the hierarchy, the class contains so little information that it is often called an **abstract** class. But, as you move down the hierarchy , more and more information (variables and methods) are added to the classes. In other words, each class is defined for a specific purpose.

Staff inheritance hierarchy

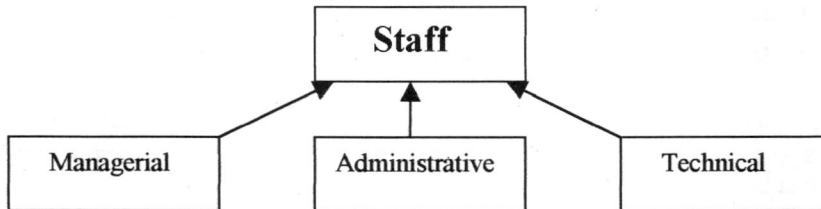

Figure 4

• As an example, consider Staff database system, which maintains managerial, administrative and technical staff monthly salary information. The system computes performance related bonuses for all employees in these categories.

• The above diagram depicts this system as staff inheritance hierarchy. The Java program will require Managerial, Technical, and Administrative classes as well as the superclass called Staff.

• The database will store the information on all three types of employees, and it will access them by referring to these through the superclass or parent class Staff.

• To calculate the bonus for each class object, the common method, that is applied to all subclasses is:

CalculateBonus ( );

• It needs no explanation to say that bonuses are calculated for each class object in all subclasses, by applying this method. But the big question is:

• How to apply this common formula to the parent class Staff ?

• It is not possible to implement this method in the parent class. It is due to the fact that the superclass Staff is an abstract class with hardly any specific information in it. It raises an important question:

• Why do we have this abstract class anyway?

• The OOP technique requires to have levels of abstraction in order to develop class hierarchy. It does make class relationship easier to follow.

• How do you relate this method to the superclass?

•When a method cannot be specified in the superclass, the keyword **abstract** is used to declare the class as an **abstract class** as shown below:

```
public abstract class Staff
{
    code
    public abstract  void CalculateBonus (   );
}
```

• You can have several abstract methods in a class. The implementation of an abstract method is in subclasses of the class that contains the abstract method.

• Anyway, what is the purpose of an abstract class?

The prime reason for an abstract class is to make available common information to subclasses. This is one of the features of OOP. Thus, it enables subclasses to share the common information.

• Like the abstract class, the abstract method provides you with the facility to factor common information into the superclass. This information is shared by subclasses.

• An abstract class cannot be instantiated. It simply means that once you have declared a class as an

abstract class, you cannot create any instances of this class. However, you can create **object variables** of an abstract class. These variables must refer to an object (instance) of a subclass.This is demonstrated below by a statement.

Staff sup = Managerial ("John Smith");

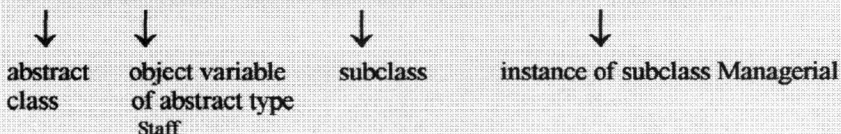

| abstract class | object variable of abstract type Staff | subclass | instance of subclass Managerial |

Casting primitive types

In its simplest term, it means the process of converting one type of data/information to another type of data/information. For instance you want to convert data stored as float type value into integer type value.

The casting process will generate a new value whose type is different than its source. The following two rules should guide you to decide when casting of simple (primitive) variables is applicable:

Rule 1:

When the destination variable holds a larger type value than the source variable, in such a case, there is no need to cast explicitly. **Why?**

• The answer is simple, the larger type storage location can accommodate a smaller type. **For instance:**

Simple casting from smaller type value to larger type value

```
int x = 25;                    // x is the source variable
double z = ( x * 2.14 );       // z is the destination variable
```

In this example, the destination variable is larger type, as double has 8 bytes of storage and can accommodate fractions with 15 significant digits. On the other hand, the integer type source variable x is only 4 bytes long storage. Thus, there is **no** need to convert it explicitly. It is converted for you automatically by the system.

• **How about precision level when converting from smaller type source to larger type destination?**

You do not suffer any loss of data, as the destination variable has more storage space than the source variable.

Rule 2:

When the destination variable holds a smaller type value than the source variable, in such a case, the casting is downward, and it should be done explicitly. **Why?**

• The answer is simple, the smaller type storage location cannot accommodate a larger type value . For instance:

Explicit casting from larger type value to smaller type value

```
double x = 4.55 ;          // source       - original type data
int y  = ( int ) x;        // destination  – new type data
```

This code will result in converting the double variable **x** into an integer value.

• **What will happen to the fractional part of the value stored in x?**

The fractional part, that is . 55 would be discarded. The value to be stored in variable y is 4, and its type is now integer. Thus, you can see that the casting has resulted in creating a new type.

It should be noted that the casting procedure does not change the value, instead it creates a new type. Think!

• The general casting format for primitive type data is as follows:

> **new type and name of variable = (new type) source variable**

As in the above example:

$$\textbf{int } y = (\textbf{int }) X;$$

```
----    ---        ----    ----
 ↓       ↓          ↓       ↓
new     new        new    source
type    name       type   variable
```

• Does explicit casting cause loss of precision? Yes, in this case , **.55** has been lost. The value is truncated, because there is not enough space in **int y** to hold all digits. Note that the fractional part is truncated, not rounded. The casting method does not round a figure, but it truncates/ discards it in order to fit it in store.

• What will happen if your source variable is not acceptable in the destination variable? Java will convert the value, but the result will not be the desired output.

• Is it possible to cast boolean values? No. It is not allowed. Casting occurs between numeric types.

• Is it possible to use a primitive type variable in a different format without casting it? Yes, you can do so. For instance, there is no need to cast **char** type variable into **int** type variable. **Why?** A character variable can be used as an int variable. Similarly, an int variable can be used as a char variable.

• When calculating, involving casting, you should use parentheses as casting has a higher precedence than arithmetic; otherwise, your computing value will be wrong. For instance:

```
double x = 12.4
double y = 9.3
int z = ( int ) (x/y)        // ( ) is required in order to avoid casting of x first.
```

Casting Objects

• For casting objects, it is essential that a class is a subclass of the other, i.e., cast takes place within an inheritance hierarchy, so that the source and destination are within an inheritance hierarchy.

• When casting an object from a subclass to its superclass, you must do so **explicitly**. It is because the subclass has more information in terms of arguments and methods than its superclass possesses.

This explicit cast causes loss of information, which the subclass possesses. For instance, the subclass may have more variable than the superclass has in it. You might lose some of these variables.

• Now consider Figure 5, in which Team is the immediate superclass for Hockey and Tennis subclasses.

Student inheritance hierarchy

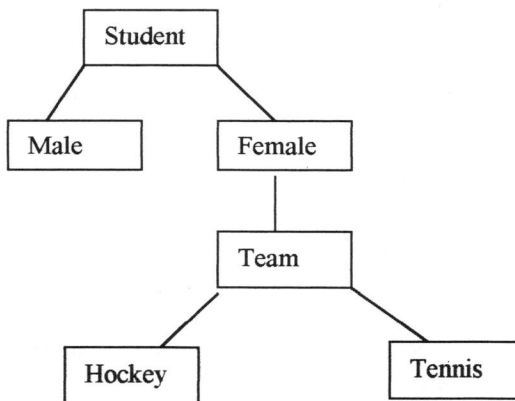

Figure 5

You can cast an object of the Hockey subclass to its superclass Team. You can also cast an object of the superclass Team to any of its subclasses namely Hockey and Team. It is allowed to cast an object to an object of its class own superclass or subclass only.

However, you cannot cast an instance of the Tennis class to an instance of the Male class, because the Hockey class is not a subclass of the Male class.

Example 1: casting an object from the sublcass to its superclass

```
Hockey p1;                      // p1 is an instance of  the subclass Hockey
Team player1;                   // player1 is an instance of the immediate superclass Team
p1 = new Hockey ( );            // p1 is a Hockey object
Team player1  = ( Team) p1;     // this casts a Hockey object called p1 into a Team object
```

There is some loss of information when you cast an object from the subclass into its superclass. Thus, this cast will result in the loss of information.

Further breakdown of the casting statement for your benefit:

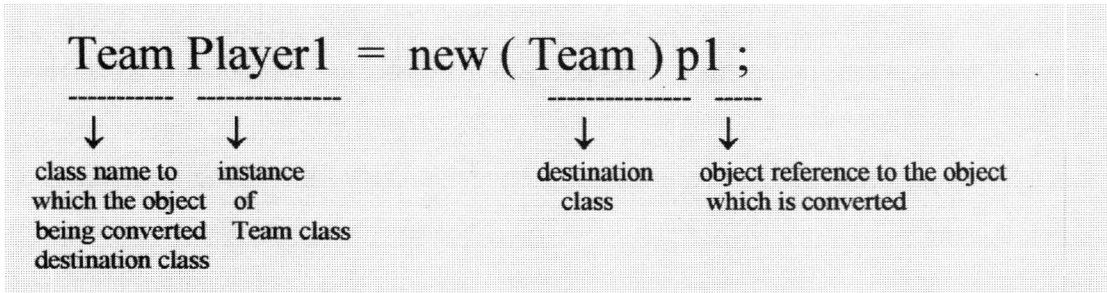

Team Player1 = new (Team) p1 ;

class name to	instance	destination	object reference to the object
which the object	of	class	which is converted
being converted	Team class		
destination class			

In fact, it is the same casting operation , which has been demonstrated above for casting primitive type variables.

Example 2: Casting an object from the superclass to its subclass

```
train t1 = new train ( );        // train is the superclass
  goods g1  = new goods ( );      // goods is a subclass of train class
  goods g1 = new ( goods ) t1     //  train object is converted into a goods object g1.
```

In this cast, there will not be any loss of information. On the other hand, there will be some gain as now all variables and methods of the subclass are available to the **object t1** of train class.

It is to emphasise that:

• there is no need to cast an object of a class to an object of another class, if the subclass and its superclass have the same set of methods and arguments.

• the casting of an object from the superclass to the subclass in the class hierarchy is carried out automatically, because the subclass contains more information than the superclass.

• casting method does not change the actual value or the object. It converts the object or the value to a new type value or object.

• When casting an object, the existing object exists at all times, because the cast creates an object reference, as shown in the above examples.

• in Java, objects are subclasses of the **object class**. Therefore, an object can be used without casting it in a class, in any place where a superclass is expected.

• When you cast an object from the subclass into the superclass, which has no method (s) that the subclass will require, in that case, the Java system will generate an error message.

Converting variables to objects and vice versa

Objects and variables are not the same thing. You cannot use an object as a substitute for a variable and vice versa. The good news is that **Java . lang package** has classes for these primitive types. These are outlined below.

Java . lang class	Primitive type equivalent
Boolean	boolean
Byte	byte
Character	character
Double	double
Float	float
Integer	integer
Long	integer
Short	short

Note that class name begins with the capital letter. This method of writing enables us to make a clear distinction between these two types.

. How to create an object using the value of the variable?

. You have to use the operator **new,** and class methods that are defined in each of the above listed classes.

. The following example shows you how to create an object from an integer value by applying the **Integer ( )** class method for creating an Integer object.

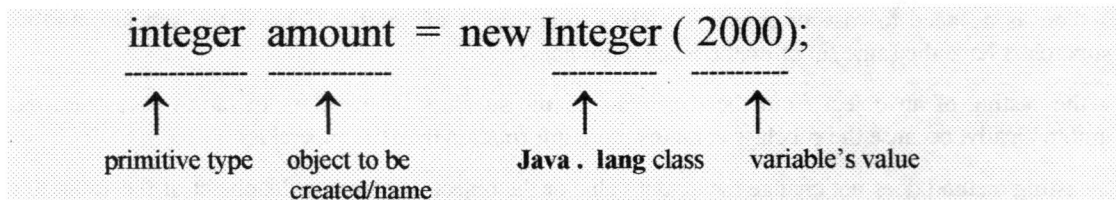

$$\text{integer \quad amount \quad = \quad new \; Integer \; (\; 2000);}$$

↑	↑	↑	↑
primitive type	object to be created/name	**Java . lang** class	variable's value

. **Integer ( )** is the class method for converting/ creating the **Integer object called amount**.

. **General format** for converting from an integer type to an integer object is as follows:

integer object to be created = new Integer (variable's value) ;

↑
name

. How about converting back the object into the simple variable?

You can convert the object into the simple value in order to use it . The Java . lang also has methods for this purpose as shown below. For converting the Integer object, the classs method is **intValue ( )**. The following assignment statement illustrates this technique.

$$\text{int money} = \text{amount . intValue ( );}$$

↑	↑	↑	↑	↑
type primitive	variable	object	point is essential here	method which extracts integer value from the an integer object amount

This assignment statement will return 2000.

Testing the class of an object

• The *Instanceof* operator can be used to find out the class of an object. Why is it necessary to carry out this test? It is a good idea to find out the class of your object. This way, you can avoid a run time exception error generated by the system, and get to know the class of the object before performing the cast.

• The instanceof test return true or false in accordance with:

> . if the object is an instance of the named class than the test returns **true**.
> . if the object is not an instance of the named class than the test returns **false**.

• The **general format** of the test is given below.

operator *instanceof* named class

.**Examples** of the use of *instanceof* operator to test whether or not the object is an instance of the class named.

1)   C++ instanceof computerBook ;   // it will return true

2)   fashionMagazine instanceof computerBook ;   // it will return false because
                                              fashion Magazine is not sold at a this bookshop

In case 2), the compiler will not allow you to cast, as there is no chance for the cast to be successful.

A package

A package contains a number of related classes. These classes have some common objectives. The Java library consists of a number of packages. Because classes in different packages have some specific purpose, your Java classes can have access to only classes in **java . lang** package. It is the base language package inside the Java package, supplied with the JDK. Packages are organised in hierarchical order. This is why **java . lang** package is inside the Java package. The hierarchy of packages guarantees uniqueness of package names, and thus avoids conflicting situations.

. How to refer to a package in your source file?

Example 1:

The code: **import java . awt.* ;**

This statement in your program means that you are referring to the Java package, which contains **awt** (Abstract Windows Toolkit) package. So, this is a package within a package. This will make available all classes in the Java awt package for use in your program. The **java .awt** pakage is part of the source code supplied with the JDK.

. Note the use of period '.' and an asterisk '*' in correct places.

. **Import** is a keyword. When you use the import statement in your program, it implies that you want to make classes of the package, to which you have referred in the import statement, available for use in your program.

. The import statement is listed at the top of your source file.

.The **asterisk** is used when you want all classes in a particular package available for use in your program. Use the asterisk to import the whole package.

. The **asterisk** is used only when you want to import just one package.

. Will all imported classes in your program have any adverse effects on your program? No. Therefore, you can import all classes of a package in your program.

. What happens when you have imported two packages, all of them having classes of the same name? There is a problem of name conflict. It may be that both names refer to two different things. The compiler will get confused, and would not compile your program. How do you avoid this situation?

In such circumstances, in addition to the import statements at the top of your source file, you must also refer to the required class in your program by its full package name. For instance:

import Bridclasses.*;   // Brid package contains a class called Town

import Yorkclasses.*;   // York package contains a class called Town

To use class Town from these packages , you must refer to each class by its full name:

    Bridclasses . Town Seaside = new Bridclasses . Town ("Bridlington-by-the sea");

    Yorkclasses . Town City = new yorkclasses . Town ("York City");

Example 2: The code: **java . awt. Graphics ;**

This statement means that you want to import only Graphics class of AWT (awt) package in your program.

. Can you make your own package?

Yes indeed, Java allows you to make your own package. Thus, you can group all those classes, which have some common purpose. This way, you can keep your classes separate and when necessary use them in your programs. I must add that this activity requires a long program. There is no space for it in a book of this size.

. Can you use your own classes in your programs, if you do not group them in your own package?

A class in your own program, which is not inside any package, can also be used in your other programs. You just refer to any of these classes by their names in your other programs.

. What is a default package and when to use it?

The **java .lang** package is inside the java package. It is the base language package. It is therefore the default package. It simply means that when your program is being compiled, the compiler searches the **java. lang** package. Thus, there is no need to refer to it explicitly in your program. All classes in this package are available to be used when required in your program.

On the other hand, if you have to use classes from other packages in your program, then you must include the import statement in your source file.

. Is it possible to import more than one package with * in the import statement?

No. it is not allowed. Only one package in the import statement is permitted.

Exercises

1. The computer book section at your library has its own subject classification. The Java programmer has called this classification, class types. These are ComputerBook class , Programming class, SystemsAnaysis class , GeneralComputing class. Which of these four classes would you consider as an abstract class? Justify your answer. Sketch a diagram to illustrate the relationship of these classes.

2. **Student JavaEveningProg = new Student (   );** What is the purpose of the above Java code? Also, analyse this code.

3. **ToyotaCar. CorollaSportif = " 5- door saloon";** This statement gives three pieces of information that can be identified by using the Object Oriented Language terminology. Write down against each item of information its name.

4. What is essential for casting an object? Refer to figure 3 in this chapter and cast a MinisterA to Central Government. For this purpose, you can write CentralGovernment.

5. Write the code in 'skeleton form' for deriving a class from the existing class. Your code must include the keyword extends, to mean that one class inherits from the other class. You can use Figure 1 of this chapter for classes of your choice.

6. Is it true to say that often the difference between an object and a class is blurred? If your answer is **true** then sketch an inheritance hierarchy diagram to illustrate your answer.

7. When will you add the following code to your program?

    a)   import java . awt .*;
    b)   import java . awt;

8. What does the word behaviour mean in the context of Object Oriented Programming? Explain it giving an example.

9. Is there any difference between an object and an instance? Explain your answer.

10. a) When will you call this code or identical code in your program?

```
public Temperature (   )
  {
    TempRecorded = 40;
    patient = " Smith";
  }
```

Give an example of the code which will call the above code during the execution of your program.

b) Construct an example of a class method.

Chapter 7
Applets Basic Understanding

An applet is a program, which is embedded in a Web page. In a Web page, an applet has some space. This space is measured in pixels. It can display buttons, boxes, and more. It is dynamically downloaded by a Java-enabled browser from the Internet on your own computer system to run it. This chapter lays the foundation for developing basic applets. Here, the relationship between AWT and the Swing is also outlined so that you can appreciate their vitally important roles in developing programs for the Internet.

A partial AWT class hierarchy

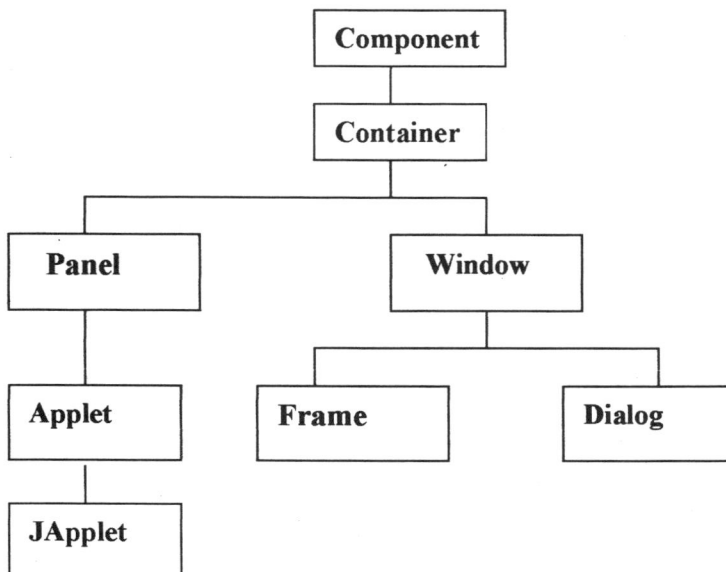

Diagram 1

An applet

An applet is a Java class. It is derived from the **Applet** class. The Applet class is in the **java . applet** package. The **java . applet** package has classes that are necessary to create an applet. It also has classes that are used by an applet in order to communicate with its applet context. The **java.applet** package is **not** part of the **AWT** package, but the applet class is an AWT component. AWT stands for Abstract Windowing Toolkit. As stated earlier the Java class hierarchy is very complex, therefore, diagram 1 shows a partial AWT hierarchy.

The purpose of this diagram is to show you that the **java . applet . Applet** class is itself a subclass of **java . awt . panel**, and that your applets are in the hierarchy of components in the AWT package.

The awt package

The **Java . awt** package contains classes and interfaces, which constitute the Abstract Windowing Toolkit **(awt or AWT)**. This package includes:

. **Graphics class** - for graphics context, drawing and painting shapes and objects
. **Components class** – for all GUI (pronounced *gooey* - graphic user interface -) components such as menus and buttons
. **Container class** - for components that can hold other components or containers, such as Frame
. **Font class** – for representing font
. **Frame class** – for representing a top-level window with a title

These are just a few out of many classes in this package. This package also has the following sub packages:

. **java . awt . event** - contains classes and interfaces that implement the new event.

. **java . awt . image** - contains classes and interfaces for managing bitmap images

. **java . awt . datatransfer** – contains classes and interfaces for data transfer

. **java . awt . peer** - contains (hidden) classes and interfaces for specific platforms such as Windows 95

The AWT enables a programmer to design interface in an abstract manner. This way, a program can be run across different platforms, and thus applets can be run on the World Wide Web. This approach has worked well for simple programs, but it needed enhancement so that high quality programs can be run across different platforms.

The Swing

Sun and Netscape has developed the **Swing**, which is now part of the **Java Foundation Classes (JFC)**. **JFC** is a vast library, which also includes Swing toolkit. The Swing classes are inside a package called **javax . swing**. It has lightweight and rich user interface components. The superclass for the Swing applets is **Japplet** class. In this book, all applets extend the Japplet class.

In practical terms, the Swing has not replaced the AWT, but it has enhanced user interface components. The Swing classes include everything that you will need to develop GUI based programs. For instance, the Swing can enable you to create buttons, text fields, dialogue boxes, pull-down menus. You can also include GUI in your applets. The Swing classes also include fonts, colour and many other graphics facilities. The Swing is a huge package.

This is a new development, and thus only recent versions of the Java language can let you use the Swing GUI toolkit. The Swing class library is a GUI library. This library has enhanced the quality of GUI. With the help of Swing classes, one can develop high quality portable programs that use a GUI. The Swing class library promises consistency across platforms, and less different bugs on different platforms. Note that before the swing library, there were different bugs in the AWT GUI kit on the different platforms. Through the inheritance hierarchy as shown in diagram 1, your applet can make use of these components. Thus, your applets can make the best use of many capabilities of awt package, and Swing.

Applets essential methods

The following important point must be remembered:

- Applets do not have a main method as application programs have. Instead, applets have sections for doing different things.

- Applets inherit the following built-in methods:

     . init ( )   **. paint ( )**   **. start ( )**   **. stop ( )**   **. Destroy ( )**

- Depending on the nature of your program, you have to override one or more of these methods with your own version. These methods are outlined below. But, firstly:

. What is override or overriding in this context?

Classes have some built-in methods for performing some specific functions. Classes also have built-in variables and constants. These different class components are collectively known as **class members**. An inherited method or the built-in method has some basic behaviour patterns. These may not be enough for your requirements, and by means of overriding you can customise the behaviour patterns from the base or superclass as you want them in your class, which is a derived class. You will learn more about the derived class soon.

. The init ( ) method

The purpose of this method is to initialise the applet. This initialisation may be to set up fonts, colours, and initial values to variables. For instance, the following is an illustration of overriding the init ( ) method in your applet class:

```
Public void init ( )     // note no ; is needed here
{
  your code here
}
```

You can initialise an applet only once. On the other hand, an applet can be started many times during its lifetime.

. The start ( ) method

When a program begins for the first time, the **init ( )** method is processed first, and then the **start ( )** method is called automatically. However, if for some reason, the applet was stopped, it can start all over again by calling the start ( ) method. Its use is more common in animation. The following is an illustration of overriding the start ( ) method in your program:

```
Public void start ( )
{
  your code
}
```

. The stop ( ) method

The stopping happens when the applet has ceased execution because of any of the following:

- when you have called the stop ( ) method in your program
- when you have opened another page on the Web, and left the current page

You can override it in a program as shown below:

```
Public void stop  (  )
{
    your code
}
```

Like **start method**, its use is common in animation.

. The paint (   ) method

It is a very important method, because without it your applet cannot display anything on the screen. Painting can happen many times in the life of an applet. For instance, when the browser is minimised and then maximised, or the browser window is moved to a different place on the screen. You will normally override it. The term **painting** in this context refers to something on the screen, which is drawn by the applet. This something on the screen may be a line, an image, some text or just a coloured background. Indeed, it enables your applet to display or re-display something on the applet window. It is called when the Web browser informs the applet to create its display on the screen. It should be noted that unlike the other methods, the paint (   ) method takes an argument. For instance:

```
public class paint ( Graphics g )

{
   your code here
}
```

In this example, the argument is an **object g** of the **Graphics class**.

• I have used the **Swing** to implement applets, therefore, applets have extended the **JApplet** class, which is the superclass for Swing applets. **Why** ? If you do not do so, your Swing components may not paint as required.

• You must include in your program all the required packages for all classes that are needed. This is done through import statements at the top of your program.

. The destroy (   ) method

Like the start, stop method, it is most use in animation. Its purpose is to free the resources when the applet has stopped. It is rare that you will override it. You will do so only when there are some specific resources that you want to free. It can be overridden as follows:

```
          Public void destroy (  )
          {
            your code
          }
```

- **An example of applet designed to do nothing**

```
     Public class  Donothing  extends  JApplet
     {
               // no code
     }
```

It will do nothing as it has no code in it to do anything. Nevertheless, it is an applet.

Your first applet

Applets differ from applications. Applets are designed for presentation on the World Wide Web. This first applet is created, compiled and saved in a file called **FirstApplet . java.** This is the simplest applet, which displays a message, "My First Applet".

. **Java applets** are programs that run on Web pages as **HTML documents**. Thus, for this applet, you have to create an HTML file called **FirstApplet . html**. For the sake of simplicity, I have chosen the same name as for the applet.

. You can give any name of your choice, as long as both files have their own specific file extensions. The applet file has "**. applet**" extension, and HTML file has "**. html**" extension. Thus, the system can easily distinguish these two files, and link them when the applet is run. **How?** You will find out soon.

. You can use the **appletviewer** tool to test your applets. The appletviewer tool comes with Java development Kit.

. As applets are placed on a Web page the **Web browser** loads it along with the other parts of the page. This section is discussed towards the end of this chapter, along with **Java Plug-in** that runs applets, which cannot be run by a Web browser.

Explanation

The program **FirstApplet . java** is shown in diagram 2, and now I will analyse it for you.

. The following two **import** statements are required at the beginning of the program.

import java . awt.* ;   // contains classes for creating user interfaces, painting graphics and images.

import javax . swing.* ; // contains classes for the creation of graphical user interface. The **JApplet**
class is in this package.

These import statements bring the required code into this program. If you do not use the required package(s), your program will not be compiled successfully, and you will get an error message, similar to the one shown below.

Just to remind you that class libraries are in fact packages. One of them is called **java . awt**. This library has the Graphics class. This class handles the graphics work. These packages have built-in functions, which make your programming task much easier. Without these packages, it would have been much more difficult to write the code from scratch. So, these libraries make a programmer's life easy.

An Error Message

```
C:\Examples>javac FirstApplet . java
FirstApplet.java:4: Superclass JApplet of class FirstApplet not found.
public class FirstApplet extends JApplet
                                 ^
1 error

This is the effect of excluding from the import list of statements, import javax . swing.*; statement.
This experiment was conducted in order to demonstrate to you the likely effects of not having the correct package in a program.
```

Remember - if you are using several classes, which are in the same package, you should include in your import statement " **.*** ". The import statement with " **.*** " makes available all classes in a particular package. For instance: **import javax . swing.*;**

.   **public class FirstApplet extends JApplet**

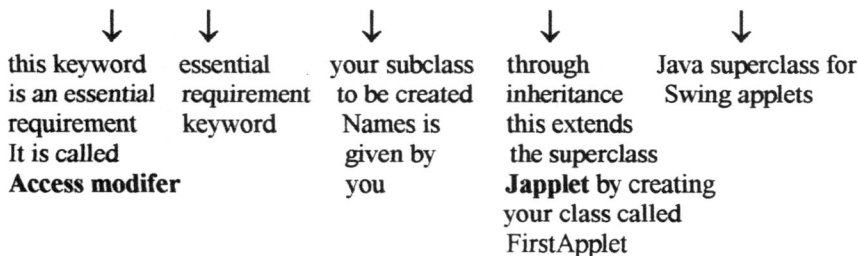

↓	↓	↓	↓	↓
this keyword is an essential requirement It is called **Access modifer**	essential requirement keyword	your subclass to be created Names is given by you	through inheritance this extends the superclass **Japplet** by creating your class called FirstApplet	Java superclass for Swing applets

In fact, your applet starts here. You must note that the applet class must be declared as **public**; otherwise it will not be executed.

. public void paint (Graphics g)

This is to implement the paint ( ) method, which is one of the essential methods described above, under applet's essential methods . In fact, the idea is to override the default paint ( ) method. The argument, which is within the ( ) is a Graphics object **g**. The graphical object represents the physical display of an applet. The Graphics class is in the Java AWT package. This Graphics object represents the physical display of the applet. Through the Graphics class of objects, you can have graphics environment such as a window for this applet. That is why you have to use a required built-in method of this object. For instance, you can use:

• **drawString ( )**   • **drawImage ( )** • **drrawLine ( )**   • **drawOval ( )** and • **other methods**.

The **drawLine ( )** method is implemented in this program. Once again, I repeat that applets do not have the main ( ) method, which is in application programs. It should be **remembered** that:

the paint ( ) method includes a Graphics object, which is the only argument. This object represents applet window.

. Is it always necessary to declare paint ( ) method as public?

If your applet uses your own classes , in that case, you do not have to declare your paint ( ) method public. You can declare a class method as:

                 • public   or   • private   or   • protected

The advantage of declaring a class method as **public** is that you can call it from anywhere in the program. This way, the call to a method is not limited to the class in which it is defined.

If you declare a method as **private**, then it may be called only from the class in which it is defined.

If you declare a method as **protected**, then it may be called only from the class in which it is defined, and the class derived from that class.

• **super.paint (g);** - this statement is a **call** to the paint ( ) method of the superclass. It sends the Graphics object **g** to the paint ( ) method of the superclass. You should notice that the **g object** is the same object, which is being sent to this applet's paint ( ) method. It is the object that represents applet window. Here, dot is essential between super and paint.

. Is it necessary to have a call to the paint ( ) method?

It is required to include a call statement as first statement in the paint (   ) method, because it handles the task of making sure that your applet window is set up correctly. It is a built-in method.

• **g . drawString ("My First Applet ", 50, 100) ;** - the task that is performed by this applet is to display the string: **My First Applet !** This task is carried out by the paint (   ) method. As the text has to be displayed in the applet window, the **drawString** method of the Graphics class is implemented. Yes indeed, the text appears in the applet window. Here, it is important to know the answer to the following question:

• **How do you implement or reach the method of the object g of the Graphics class ?**

In order to reach or implement such a method, you must make use of a dot operator, which is a **dot " ."** sign. The general format is **g.drawString (   )**. It takes three parameters (see below).

This statement sends the following three arguments/parameters to drawString ( ) method:

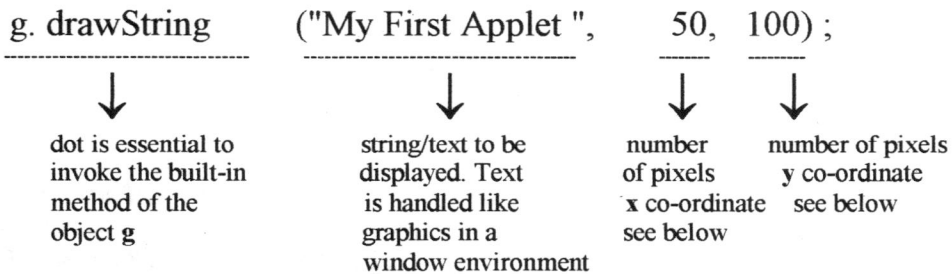

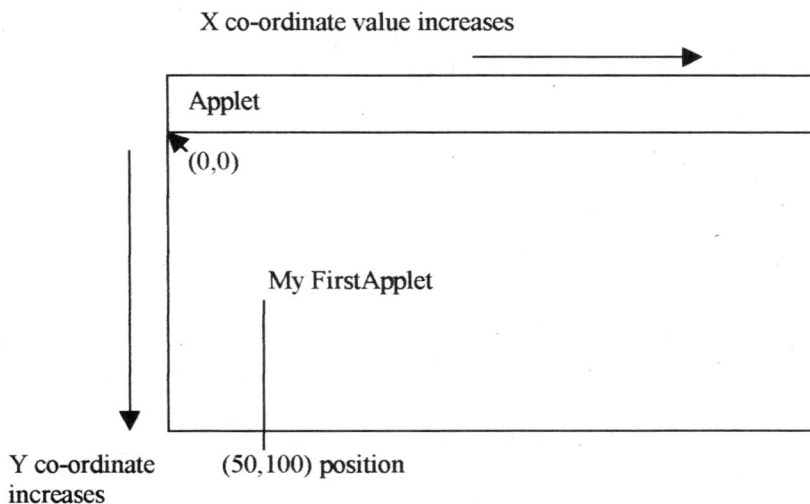

g. drawString   ("My First Applet ",   50,   100) ;

↓	↓	↓	↓
dot is essential to invoke the built-in method of the object **g**	string/text to be displayed. Text is handled like graphics in a window environment	number of pixels **x** co-ordinate see below	number of pixels **y** co-ordinate see below

Figure1: Drawing a string at (50, 100) position

• The (x, y) co-ordinate system in Java is used to position things in applet's window. The top left corner of an applet window is just below the word Applet in the applet window. Its position is at (0,0) pixels. From this place, the original position of the applet is stated. For this applet, the above statement says that the text, which is **My First Applet** has to be displayed in the applet window, starting at 50 pixels from the top left, and 100 pixels down from the top left.

• You have to state three parameters to the drawString ( ) method as shown above. These are:

   • the text which you wish to display in the applet window

   • the location of the text/string's lower-left corner, which is the starting position of the string. It is the (x, y) co-ordinate. It is stated as two integer values.

. Is the drawString ( ) method a print method?

Certainly, it is just like the **System . out . println ( ) method** whose function is to display the output to a system's standard output device. Similarly, DrawString ( ) method is used to display the text in an applet window.

• All lines in the program shown in diagram 2 have been analysed, except { }. However, you have already met these brackets or braces in application programs.

The source code file

The source code shown in Diagram 2 above was prepared by using the **WordPad** text editor in exactly the same way, as it was used for application programs. You must save it in the same way as you have been saving your application programs. I saved it as **FirstApplet .java**. Of course, FirstApplet is my class name for this applet.

. Do you have to include the word applet in your class name?

No. It is my own choice. If I wanted, I could have called it **Test1**, etc. Like the application program, the class name begins with a capital letter.

Compiling the source code

Compile it just like the application program. **As a reminder:** Use MS-DOS Prompt for compiling the applet : The command line should read: **javac FirstApplet . java**. As you already know that **javac** is the compiler that converts the source code into the Java byte code.

You may get error messages. If so, make your program error-free by editing the text and re-compiling it as many times as necessary. **A word of warning:** pay special attention to lower case and capital case letters , spelling (Colour is not the same as COLOR or colour) and insert symbols such as ". ", " * ", where necessary. Many error messages are due to these minor typing mistakes.

FirstApplet .java

```
import java.awt.*;
import javax.swing.*;

public class FirstApplet extends JApplet
{

  public void paint (Graphics g )

{
  super.paint (g);
  g.drawString ("My First Applet", 50, 100);
}
}
```

Diagram 2

Testing your applet

Unlike application programs, the compiled applets cannot be tested through the **Java interpreter** tool. **Why?**

It is due to the fact that applets are designed to place them on a Web page so that they can be viewed.

The only way, one can run an applet on the Internet is from within an HTML document. For this purpose, you have to use a special HTML tag in order to create a Web page, which will load the applet.

A Java -enabled browser uses the information, which is within the HTML tag in order to locate the compiled program, and finally execute the applet. It is therefore, highly desirable to have some basic working knowledge of HTML. The HTML is mentioned in chapter 1.Here, I give a brief description, so that you can prepare an HTML document.

Once you have grasped it, you will begin to think that the HTML is an essential component of the nuts and bolts of the World Wide Web **(WWW)**.

The HTML document

The HTML documents contain plain text **(ASCII)**. These documents use special **markup codes**, which are embedded in the text. I have used Windows 98 WordPad for my HTML documents. If I wanted to use, say Microsoft Word for producing the HTML document, I could have done so. Thus, you can use whatever word processing tool is available on your computer. If you allow yourself, sufficient time, you can learn the basic skills of HTML as you prepare a few documents.

. How can you distinguish the HTML document from any other plain document?

The HTML document has HTML **tags**. HTML tags are markup codes, which are typed into the document. These markup codes are surrounded by special markers, which are the **angle brackets**, < and >. The following tags must be included in all HTML documents:

. The <HTML > tag

Your document must begin with the **declaration or opening** tag < **HTML**>, and it should end with the **closing** tag </ **HTML**>. It should be noted that the closing tag has a forward slash within the < >. If you omit it, you will get an error message.

. The <HEAD> and <Body> tags

An HTML document must have a **head** and **body**. These divisions of the document enable the browsers to interpret the document correctly. What is included in the **head** of the HTML document?

It includes nothing more than some general information concerning the document. It looks like the following example:

Example of <HEAD> tag

```
            <HEAD>
            learning to create an HTML document
            </HEAD>
```

Example of <Body> tag

```
            <BODY>
            This is my first HTML document for my first applet
            </ BODY>
```

The **body** of the HTML document can have the bulk of the information that makes up your applet. It looks as demonstrated shown above.

. The <TITLE > tag

It is written within the <HEAD> section of an HTML document. Each document that is displayed by the Web browser should have its title shown in the top border of the browser window. Like other tags, it has an opening tag and a closing tag, as demonstrated by the following examples:

Example of <TITLE> tag

<TITLE>
My first applet
< / TITLE>

The <APPLET>tag

The applet tag is a special tag of HTML, aimed at including applets on Web pages. It also has its own closing tag, which is < /APPLET>.

In summary, each of these tags is in pairs: **<HTML> and </HTML>**. The HTML markup codes are **not case-sensitive**. I have used uppercase; but you can use lowercase, if you wish to. Also, some people write HTML tags on the same line with other tags, such as **<html><head>**. I have not done so, because in my opinion it makes editing the document difficult. Now it is time to put theory into practice by preparing a workable HTML page.

The HTML page (document)

I have used Windows 98 WordPad to prepare all HTML documents, including the HTML page/document for displaying the applet shown in diagram 2. This document has to be saved by using the **Save As** feature in plain **ACII** code, which is **save type: Text Document**. The file extension is: **.html**. The document was saved as: **FirstApplet.html**, as shown in diagram 3. For the sake of simplicity, I have called this HTML page by the same name as already given to the program in diagram 2. You call it what you like. Because of different file extensions, the system knows which is which.

Explanation

. In diagram 2, the HTML code starts with an **<HTML> tag**. It declares that it is HTML document.

. **<HEAD>** tag - it has no other information about the document, except to include the title tag.

. **<TITLE>** tag - it is followed by the title of your applet. The title is followed by the closing tag **</TITLE>**.

. **</HEAD>** tag - There is no other information to go into the **head section** of this HTML document,

and thus the next line contains nothing except the closing tag for this section.

. **<BODY>** tag - it begins the body section. In this case, it has only the applet tag.

```
. <APPLET CODE = "FirstApplet.class" width = 300 height = 200>
  </APPLET>
```

These two lines are vitally important. Here, <APPLET> and <APPLET> tags contain the code that handles the applet.

. **CODE = "FirstApplet. class"** - it shows the name of the class file which contains the applet to be run. The class file and the HTML file must be in the same directory.

. **width = 300 height = 200** - these two measurements indicate the size in pixels of the window in which to run the applet on the Web page. These measurements will draw a grey rectangle on screen. It is important to remember that the area should be large enough to display the applet; otherwise your applet will be hidden. You can resize the rectangle, if your applet is outside the set boundaries.

. There is nothing else in the <body> section of this document. Thus, </BODY> is used to close this section. It is then followed by the HTML closing tag: </HTML>.

. **Displaying the applet** - The text between the **<APPLET>** and **</APPLET>** is displayed by the browser.

HTML Document: FirstApplet.html

```
<HTML>
<HEAD>
<TITLE><First Applet</TITLE>
</HEAD>
<BODY>
<Applet CODE= "FirstApplet.class" width=300 height=200>
</APPLET>
</BODY>
</HTML>
```

Diagram 3

Testing your applet

The **appletviewer** tool is part of your Java Development Kit. You can test your applets with the

appletviewer tool. How to apply this test?   In the MS-DOS Prompt window, just type in as shown below:

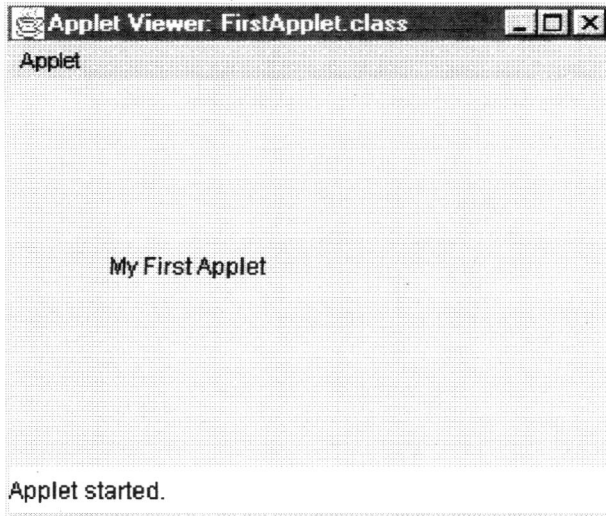

Diagram 4

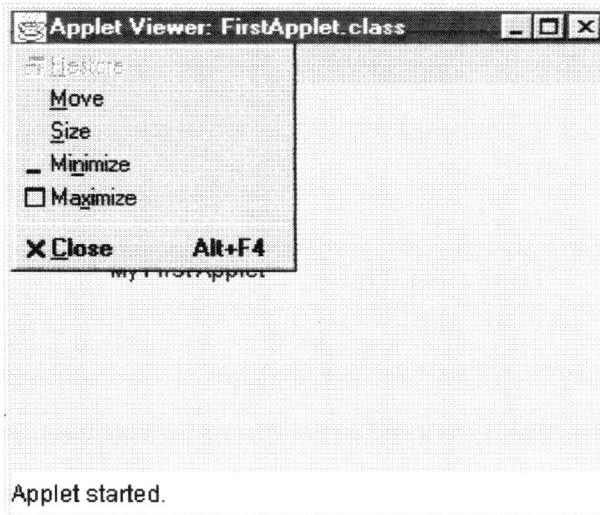

Diagram 4A

C:\Examples>appletviewer FirstApplet . html.

Just to remind you that **Examples** is the name of my folder in which all my Java programs are stored.

You must write the name of the folder in which you have stored all your Java files (HTML files included). The screen capture of FirstApplet started into the appletviewer is shown in diagram 4 above.

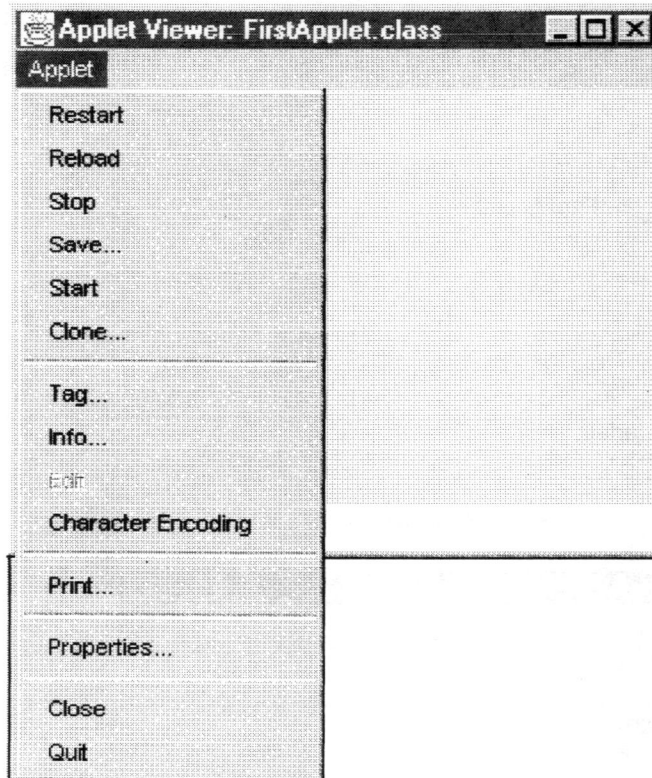

Diagram 4B

The diagram 4 shows an applet in the applet viewer. In this diagram, in its top right-hand corner , you can see its ' **close box** '. If you click it, you will close the applet viewer. In the top left-hand corner of this diagram, you can see an icon. If you click it, you will open a menu. This menu is depicted in Diagram 4A. You can also close the applet viewer by selecting **Close** from this menu.

In diagram 4, just under the top left-hand corner, you can find the word **Applet**. By clicking Applet, you can open a pull down menu. This pull down menu is shown in diagram 4B above. You should experiment with these menus to learn more about them. For example:

●**Clone** - it allows you to view a copy of the applet. You will end up with as many copies as the times you click this option.

.Tag - it shows the <APPLET>.......</APPLET> tag. This is where the applet resides.

Finally, the lower part of this applet viewer window has a white strip. This is its status bar, where applet viewer tool displays messages and gives information, such as Applet started, Applet loaded, etc. This is where, you will be notified, if your applet cannot be run ...

Exercise

Write an applet called **FirstTrial . java** in order to display in its window the following information.

Contact me at

WWW. NOBODY. COM

You should display this information in the same format as shown above. Start your text at (165,100), Create an empty line (space between two lines) at (150,115), and start a third line at (150, 130), so that your layout looks like the layout as shown above. You must also create and store the required HTML document in order to test your applet with the applet viewer Java tool.

Chapter 8

Fonts and Colours

Applets are designed to be displayed on the screen. .Java enables you to control the appearance of your applet. In this chapter, you will learn about the **Font** and **Colour** classes. You will soon learn that you can present text by using different fonts, and colours, which make applets visually attractive.

Fonts class

In the last chapter, you have already learnt that using the Graphics class, you can print text on the screen. The Font class **java . awt . Font** is in the AWT package. The appearance of text is determined by its font, which has the following three properties.

. Name - a font has a name. The AWT package has five logical names for fonts. These are:

- **SansSerif**   **Serif**   **Monospaced**   **Dialog**   **DialogInput**

When the program is executed on the host (user) machine, these names are mapped to fonts that are available on the host machine. Fonts do vary, as they are dependent on the host machine. In reality, the name is the face name or the **typeface** of the font. There are other names for fonts, which are trade names given by their manufacturers. So, it creates some confusion - too many names. The following names are commonly used and matched with three of the above names:

. **Helvetica** $\rightarrow$ **SansSerif**. On your Windows 95/98 system, it may be displayed as **Arial**.

. **TimesRoman** $\rightarrow$ **Serif**. On your Windows 95/98 system, it may be displayed as
Times New Roman.

. **Courier** $\rightarrow$ **MonoSpaced**. On your Windows 95/98 system, it may be displayed as
Courier New.

These are standard fonts. You can use a logical name of a font in your program.

• **Style** - You must also specify the style of the font. It can be plain, **bold**, *italic*, or ***bold italic***.

• **Size** - The size is given in points, but in reality the display is in pixels.

. How can you create a font object in your program?

In order to display text by using a specific typeface, style and size, you must first create an individual font object. It is created by using the font class's new constructor as shown below:

Font heading = new Font ("TimesRoman" , Font . BOLD , 18);

The above statement (constructor) creates a 18 point **bold** Times Roman font object. The font, which you have included in your applet may not be available on the system, where your applet may run. However, if your font is not available on the host system, which is running your applet, Java will re-place it with a default font.

• You can also use the logical name of a font in Font class's new constructor as illustrated below.

Font title = new Font (" SansSerif ", Font . ITALIC, 12);

• Is it a good idea to use the logical name in Font class's constructor?

If you use the logical name in your Font class's constructor, it can enable the host machine to map the stated logical name with one of its own fonts, which is the nearest match/map. It is almost impossible to know what fonts on an unknown user's system are installed, but all parts of Java are supposed to support Helvetica, Courier, TimesRoman, and Dialog fonts.

FontMetrics class

The package is **java . awt . FontMetrics.**

The FontMetrics class contains information concerning fonts. The terms used in FontMetrics class are the same as used by typesetters. These terms are as follows:

. **baseline** - it an imaginary line, where the lower part of characters such as **e** rests.
. **ascender** - it is the upper part of a character.
. **ascent** - it is the distance between the font's baseline to the top of an ascender.
. **descender** - it is the lower part of a letters such as **p**, which drop below the baseline.
. **descent** - it is the distance between the font's baseline to a descender.
. **leading** - it is the space between the descent of one line and the ascent of the next line.
. **height** - it is the sum of descent + ascent + leading. It gives the height of the font.

The **FontMMetrics** class has the following **methods:**

. int getAscent ( ) - it returns the ascent of the font.

. int getDescent ( ) - it returns the descent of the font.

. int getLeading ( ) - it returns the leading for the font.

. int getHeight ( ) - it returns the total height of the font.

These methods are platform independent, and thus you can use them in your program.

Color class

The color class **java . awt . Color** is in the AWT package. It has 13 standard colours, which are given in table 1 below.

Table 1: Standard Colours

black	blue	cyan	darkGray	gray	green	lightGray
magenta	orange	pink	red	white	yellow	

If the colour of your choice is not one of the standard colours, you can create your own **color object**. **How?**

In computing filed colours are created by any combination of **red, green** and **blue (RGB)**. You can also specify **colour intensity**, which is between the range of **0-255**. In accordance with this scheme **255** represents the maximum intensity of the chosen colour, and **0** means no intensity of the chosen colour (colour is off). Thus:

. (255, 255, 255) - it is white colour

. (0, 0, 0) - it is black colour

You can create, beyond one's imagination, countless colours using RGB colour scheme. However, it depends on your own graphics system. If your screen has a limited capability of displaying graphics, in that case, you cannot have very many colours. In order to use a particular colour, you must create an instance of the **Color class**. If you know the RGB values, you can use these within ( ) to specify the intensity of the colour required. Furthermore, if the required colour is not one of the standard colours, you can use RGB values to create a colour object. The following examples show you how to create a colour object.

-        **Color blue = new Color (0 , 255 , 0);**

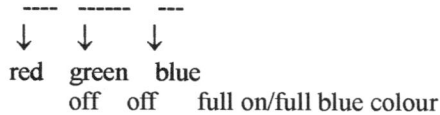

                      ↓   ↓   ↓
                    red   green   blue
                    off   off   full on/full blue colour

-        **Color choice = new Color (150, 70, 100);**

This will generate a colour of my own choice by mixing the amount of red, green and blue colours in accordance with the amount of intensity of each colour stated in ( ).

Using fonts & colours

The program **SecondApplet .java** shown in diagram 1 is designed to demonstrate how to use fonts and colour. This program is an applet, which displays a message in the following format:

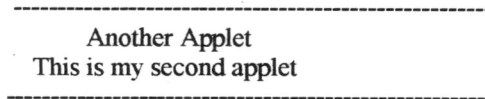

           Another Applet
        This is my second applet

The colour used is **black**.

Explanation

This program is similar to the program discussed in chapter 7. The statements which you have not yet met are described below.

-    **Font f = new Font ("TimesNewRoman", Font . BOLD, 20);**

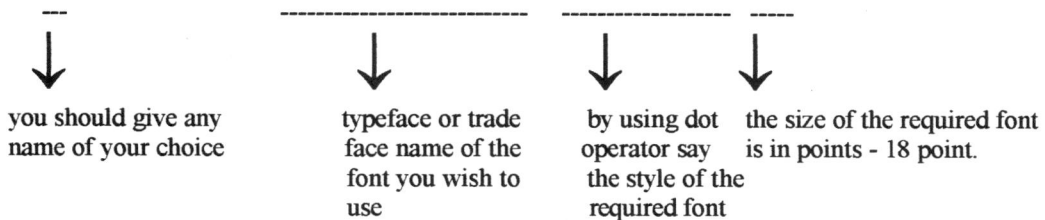

      ↓   ↓   ↓   ↓

you should give any name of your choice	typeface or trade face name of the font you wish to use	by using dot operator say the style of the required font	the size of the required font is in points - 18 point.

This statement is a font constructor, whose purpose is to create a new font object called **f** for the specification given within the ( ), as explained above.

- The text is drawn on the screen by using the **drawString ( )** method, as explained in chapter 7. It is, therefore, essential to set the current font object to your font object **f** by using the **setFont ( )** method. This is achieved by **g . setFont (f)**; You must set the font before drawing the text on the screen.

. What is this current font?

The Graphics object on which you are drawing text maintains the current graphics state. The current font is an element of this current graphics state. In order to change the font of the text, it is necessary to change the current font.

• As you have just set the current font to the font in which you wish to draw the text, you must also set the current colour to the colour in which you wish to draw the text. This is achieved by applying the **setColor ( )** method for Graphics object. Therefore, the following code:

g . setColor (Color . black);

is in the program. This sets the current colour black.

• The explanation of other statements in this program is similar to the explanation of statements in the program in the previous chapter. Compare and contrast this program with the program in the previous chapter, so that you can learn more by analysing, and by running these programs on your machine.

•The HTML document/ Web page **SecondApplet.html** for connecting the applet **SecondApplet .java** is shown in diagram 2. It is suggested that you compare it with the HTML document in the previous chapter, to find out in what ways these two documents differ. The difference is minimal. Look for it!

HTML document

In order to link the SecondApplet.java with that of the Web page, you need to have the HMTL document. It is shown in diagram 2.

HTML Document:SecondApplet.html

```
<HTML>
<HEAD>
<TITLE>Applet2</TITLE>
</HEAD>
<BODY>
<BR>
<APPLET CODE= "SecondApplet.class" width=300 height=200>
</APPLET>
</BODY>
</HTML>
```

Diagram 2

SecondApplet .java

```
import java.awt.*;                    // Graphics class is also in it
import javax.swing.*;

public class SecondApplet extends JApplet
{

 Font f = new Font ( "TimesNewRoman",Font.BOLD, 20 );
 public void paint (Graphics g )

{
  super.paint (g);
  g.setFont (f);
  g.setColor (Color.black);
  g.drawString(".........................................", 20,80);
  g.drawString ("Another  Applet",60,100);
  g.drawString ("This is my second applet", 20,130);
  g.drawString (".........................................", 20,150);
}
}
```

Diagram 1

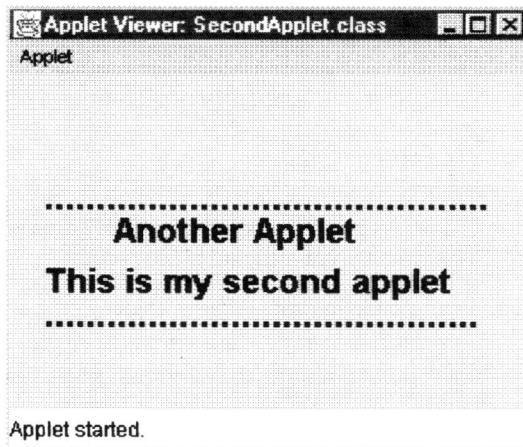

Diagram 3

Program output

The applet was viewed and tested with the **appletviewer** Java tool successfully. It is shown above in diagram 3. The command for viewing and testing the applet is:

appletviewer SecondApplet . html

Just to remind you that the file extension is **. html** (not java).

Using various fonts and colours

The purpose of the program **DifferentFonts. Java** , which is shown in diagram 4, is to demonstrate how to use different fonts and different colours in the same program. For this reason, the applet is designed to display a block of text consisting of three lines of text written in three different typefaces, styles , sizes and colours. The block of text has one black dotted-line drawn above it, and the other white dotted -line is drawn just below it.

Explanation

- ## In what ways does this program differ from the last program?

Basically, there is not much difference between the structures of these two programs. But even so, this program extends your knowledge of Java programming in the following ways.

- This program has three constructor statements, because it is required to display three lines of text.

Each constructor method has its own specific parameters. These parameters/ arguments specify the face name of the font, its style and size. These are listed below.

```
Font f  =  new Font ( " TimesNewRoman ",Font .BOLD , 20 ) ;
Font f1 = new Font (" Britannic", Font .PLAIN ,14 ) ;
Font f2 = new Font (" Impact", Font . ITALIC ,20 ) ;
```

This is required so, that each line of text is drawn in accordance with its own parameters. This is why each text is kept in a separate Font object namely, f1, f2 and f3.

- In program 1, there is only one line of code to draw the text object in the current colour. In this program, there are four such lines. You must first set the colour before you can draw the text and dotted lines as required. For this reason, in this program, there are 4 following setColour ( ) methods:

g . setColor (Color . black) ;
g . setColor (Color.white) ;
g . setColor (Color.darkGray) ;
g . setColor (Color . white) ;

These methods are for Graphics objects, which are to be drawn. Remember that you cannot begin successfully all drawing operations without first setting these methods. These must be set in the correct places in your program (not together as shown above) as shown in diagram 4. For instance:

```
g.setColor ( Color . white ) ;
g.drawString (".................................................", 58 ,200 ) ;
```

Here, the current colour is set to white colour, and the drawing of the dotted-line occurs in the white colour. Integers 58 and 200 correspond to (x ,y) co-ordinates (see chapter 7). The rest of the code is similar to the code for applets discussed so far. You should try it on your own machine.

DifferentFonts. Java

```
import java.awt.*;            // Colours are also defined in it
import javax.swing.*;

public class DifferentFonts extends JApplet
{
  public void paint (Graphics g )
  {

  Font f = new Font ( " TimesNewRoman ",Font .BOLD , 20 ) ;
  Font f1 = new Font (" Britannic", Font .PLAIN ,14 ) ;
  Font f2 = new Font (" Impact", Font . ITALIC ,20 ) ;

  Super . paint ( g ) ;
  g.setFont ( f ) ;
  g.setColor ( Color . black ) ;
  g.drawString ( ".................................................", 58 ,80 ) ;
  g. setColor  ( Color.white ) ;
  g.drawString  (" This is a New Roman bold font size 20 ", 60 ,110 ) ;
  g.setFont ( f1 ) ;
  g.drawString (" This is a Britannic Plain font size 14", 60, 140 ) ;
  g.setFont ( f2 ) ;
  g.setColor ( Color.darkGray ) ;
  g.drawString (" This is an impact Italic font size  14 ", 70, 170 ) ;
  g.setColor ( Color . white ) ;
  g.drawString (".................................................", 58 ,200 ) ;
}
}
```

Diagram 4

DifferentFonts . html

```
<HTML>
<HEAD>
    <TITLE>Applet2</TITLE>
</HEAD>
<BODY>
<BR>
<APPLET CODE= "DifferentFonts.class" width = 500 height = 300>
</APPLET>
</BODY>
</HTML>
```

Diagram 5

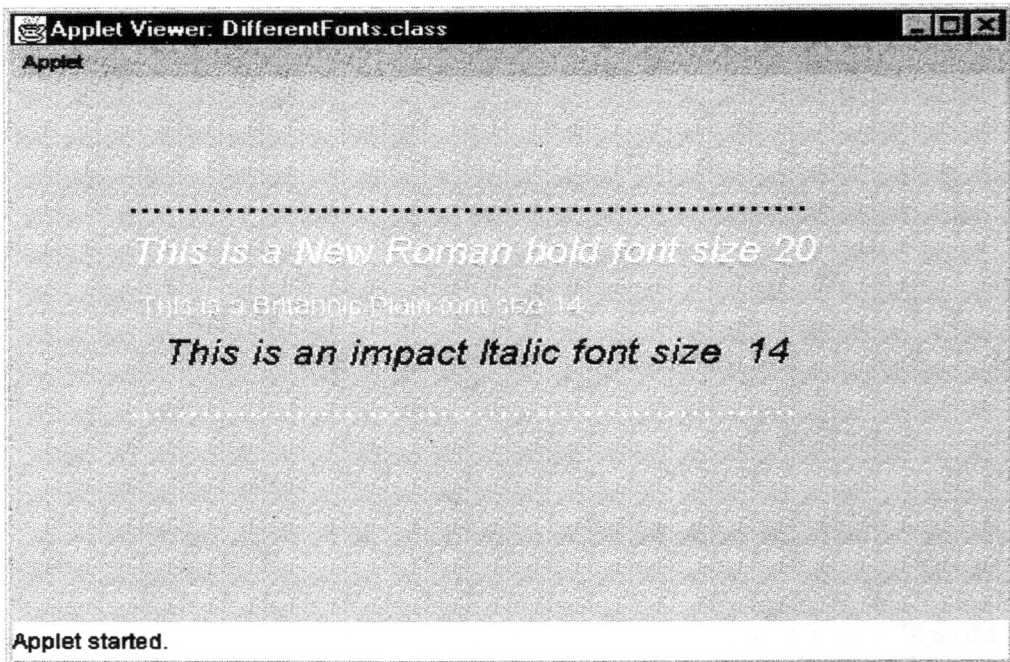

Diagram 6: Applet Viewer displaying the applet

DifferentFonts.html

The diagram 5 contains the above required html document for running the applet DifferentFonts . java. You should compare it with the html document shown in diagram 2.

Program output

The applet was viewed and tested through the **appletviewer** Java tool successfully. It is shown below in diagram 6. The command for viewing and testing the applet: **appletviewer SecondApplet. html**

. What is the standard range of fonts sizes in point?

The typical range is between 9-48 point. You may have to experiment first to find out which is the correct size for your own requirements.

. Is it possible to set the background and foreground colours for an applet?

Yes, you can set the background and foreground colours for an applet.

. To set the background colour for the applet, you must apply the **setBackground ( ) method**. It does not change the colour of containers and components within an applet.

. To set the foreground colour for the applet, the method is **setForeground ( )**. The effect of the foreground colour is that whatever has been drawn on the applet, in whatever colour, is changed to the foreground colour. The foreground colour method is useful, if you wish to change the colour, which Java uses to display text on the applet.

These methods are defined in the **java. awt. Component** class, and therefore, you must include this class in your program as an import statement.

. Are there some more pre-defined colours ?

In the **SystemColor class**, there are 26 pre-defined colours. It is a subclass of Color class. It encapsulates colour data structure for the user's system. The idea is to shield you from platform dependencies. Among other facilities, this class lets you increase or decrease the brightness of a colour. On the whole, it provides access to prevailing desktop colours on the user's desktop. Some of the predefined colours are listed in table 2 at the end of this chapter.

FontsColours . java

This is another applet designed to illustrate:

• combining the basic RGB (red, green and blue) colours in order to produce any colour of your choice

• how to set background colour for the applet

• how to implement fonts by using their logical names instead of their typeface names

• The applet displays three lines of text in three different colours of my choice. These are a sort of light green, a kind of light red and dark grey.

Explanation

```
public void init ( )
{
  setBackground ( Color.red );              // red background colour

}
```

• The purpose of the above code is to set the **background colour** of the applet. Since the initialisation happens when the applet is loaded or re-loaded, this method is the right place to set up the background colour. In fact, you should also set up the foreground colour in this method.

•   **public void paint (Graphics screen)**   // graphics object screen

In the previous program, the graphics called **g** is used. This time, I have used the graphics object called screen in the paint ( ) method. In fact, you can send either of these objects to the paint ( ) method.

• Once again, it is to emphasise that you must include **super . paint (screen);** in the point method. This statement is a call to the paint ( ) method of its superclass. It makes sure that the applet window is up-dated correctly.

• **Font f = new Font ("SansSerif", Font . BOLD, 30);**

                         ↓
          Logical name of the font instead of its typeface name

It is required to use logical names in this program. These names are used in this code, where they are required.

- **Color b = new Color (100, 255, 135);**   // a sort of light green colour

$$\downarrow \qquad \downarrow \qquad \downarrow$$
red   green   blue

These colours are combined in this ratio to produce a sort of light green colour. First, you must create a new colour object as shown by this new colour constructor, and then use the **setColor ( )** method.

screen.setColor (b);

It is should be noted that within the ( ) is the colour object, that is **b**.

FontsColours . java

```
import java . awt.*;
import javax . swing.*;

public class FontsColours extends JApplet
{
 public void init (  )
{
  setBackground ( Color.red );              // background colour
  }
  public void paint (Graphics screen )          // graphics object screen
{
  Font f  =  new Font  ( "SansSerif",Font . BOLD, 30 );
  Font f1 = new Font ( "Serif", Font . PLAIN, 28 );
  Font f2 = new Font  ( "Monospaced", Font . ITALIC, 20 );
  super. paint ( screen );                       //  call to the paint method ( )
  screen.setFont ( f );
  Color b = new Color ( 100,255,135 );                // a sort of light green colour
  screen.setColor ( b );
  screen.drawString ( "This is a SansSerif font size 30",60, 110 );
  screen.setFont ( f1 );
  Color w = new  Color ( 200, 140, 150 );               // a sort of light red colour
  screen.setColor ( w );
  screen.drawString ( " This is a Serif font size 28", 60, 140 );
  screen.setFont  ( f2 );
  screen.setColor (Color. darkGray );               // dark Grey  clour
  screen.drawString  (" This is a Monospaced Italic font size 20",  60, 170 );
}
}
```

Diagram 7

. Using this technique, I have created another colour. This colour looks like a light red colour. See the program in diagram 7. You should try this program on your machine.

DifferentFonts . html

```
<HTML>
<HEAD>
    <TITLE>Applet2</TITLE>
</HEAD>
<BODY>
<BR>
<APPLET CODE= "DifferentFonts.class" width=  500 height =320>
</APPLET>
</BODY>
</HTML>
```

Diagram 8

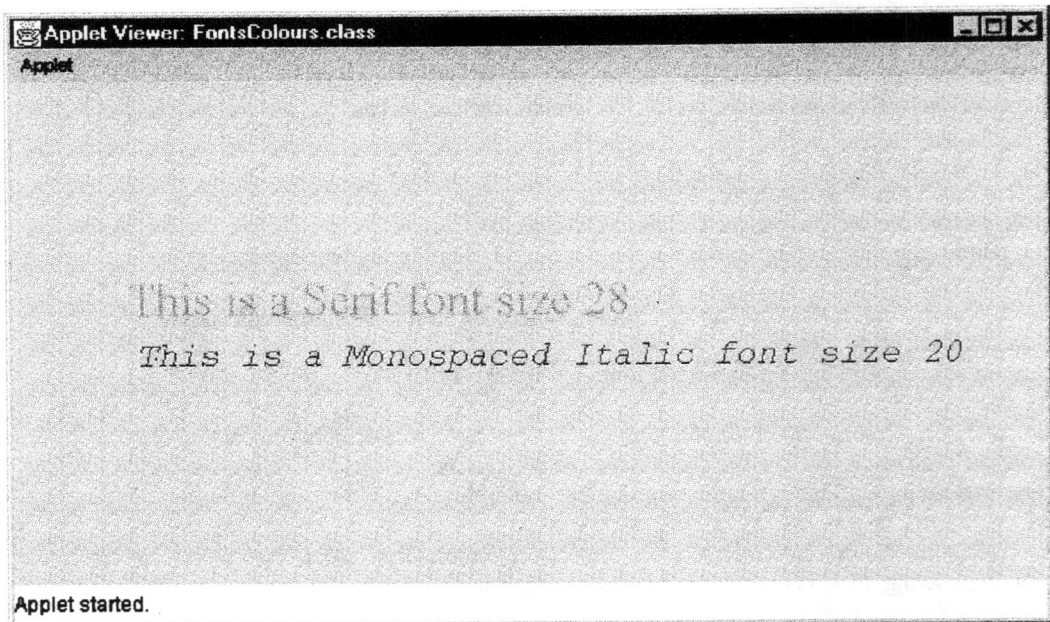

Diagram 9: FontsColours Applet displayed with the appletviewer
(You cannot get the full effect of colours in black and white)

Linking HTML and Java files

The html document for viewing the applet is **FontsColours . html**. This is shown in diagram 8 above. As usual, you can test it with the appletviewer Java tool. By now you should be able to find out how this html document differs from the previous html document. You cannot see in black and white the effects of colours on this applet. Nevertheless, you can load it into a Web page using appletviewer. The applet is in diagram 9 below.

Use of FontMetrics

The **FontMetrics** class let you specify specific information concerning a font in terms of width, height, the leading between lines, ascender and descender lengths. Some characters extend above the normal ascent, and some characters may overlap with descenders from the preceding line. The sizes of characters are different. For instance, **I** takes smaller room than **P**. It is likely that the total sum of sizes of characters in a word is not equal to the size of the word itself. This is because some fonts place pairs of characters closer together than other fonts do. This placing of characters is called **kerning**.

In order to work with the attributes such as character, string width, string height, ascender and descender lengths, you have to create a fontMetrics object (s) and apply the relevant FontMetrics class methods. The program **CetreFont . Java** is designed to illustrate the use of FontMetrics class.

CentreFont .java

The code in diagram 11 creates an applet. The string, **"An example of FontMetrics"**, is automatically centred horizontally and vertically inside the applet.

Explanation

• It is required to create a FontMetrics object. This is achieved by the following segment of the code:

```
Font f = new Font ("SansSerif",Font.BOLD,30);
FontMetrics f1 = g . getFontMetrics ( f );
g . setFont ( f );            // to set the current font to font object f
```

In the above code, **f** is the font object with its three parameters, which are logical name, style and size. This font object is then linked to the FontMetrics object called **f1** by means of the FontMetrics method get FontMetrics ( ). It is important to use the **dot** operator so that it is associated with the Graphics object **g**. The graphics object keeps track of the behaviour and attributes which are required to display information on the screen.

. The following code is for centring the string in the applet, and calculating the width of the string:

String s = "An example of FontMetrics";

```
int a = f1.stringWidth ( s );
Dimension d = getSize ( );
int b = ( d.width - a )/2;
int c = ( d.height - f1.getHeight ( ) )/2 + f1.getAscent ( );
```

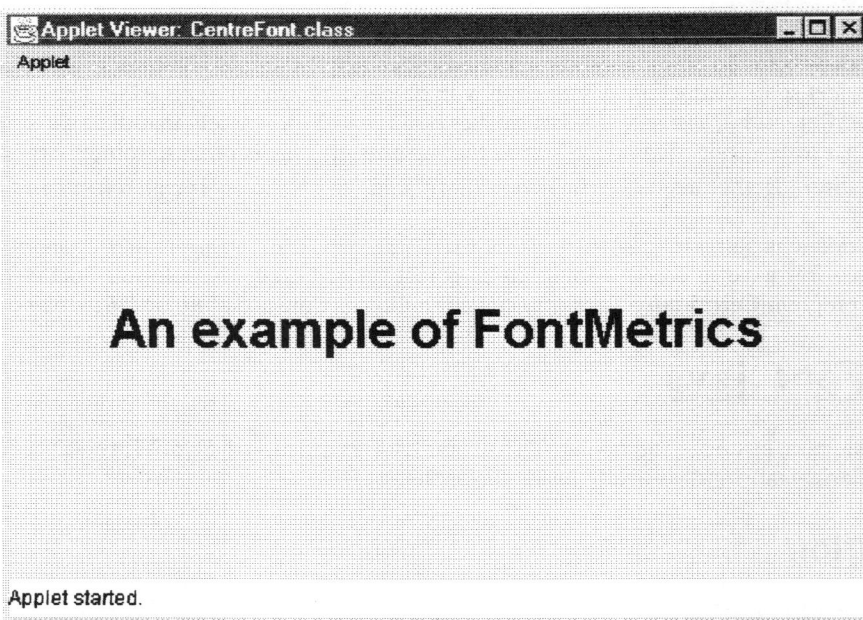

Diagram 10: **The CentreFont applet running under appletviewer**

The overall applet area is taken as a dimension object. The Dimension class is a pure data structure. Since the size of a word is not necessarily equal to the sum of the sizes of its characters, this code also calculates the individual width and height. The Dimension class object **d** stores the height and the width variables. The following FontMetrics class methods are implemented in this code:

    . stringWidth ( ) . getSize ( )   . getHeight ( )   . getAscent ( )

The calculation takes into account any **kerning**, which might have happened.

. In the statement : **g . drawString (s, b, c);** s is the string, b is the width and c is the height.

CentreFont .java

```
import java.awt.*;
import javax.swing.*;
public class CentreFont extends JApplet
{
   public void paint (Graphics g)
  {
   super.paint ( g );
   Font f = new Font ("SansSerif",Font.BOLD,30);
   FontMetrics f1 = g.getFontMetrics ( f );
   g.setFont ( f );               // to set the current font to font object f
   String s = "An example of FontMetrics";
   int a = f1.stringWidth ( s );
   Dimension d = getSize (   );
    int b = ( d.width - a )/2;
    int c = ( d.height - f1.getHeight ( ) )/2 + f1.getAscent ( );
   g.drawString ( s,  b, c );
  }
}
```

Diagram 11

CentreFont . html

```
<html>
<head>
<title>
      FontMetrics
</title>
</head>
<body>
<applet code= "CentreFont . class" width = 500 height = 300>
</applet>
</body>
</html>
```

Diagram 12

Program output

The applet is shown in diagram 10. You can now experiment with this applet. It may appear to you that the string/text is not vertically centred in the applet window. The baseline is the imaginary line. This code centres the baseline inside the applet. Thus, it requires you to imagine the middle of the baseline of the text. (Difficult concept to follow!).

Some System Colors

Colour	Purpose
(SystemColor . window)	background colour for windows
(System Color . desktop)	desktop's background colour
(SystemColor . windowText)	text colour inside windows for things, say a folder
(SystemColor. text)	background colour for text
(SystemColor . textHighlight)	background colour for highlighted text
(SystemColor . textHighlightText)	text colour for highlighted text
(SystemColor . scrollbar)	background colour scrollbars
(SystemColor . menu)	menu's background colour

Table 2

Exercise

Write an applet in order to display the information in the following format:

****

Colour inside Windows - this one

Background colour for text - this one

Text colour for selected text - this one

****

. You must apply the following rules:

. use "background colour for Windows" for the applet's own background (surface).

. use blue colour for both lines of equal length. Draw these lines by using the SansSerif Font bold face, size 25.

. implement Java subclass called System colors whose superclass is color class as required below:

. first text line - apply "text colour inside windows". Text to be written in Helvetica font bold face, size 20.

. second text line - apply "background colour for text". Text to be written in Monospaced font bold face, size 20.

. third text line - apply "text colour for selected text". Text to be written in SansSerif font bold face, size 25.

. Write the html document so that you can test your applet : **Exercise 8. class** by loading it into a Web page using appletviewer. Thus, you can run it without the use of any browser. In the appletviewer you can see different colours which may not be visible in black and white in this book.

. A practical hint: start your program with import java . awt.*; and import javax.swing.*; statements. These packages contain all the relevant classes that you will require for completing this exercise successfully.

Chapter 9
The Graphical User Interface - GUI

The modern trend is to design programs that have graphical user interface, and use mouse to control it. The program design methodology that uses this technique is called **windowing software**. The swing library is here to enable you to develop windowing programs. The aim of this chapter is to introduce you to some basic skills of graphics programming.

Introduction

The starting point is to say that your computer console screen is composed of **pixels**. Today's computer graphics systems are capable of over 16 000 pixels horizontally and vertically. Usually, a display is set to 800 by 600 pixels. You have already seen in the last chapter that the top left corner of the display unit is described as at (0 , 0) position. In other words, its **co-ordinates** are **0, 0** (horizontal and vertical). When you draw a component that constitutes a window interface such as buttons, scrollbars, etc ,

its position is also stated by reference to the top left corner of the screen. A **component** is an item in the window environment, which can be manipulated by a user . For instance, a user can scroll a scrollbar or click a button.

The GUI components

The followings are the standard components that enable you to design user-friendly interfaces.

. Buttons - Click here - this is an example of a button. They are mainly for clicking that lead to some further actions.

. Canvas - it is a defined space, where one can make graphics images , or draw pictures.

. Check box – a box which is next to a line of text. It can be checked or unchecked by the user.

Example:　　☐ √ ☐ calculate VAT

. Group Check Boxes – A group of boxes. Each box has a line of text, which can be checked or unchecked as may be required. This component is useful, when there are a number of mutually exclusive choices to offer to a user. Only one of the choices can be checked or unchecked at a time.

Example:

o **Agree**   o **Disagree**   o **Don't know**

. Choice – This component consists of a drop-down list of choices from which the user can select any one of them. **Example:**

Choice 1 ▼
Choice 2
Choice 3
Choice 4

Note : this is not generated as a graphics component. It is drawn here only to give you an example of **choice** type component.

. Label - a label is the simplest component. Its purpose is simply display any text which gives instructions or information on other components. It is exemplified below:

Please have your identity card with you

This label is instructive. A label cannot be edited.

. Layouts - the arrangement of components on the screen is called layout. There are different layouts. You will meet them again.

Since Java is a cross-platform language, its GUI may be displayed on different window systems on different screens having different resolutions. These different systems may have many different kinds of fonts of many different sizes. Therefore, Java has layout managers that enable you to position the GUI components in such a way that they are viewed on different screens of different platforms suitably. The default layout manager is the **FlowLayout** class.

. List - it is like any other list of things. The difference between a list and a choice lies in the selection criteria allowed. You can select one, or more items from a list at a particular time. The choice allows you only one selection at a time.

. Combo Boxes - a drop-down list box. It is similar to a Choice. When the user clicks on the field, a list of choices appears, and the user can select from the choices.

. Panel – a panel is an area, which contains controls, that contain other controls. Panels are derived from the Container class, and thus can be used as small containers for interface components. Panels can also be arranged inside a larger panel, under the control of a layout manager (more later on).

. Text Area – a component that allows you to enter and edit more than one line of text. You can have in this area as much text as you wish to enter. You can have scrollbars for reading the text at your ease. It allows you to enter multiple lines of text. The class for text area is called **JtextArea**.

. Text Field - it allows you to enter or edit a single line of text. The length of the text field is fixed. Thus, if you exceed the fixed length, characters are scrolled off, that is out of your sight. In this case, you cannot easily access them for editing purpose. It allows you to enter only one line of text. The class for text field is called JtextField.

The JFC Swing Components

The Java Foundation Classes (JFC) has a package which contains components. These components are known as the Swing components or Swing Set or just the Swing. It is called **java . awt. swing** package. This package is enormous in size, it contains eight sub-packages , about 75 classes and some 20 interfaces. Any reasonable discussion of this package would require several hundred pages. For our purpose, it is important to learn about the following components:

. JFrame   . JButton   . JLabel . JCheckBox   . JComboBox   . JTextField

The JFC class name begins with the letter **J**. The JFC classes are richer than the classes in the AWT package.

JFrame Class

In Java, a frame is a window, which has its own window features, such as title and menu bar. In the Swing library, **JFrame** extends the Frame class through the following inheritance hierarchy:

Component →**Container** → **Window** →**Frame** →**JFrame**

In the above, the arrow indicates the direction from component to the JFrame.

In accordance with this inheritance hierarchy **JFrames** are containers. What does it mean? It means that as a container, a frame can contain user interface components. These components may be buttons, labels, text fields, pull-down menus and the like. For instance, an applet is a container, as it can hold other components.

First, I want to demonstrate how to create a simple frame, which has nothing inside, except its name in the title bar.

TestOne . java

The program shown in diagram 1 illustrates the technique of creating a frame, which has nothing inside except its name in the title bar.

Explanation

You have already met some of these statements more than once in this book. There is no harm in explaining again. Indeed, it will serve as a revision exercise.

• **import Javax . swing.* ;** At the beginning of this program this statement is essential. If you do not list it, you will get the following error.

```
C:\Examples>javac TestOne.java
TestOne. java:4: Superclass JFrame of class DesignOne not found.
class DesignOne extends JFrame
               ^
TestOne. java:20: Class JFrame not found.
 JFrame frame = new DesignOne  (  );
 ^
2 errors
```

• **class DesignOne extends JFrame** - It is the class definition (or declaration), which defines the frame . My frame is called DesignOne. I have chosen it, because it is my first design. You can give it any other suitable name.

 The keyword **extends** is required here, so that DesignOne is linked to the **Jframe** class, and behaves just like it.

• **public DesignOne ( )** – constructor method declaration, which is followed by its body with { }.

> . **setTitle ("My First Window Design");**

This statement sets the title to the string within the " ".   It is **setTitle** method for inserting the text in the title bar.

> . **setSize (400, 400);**

The purpose of this statement is to set the size of the required new frame (window). It is 400 pixels wide and 400 pixels high. It is setSize method.

• public class **TestOne** - this class is defined to create the frame called DesignOne. The program is saved under this class name. If you try to store under the name of the class that defines the frame, your program will not be saved, and you will get an error message as shown on next page.

```
C:\Examples>javac DesignOne.java
DesignOne.java:16: Public class TestOne must be defined in a file called "TestOne . java".
public class TestOne
            ^
1 error
```

• **public static void main (String [   ] args)** - main method of the class TestOne. Here:

>   **. JFrame frame = new DesignOne( );**

The purpose of this code is to create the frame object called DesignOne.

>   **. frame . show ( );**   // it is the show method

This code makes the frame DesignOne visible on the screen. Without this show ( ) method, your frame will not appear on the screen. If your frame is behind another window, it will bring it to the front, so that it is visible.

Program TestOne . java

```
import javax.swing.*;

class DesignOne extends Jframe          // defines the frame class
{
   public DesignOne ( )

   {
     setTitle ( "My First Window Design" );
     setSize ( 400, 400 );
}
}
   public class TestOne       // defines the class for creating and making frame visible on the screen
 {
   public static void main ( String [   ] args)
{
  JFrame frame = new DesignOne (  );
   frame.show (  );                           // show method
}
}
```

Diagram 1

Program output

The required frame with its heading in the title bar appears on the screen. It is shown in diagram 2. It is empty. If you click on the upper left-hand corner of this frame, you will open its own pull down menu, as shown in diagram 2A above.

• If you select **Close option**, which is the last option, you will make this frame invisible, but the program will not be terminated.

• If you click the upper right-hand corner, you will have the same effect as before, and again the program will not be terminated.

. How do I know that the program is still running?

My computer system is under Windows 98. I have used DOS shell or MS-DOS PROMPT to run this program. This program was executed, when I entered from the keyboard **java TestOne** as shown below.

C:\Examples>java TestOne

Indeed, the program has run successfully; but there is no **C:\Examples>** prompt in this shell. Thus, now I cannot enter anything in this shell from my keyboard. The cursor is still flashing, but there is no shell prompt, and I cannot enter anything in this shell. It means that the program is still running in the background.

.How can you terminate this graphics program?

This program has no built-in mechanism to close it. However, under Windows 95/98, you have the following two options to terminate this program.

. Option 1

Press **Ctrl + ALT + Del** keys simultaneously. Make sure that you do not press these keys twice. If you do so, your computer will reboot, and you will not only close this program, but also lose all your unsaved data/information. The Close Program window will appear on your screen. Select **JAVA**, and click **End Task** button to close this program.

. Option 2

Press CTRL+ **C** keys simultaneously. This will close this graphics program.

There is a better way of closing a graphics program. It will be demonstrated later on in this chapter.

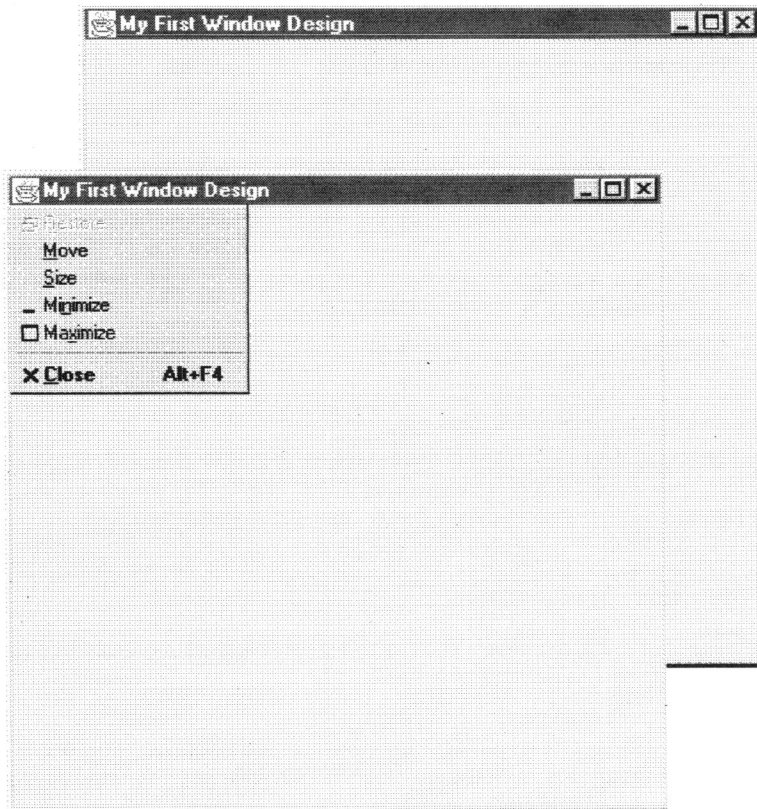

Diagrams 2&2A: A frame and its two screen captures

Panel and Pane

A panel can have user interface components such as check boxes. Since panels are derived from the **Container class**, we can use panels as containers for such components. You can have multiple panels, which can be placed inside the applet. Usually, you draw on a panel, which you add to the frame. The positioning of the panels is arranged by a layout manager.

. Should you not draw directly on the frame?

The idea is to design a frame as a container for user interfaces. Therefore, you draw on a panel. The panel is also a component. The panel containing the drawing is then added to the frame. Of course, you can draw on the frame itself, but it is considered as poor programming.

. <u>**Where do you place the components in the frame?**</u>

The JFrame has four panes. These are layered in a Jframe. The UGI components (and text) are added into the **content pane**.

DesignTwo .java

As before, let us put this theory into practice by means of the program **Designtwo.java**. The program is shown in diagram 3. The DesignTwo.java program is written and tested to create a frame, and then in this frame display the text , " **An example of text within the frame**".

Explanation

.   ## class DesignTwoPanel extends JPanel
             -------------------------------------   --------------
                              ↓   ↓
             the class name - you can give   Swing class in the **Javax . Swing** package
             another name

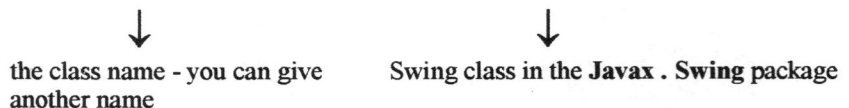

The class DesignTwoPanel extends JPanel. This way, the class DesignTwoPanel behaves like the class JPanel. Having defined our class, the next requirement is

. to override the **paint Component method**. The paintComponent method is in the JComponent class. **JComponent** classes are also in the **javax .Swing package**. For this purpose the following is required.

```
class DesignTwoPanel extends JPanel
{
    public void paintComponent (Graphics g)              // paintComponent Method
  {

    Font f = new Font ("SansSerif", Font.BOLD, 16);
    super.paintComponent (g);
    g.setFont (f);
    g.drawString (" An example of text within the frame", 50,150);   // to draw the string at 50 pixels to
                                                                      the right and 150 pixels down

}
}
```

. <u>**Where is the baseline for the text to be drawn?**</u>

The baseline for the text is at 150 pixels down. The frame size is (400, 300). Thus, the first character of the text will start at (50,150), that is half-way down.

Actually, the statements in this method are similar to the statements, which you have already met. The most important feature of this code is that it illustrates the technique of placing graphics or text messages in a panel. Now, you must know how you can create a panel on which you can draw graphics component.

. **g. drawString (" An example of text within the frame", 50,150);** this statement implements the drawString method of the graphics object g. This displays (draws the text).

. Having drawn the required text in a panel, the next thing is to add this drawing onto the content pane, which is one of the 4 panes of the JFrame. This is achieved by the following code:

```
class DesignTwoFrame extends JFrame
{
    public DesignTwoFrame ( )
  {
    setTitle ( "My First Window Design");
    setSize ( 400, 300 );                         // Frame size
    Container contentPane = getContentPane ( );
    contentPane.add (new DesignTwoPanel ( ) );
  }
}
```

By means of this code:

> . our class DesignTwoFrame extends the suprclass Jframe
> . the title of the frame is set in the title bar
> . the size of the frame is given in pixels
> . the text is added to the content pane. The segment of the code for adding the text to the
>   content pane is shown above in bold - see the last two statements above.

. The last section of the program is the **main method** for the class DesignTwo. Without this section, your program will not work. The main method is essential here. Why? This is not an applet, which does not have this method. In order to make the frame visible on the screen, the show ( ) method is implemented as **frame. Show ( ).** It is essential to make the frame visible on the screen.

. Who is the ancestor of the show ( ) method?

The show method is available to you through the inheritance hierarchy of classes. Its parent class is **Window class.** The Window class is also the parent class for JFrame class. For all Graphics User Interfaces (GUI) the superclass is the Component class.

Program output

It is shown in diagram 4. The program was executed successfully. Once again, there is further opportunity for you to experiment with this program.

DesignTwo . java

```java
import java.awt.*;
import javax.swing.*;

class DesignTwoPanel extends JPanel
{
 public void paintComponent (Graphics g)            // paintComponent Method
{

 Font f = new Font ("SansSerif", Font.BOLD, 16);
  super.paintComponent (g);                  // call to superclass
  g.setFont (f);
  g.drawString (" An example of text within the frame", 50,150);
}
}

class DesignTwoFrame extends JFrame
{
   public DesignTwoFrame (  )
    {
     setTitle ( "My First Window Design");
     setSize ( 400, 300 );
     Container contentPane = getContentPane ( );
     contentPane.add (new DesignTwoPanel ( ) );
   }
}
   public class DesignTwo
   {
   public static void main ( String [  ] args)
 {
  JFrame frame = new DesignTwoFrame(   );
   frame.show ( );
}
}
```

Diagram 3

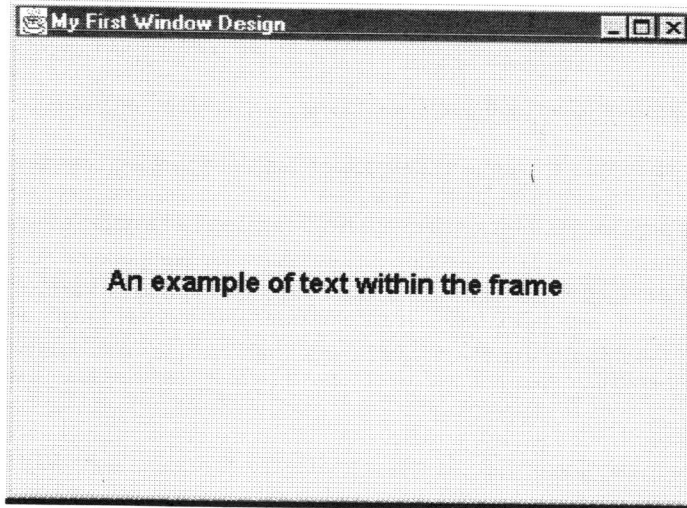

Diagram 4: **A frame design with its heading & text displayed**

JComponents

In order to use GUI components in your Java program, you must do the following things:

      . create a component object

      . apply add ( ) method to add the object to an existing component

      . display the component in the applet pane

The existing component is a container. A **container** is a component, which can contain other components in a graphical user interface. In fact, your applet is a container, to which you can add other components. The following figure 1 shows a partial inheritance hierarchy of classes.

A tiny portion of class hierarchy structure

Object ← Component ← Container ← JComponent

Figure 1

Layout Managers

At this stage, it is desirable to discuss layout managers. You have already leant that the layout for the graphical user interface (GUI) components on the screen is carried out by layout managers.

So far, you have not been introduced to some techniques of placing graphics component such as **textfield**, **buttons** and so on in your applet. Well, Java places the GUI components in your applet automatically. How? For this purpose, Java uses a default layout manager. The default layout manager is called **FlowLayout manager**. The FlowLayout manager places the components on to an area in your applet, starting from left to right. When there is no more room on the line, it starts arranging the component on the next line. It is the same process as words are placed on a printed page. It is fine, but there are occasions when you want to control the placement of components. Why? The reason for this is the fact that the FlowLayout manager does not always arrange the components as you may wish.

There is no need to worry about it, as Java has a number of layout managers. There are some half a dozen layout manager classes in the **AWT** package. The FlowLayout class is in the AWT package. In addition, there are several layout managers in the **javax . swing** package. The layout manager classes of the Swing can handle almost everything. The Layout manager classes in the Swing can assist you to customise the layout. To summarise, the layout manager is a special object, whose purpose is to arrange components in an applet.

Label Component

The label holds only one line of text. You cannot use a label for the user input. Once the label is created, you cannot edit it. The program **ShowLabel . java** is listed in diagram 5. Its purpose is to illustrate how to create a **JLabel** component. The label, "This is a label", has to be created and displayed on an applet.

Explanation

• By now, you know that you must start writing your program by listing the required import statements. This program has two import statements. My class **ShowLabel** extends the superclass **Japplet**.

• In fact, JLabel class is in javax . swing . JLabel. The import statement: import javax . swing.*; includes this class as well.

• **What will happen if you import javax . swing . JLabel ?**

Since the JApplet is not included in javax . swing . JLabel your program will not be compiled successfully. Therefore, it is necessary to import : **import javax . swing.*;**

The reason for the other import statement is given below.

• The constructor for JLabel is: **JLabel L1 = new JLabel ("This is a label");**

You know that the constructor method is applied to create an instance of a class. This constructor takes an argument within ( ). Here, the argument is the label itself. This has created the object **L1**.

• The next step is to add this new object to a container. How do you go about it ?

A tiny portion of class hierarchy structure

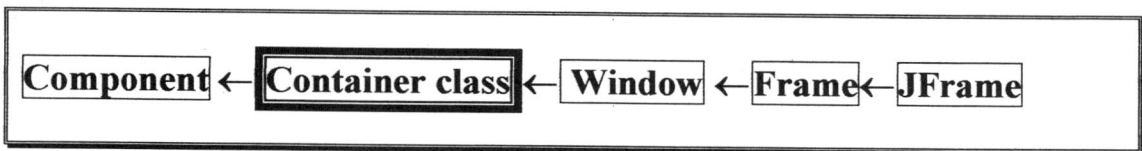

Component ← **Container class** ← **Window** ← **Frame** ← **JFrame**

Figure 2

You have already learnt that the content pane is the area of the window where you place the components for display. The superclass of Window class is the Container class, which is in the AWT package. Figure 2 above depicts a tiny portion of complex class hierarchy structure. For this reason, one of the two import statements is **import java.awt.*;** as shown in diagram 5.

• Through this complex hierarchy of classes, the pane is thus an instance or object of the container class. Since an applet is also a container, its pane is returned by the following method:

getContentPane ( )

• The statement **Container pane = getContentPane ( );** performs the following two-fold task:
     • creates a Container instance. This is called pane. - it represents the content pane.

     • initialises the applet's content pane. Note, there are no parameters in ( ).

• Having created the Container object **pane**, the next thing to do is to add to this a component. In order to do so, you have to call the **add ( ) method**. When you are adding a control such as a label to your applet, then you are using the default layout manager, which is FlowLayout manager. For this

reason, this program has the statement: **pane.add (L1);**
                                                            ↑

          The parameter is the label itself, which has to be show in the applet's content pane.

Both the Layout manager and the add ( ) method are in the AWT package. Thus, another reason for the import statement.

. How do you display the component in the applet pane?

. The **add ( )** method is used with the FlowLayout manager. This method does not place a component in a particular place on to the applet. This task is performed by the default layout manager.

In order to perform this task, you must first create an object of the **FlowLayout** manager's class. This is done by the following statement.

$$\text{FlowLayout} \quad \text{flow} \quad = \quad \text{new FlowLayout ( );}$$

```
        ------------------   --------                       -----
              ↑                 ↑                             ↑
        the name of        name of the flow layout      takes no parameters
        flow layout        object to be created
        manager            You can call it by another name
```

. It is now essential to link the container with the Flow layout manager. This link is achieved by the

following code: **pane . setLayout (flow);**

```
                                        ---------
                                           ↑
```
                          Flow layout object called flow. This parameter is essential
                          here in order to link the container with that of the flow layout manager

. **set ContentPane (pane);** this code is required to set the label in the applet's content pane.

. Now, you should study diagram 5 in order to relate this explanation to the program shown in this diagram. In order to comprehend the **control flow**, which is the sequence of execution of statements in this program. One should not only read the program, but also experiment with it on a computer system, and thus discover for oneself how each statement fits in its place, and meets the above explanation.

The new <OBJECT> tag

Until now, I have delayed the use of the new <OBJECT> tag for running your applets. So far, you have been shown the HTML documents, which, of course, have included the applet tag <APPLET>. Another reason, for delaying its application, is the fact that it is not supported by older browsers. Thus, it is better to use the <APPLET> tag. With this tag, your applets can be viewed by a much larger number of Internet users.

. What is this new <OBJECT> tag?

At one time, you can run on a Web page, nothing except Java's applets programs. So, the <applet> tag was alright to include in your HTML document. Nowadays, you can also run on a web page Active X programs, and so on. The latest version of HTML 4.0 has re-defined the <OBJECT> tag, which was first used with Active X control. This re-definition has broadened its scope, and thus it includes all kinds of objects in Web pages. These objects include HTML document besides objects such as images. This tag can be used with Java applets. This is supported by both Microsoft Internet Explorer and Net-scape Navigator. Its general format is shown in Figure 3.

```
<Object CODE = " application"   CODEBASE = "Applet1.class" HEIGHT = 200 WIDTH = 300>
</Object>
```

Figure 3

ShowLabel . java

```java
import java.awt.*;
import javax.swing.*;

public class ShowLabel extends JApplet
{

JLabel L1 = new JLabel ( "This is a label" );

 public void init ( )
{
  FlowLayout flow = new FlowLayout ( );
  Container pane = getContentPane  ( );
  pane.setLayout (flow);
  pane.add ( L1 );
  setContentPane ( pane );
}
}
```

Diagram 5

ShowLabel.html

```html
<applet code = "ShowLabel.class" height =300 width = 200>
</applet>
```

Diagram 6

ShowLabel Applet running under appletviewer

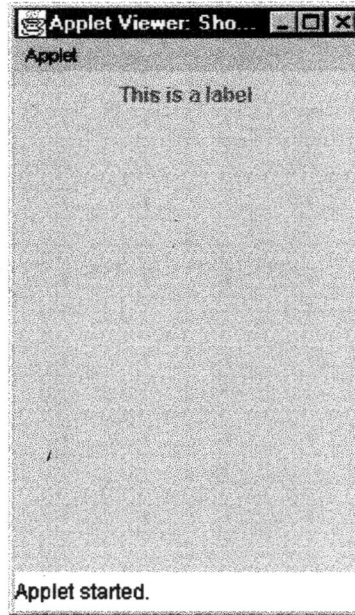

Diagram 7

Buttons

The last program demonstrated how to create and display a simple label on an applet. Next, you will learn how to create and display another control called button. You can set up an applet with one or more buttons. A button can have the caption "Click here" When the user clicks the button, it reacts accordingly. The program **ClickButton . java** listed in diagram 8 is designed to create a click button, and display it in the applet pane.

Explanation

The program's structure is very similar to the structure of the last program. However, it does no harm to highlight the following important points.

- The class ClickButton extends the superclass JApplet. The constructor method is applied to create an object called ClickMe. It is an instance of its parent class JButton.

- In the **init ( )** method:

. flow an instance of the FlowLayout manager class is created.
. GetContent Pane ( ) method is called.

     . An association between the container and the flowLayout manager is created by calling the setLayoutManager ( )method of the applet's content pane.

     . add ( ) method is called to add the component ClickMe in the applet pane.

. **ClickButton.html** document is in diagram 9. The applet **ClickButton . java** is shown in diagram 10. It is suggested that you run this program on your machine. When you can see the applet on your screen, you should click the button to see its reaction. When you click the button in your applet, an interface event occurs. See events on page.

ClickButton .java

```
import java.awt.*;
import javax.swing.*;
public class ClickButton extends JApplet
{
  JButton ClickMe = new JButton ("Click Here");
  public void init ( )
{
  FlowLayout  flow = new FlowLayout ( );
  Container pane = getContentPane ( );
  pane.setLayout (flow);
  pane.add ( ClickMe );
  setContentPane ( pane);
}
}
}
```

Diagram 8

ClickButton . html

```
<Object code= "ClickButton.class" width = 250 height = 250>
</Object>
```

Diagram 9

Diagram 10: Applet ClickButton

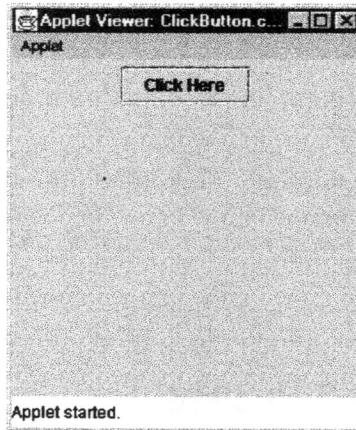

Text field Component

A text field holds a line of text. It is known to all window users. You can edit the text field. It may be that you do not wish to allow the user to edit the text in the text field. In that case, You can design a program, which will make text field read-only. The program **Text . java**, which is shown in diagram 11 is designed to create and display a text field on your applet.

Explanation

Like other programs in this chapter, the program implements the JFC Swing component called **JTextField**. In addition, it uses the FlowLayout manager of the AWT package for positioning the applet in the applet's pane. The program structure is almost the same as in the previous program.

Since the length of the text field is fixed, you have to state its length in a number of characters (to initialise it), when creating the TextField object called **text**. The following statement creates the text field:

JTextField text = new JTextField (30);

object being created   number of characters

The rest of the program follows the pattern of the previous program.

Text . java

```java
import java.awt.*;
import javax.swing.*;

public class Text extends JApplet
{

 JTextField  text = new JTextField (30);        // to create text as an instance of JTextField

 public void init ( )


 {
  FlowLayout flow = new FlowLayout ( );   // to create flow as instance of FlowLayout
  Container pane = getContentPane ( );
  pane.setLayout (flow);
  pane.add ( text );
  setContentPane ( pane);
 }
 }
```

Diagram 11

Text.html

The html document (or if you prefer Object tag) is in diagram 12. You must view it in the appletviewer to test it.

```
                          Text.html
<Object code= "Text.class" width = 300 height = 100>
</Object>
```

Diagram 12

Program Output

It is shown in diagrams 13 and 13 A. The program was executed successfully. You can see two versions of the screen capture. You must view it in the appletviewer to test it (or use a browser).

Applet: Text . java   Applet: Text . java - text entered

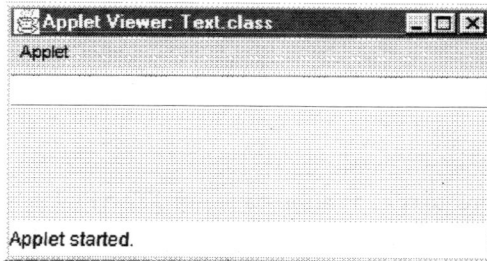

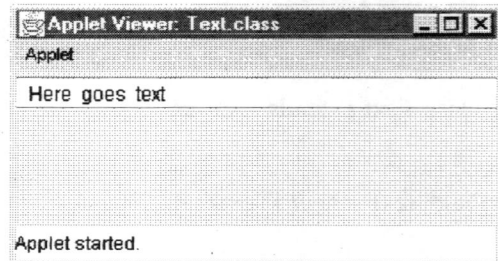

Diagram 13   **Diagram 13A**

• In what ways does a label differ from the text field?

- • You cannot edit the label, but you can edit a text field.
- • You use a label for displaying information.
- • you use a text field for data /text input from the keyboard.

CheckBox Component

A check box is a user interface component. It has two alternative states. It can be **true**, or **false**. True means the check box is checked (on), and false means, it is unchecked (off). At this stage, it is better to know the answer to the question:

• What is really the difference between a button and a check box?

When you click a button it reacts. For instance, you can design a button in such a way that when the user clicks it, it responds by displaying a message. In contrast, the check box does not display any messages, instead it indicates what action one can take. It has optional features. For example, there are 4 boxes with text next to each box, indicating its purpose. In this case, you are given 4 options to choose from. You can choose any of these 4 boxes at a time.

• Is it always possible to select any of the boxes in a user interface?

No. There are two different approaches for designing check boxes. These are known as **Exclusive** and **non-exclusive**. The exclusive approach leads to a number of boxes, but only one of them at a time can be checked. Groups of boxes created by exclusive approach are known as **radio buttons**. In figure 4, there are three radio buttons, marked 1 to 3.

Radio Buttons

Only one radio button is active in this diagram. It is button marked 3

             1   **2**   3

Figure 4

On the other hand, with the non-exclusive approach, you can design a number of boxes, and any of these boxes can be selected. Of course, any of these two approaches can be used, depending on the purpose of using these check boxes in an applet.

The program **GroupCheckBox .java** is depicted in diagram 14. This program creates a group of 4 check boxes, and displays these on your applet. This program applies a non-exclusive approach to designing check boxes. It is a group of 4 Check boxes called:

     . **Payment Method**   . **Cash**   . **Credit Card**   . **Debit Card**

This group of check boxes will be displayed in the pane of the applet: **GroupCheckBox . java**.

Explanation

. The import statement **import javax . swing.*;** is the same as used in the last program because the

     . **GroupCheckBox** class extends the superclass Japplet.
     . the Swing component for GUI JCheckbBox is implemented.

. The other import statement **import java . awt.*;** was also listed in the previous program. It is also required in this program, because the **add ( ) method** is used to add the applet in the applet's content pane. When you call this method, you must also use the FlowLayout manager for placing the components onto your applet. Once the layout manager is created, you must also call the **setLayout ( ) method** in order to link the FlowLayout manager with that of the container.

. In this program, you have 4 **JCheckBox ( )** constructor methods. The parameters within the ( ) represents the text, which will be shown along side each check box, and the state of the check box.

GroupCheckBox .java

```java
import java.awt.*;
import javax.swing.*;

public class GroupCheckBox extends JApplet
{

JCheckBox  payment      = new JCheckBox (" Payment Method " );
JCheckBox  cash         = new JCheckBox (" Cash " );
JCheckBox  creditCard   = new JCheckBox (" Credit Card ");
JCheckBox  debitCard    = new JCheckBox (" Debit Card ", true );

 public void init ( )
 {

 FlowLayout flow = new FlowLayout ( );
 Container pane = getContentPane ( );

 ButtonGroup  group = new ButtonGroup( );  // to create the ButtonGroup object called group

 group.add (payment);
 group.add (cash);
 group.add (creditCard);
 group.add (debitCard);

 pane.setLayout (flow);

 pane.add (payment);
 pane.add (cash);
 pane.add (creditCard);
 pane.add (debitCard);

 setContentPane ( pane);
 }
}
```

Diagram 14

JCheckBox debitCard = new JCheckBox (" Debit Card ", true);

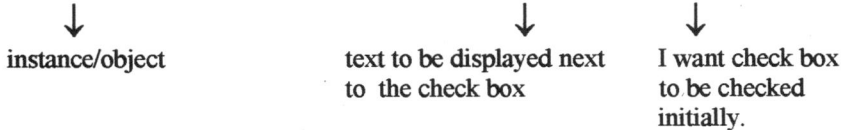

      ↓   ↓   ↓

    instance/object   text to be displayed next   I want check box

                                 to the check box   to be checked

                                                     initially.

If you do not wish to set the initial state of the check box, there is no need to include true or false in the constructor method. The effect of including false is the same as omitting it, which means unchecked initially. You must experiment to explore it.

• This program creates and displays a group of 4 check boxes. As it is a group, you must create an object of the **ButtonGroup class**. The ButtonGroup class is one of the **JComponent classes**, in the javax . swing package. Most of these classes are related to GUI creation. The following state-ment/constructor creates the group button called **Group** (you can call it what you like):

         ButtonGroup group = new ButtonGroup( );

                ↓   ↓

        group object   one of JComponent classes for creating a group

Having created this object, you must associate it with each of the components with the add ( ) method, as shown by the segment of the following code:

```
group.add (cash);
group.add (creditCard);
group.add (debitCard);
```

• The other segment of the code in the **init ( )** method section is similar to the code in programs dis-cussed in this chapter.

GroupCheckBox.html

It is in diagram 15. This will enable you to test the applet with the aid of appletviewer.

The applet

It is shown in diagram 15A. You can see that the box, which has next to it the text **Debit Card** is checked. Why? This box is checked initially because **true** is included in its constructor method. If you check one of the other boxes, the check next to the Debit Card will vanish. You can also see that the box, which you have just checked, the text next to it, is now within a box. Explore it for yourself by experiment.

GroupCheckBox.html

<Object code= "GroupCheckBox.class" width = 150 height = 300>
</Object>

Diagram 15

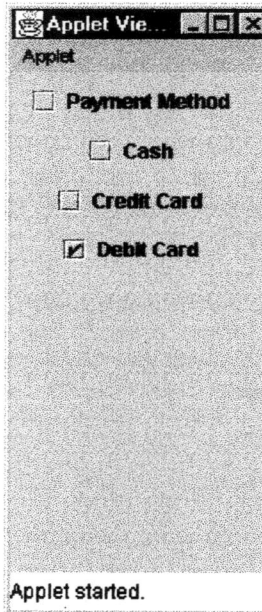

Diagram 15A Applet GroupCheckBox

Combo Box Component

A **JComboBox** is like the choice class of the java awt . Choice class. The **JComboBox class** is in the Swing package, which is implemented here. It consists of a number of data items to choose from.

The user is prompted to select any one item at a time from the list. The first item from the list is visible initially. Next to the visible item, is an arrow. If the user clicks it with the mouse, a drop-down list will appear. From this list any of the items can be selected.

ComboBox .java

```
import java.awt.*;
import javax.swing.*;

public class ComboBox extends JApplet
{

JComboBox surname   = new JComboBox ( );

 public void init ( )
{

 FlowLayout flow = new FlowLayout ( );
 Container pane = getContentPane  ( );

 surname.addItem ("Taylor");
 surname.addItem ("Smith");
 surname.addItem ("Butler");
 surname.addItem ("Johnson" );
 surname.addItem  ("Major" );

 pane.setLayout (flow);
 pane.add (surname);
 setContentPane ( pane);
}
}
```

Diagram 16

ComboBox . html

```
<Object code= "ComboBox.class" width = 150 height = 300>
</Object>
```

Diagram 17

ComboBox .java

The program shown in diagram 16 is designed to create and display a JComboBox component. For the purpose of demonstration, there are only 5 surnames in this box to chose from.

Diagram 18

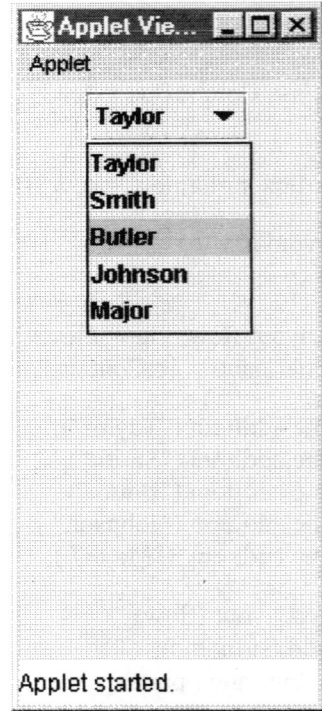

Diagram 18A

Diagram 18 shows the original form of the applet. In diagram 18A Butler is selected from the list of 5 names stored. Just click the arrow to open the list in this combo box component.

Explanation

The program starts with the required import statements.

The class ComboBox extends the JApplet. In addition, the JFC Component has to be created. The constructor method:

JComboBox surname   = new JComboBox ( );

creates a JComboBox object called surname. The surname is a list of choices. These choice items are added to the list by calling the **addItem ( ) method.** The following code adds items to the list.

```
surname.addItem ("Taylor");
surname.addItem ("Smith");
surname.addItem ("Butler");
surname.addItem ("Johnson" );
surname.addItem  ("Major" );
```

The rest of the code is similar to the code in the previous programs. By clicking the arrow in the combo box, you can open the pop-down list for selecting any surname. This selected item is highlighted by the system. You should run this program to learn more from it. I used the html document listed in diagram 17 to test this applet with the appletviewer.

The BorderLayout Manager

Unlike the flow layout manager, which controls the position of each component, the border layout manager gives you the freedom for placing the components where you want. It divides the frame into 5 areas as shown in diagram 19. These are north, WEST, CENTER, EAST, NORTH AND SOUTH. In fact, it is the default manager for the content pane of JFrame. It lays the edge component first. The remaining area is allocated to the centre. You can place your component in any of these areas. All these area do not have to filled by components

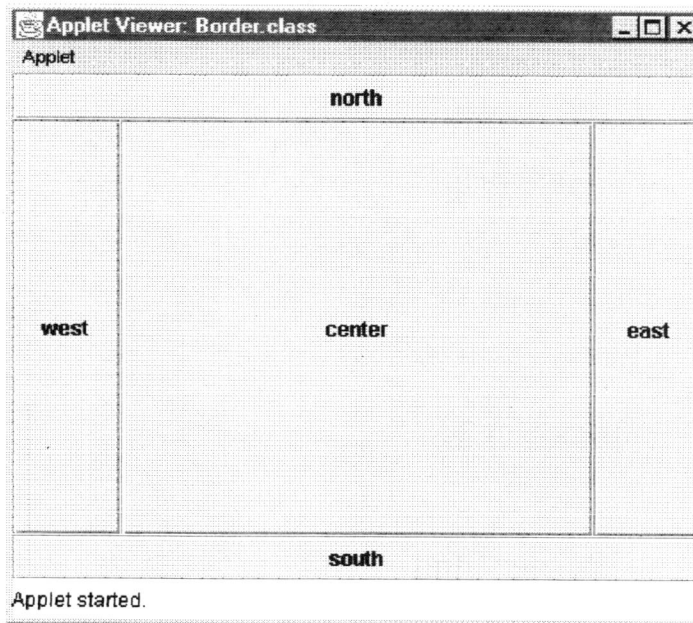

Diagram 19: BorderLayout Manager format

The program **Border . java** shown in diagram 20 is designed to produce the layout of the Border-Layout Manager. The html document for running this applet is shown in diagram 20A below. The output of this program is in diagram 19 above.

Border . java

```
import java.awt.*;
import javax.swing.*;

public class Border extends JApplet
{

JButton Button1 = new JButton ("north");
JButton Button2 = new JButton ("west");
JButton Button3 = new JButton ("center");
JButton Button4 = new JButton (" east");
JButton Button5 = new JButton ("south");
public void init ( )
 {
  Container pane = getContentPane ( );
  BorderLayout map = new BorderLayout ( );
  pane.setLayout (map);
  pane.add (Button1, BorderLayout.NORTH);
  pane.add (Button2, BorderLayout.WEST);
  pane.add (Button3, BorderLayout.CENTER);
  pane.add (Button4, BorderLayout.EAST);
  pane.add (Button5, BorderLayout.SOUTH);

}
}
}
```

Diagram 20

Border.html

```
<Object code = "Border.class", height= 300 width = 400>
</Object>
```

Diagram 20A

BorderDivision . java

The program listed in diagram 21 is designed to demonstrate the use of BorderLayout manager. This program creates 5 buttons namely:

. **Sales**   . **Production**   . **Marketing**   . **Production**   . **Transport**

These buttons are displayed in the applet pane.

Explanation

• The basic code design technique is the same as for other programs in this chapter. When you study this program, you will find out that in this program, you have to have 5 constructor methods to create 5 different instances of the **JButton** class.

• Like the previous programs, the add ( ) method is also called, but 5 times in order to add 5 different buttons (Button 1 to Button5) in the container pane(applet). Here, the add ( ) method has two parameters within ( ) as shown below.

Pane . add (Button1, BorderLayout . NORTH) ;

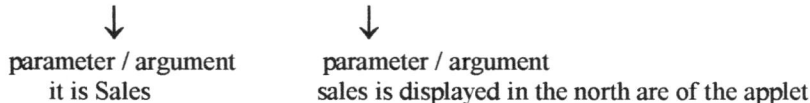

parameter / argument   parameter / argument
it is Sales   sales is displayed in the north are of the applet

The HTML document is in diagram 22. You can use this document in order to test the applet with the **Appletviewer** java tool.

The applet is in diagram 23. You can see that unlike the flow layout manager the border layout has occupied the whole area, by growing all components.

Since the border layout manager arranges components first in the border areas, and then allocates the remaining space to the centre region, the centre region has a larger area. It does so to fill the whole remaining space. There is no gap between the regions, because the border layout grows all components to fill the whole frame.

• Is it possible to add gaps to a border layout?

Yes, you can add gaps to a border layout. This is demonstrated by making the following amendment to the program listed in diagram 21. The constructor (statement) shown below is in program 21. This constructor has **no** arguments within ( ), and thus it does not produce gaps.

BorderLayout map = new BorderLayout ( );

•Therefore, for adding gaps between the components, the above constructor is amended as shown below.

BorderLayout map = new BorderLayout (10 , 10);

$$\downarrow$$

These two integers specified in pixels
vertical and horizontal gaps between the components.

• I replaced the original constructor in the program shown in diagram 21, and re-named and saved it as **SpaceBorder . java**. I also re-named and saved the html document for testing this program with the appletviewer. The program was compiled successfully. The applet is in diagram 24. You can see gaps between these 5 components.

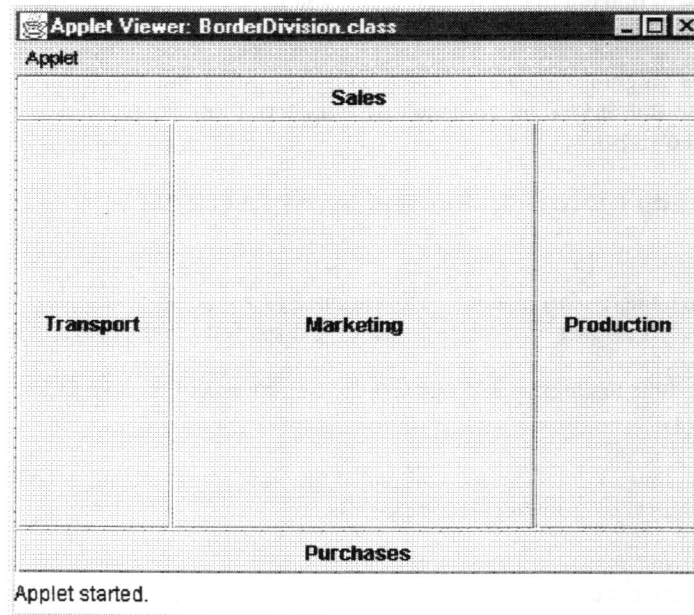

Diagram 23

+--+
| |
| **BorderDivision . html** |
| |
| <Object code = "BorderDivision.class", height= 300 width = 400> |
| </Object> |
| |
+--+

Diagram 22

BorderDivision . java

```java
import java.awt.*;
import javax.swing.*;

public class BorderDivision extends JApplet

{

JButton Button1 = new JButton ("Sales");
JButton Button2 = new JButton ("Purchases");
JButton Button3 = new JButton ("Marketing");
JButton Button4 = new JButton ("Production");
JButton Button5 = new JButton ("Transport");

public void init ( )

{
  Container pane  =  getContentPane ( );
  BorderLayout map = new BorderLayout ( );
  pane.setLayout (map);

  pane.add (Button1, BorderLayout.NORTH);
  pane.add (Button2, BorderLayout.SOUTH);
  pane.add (Button3, BorderLayout.CENTER);
  pane.add (Button4, BorderLayout.EAST);
  pane.add (Button5, BorderLayout.WEST);

}
}
```

Diagram 21

Applet SpaceBorder with spaces between components

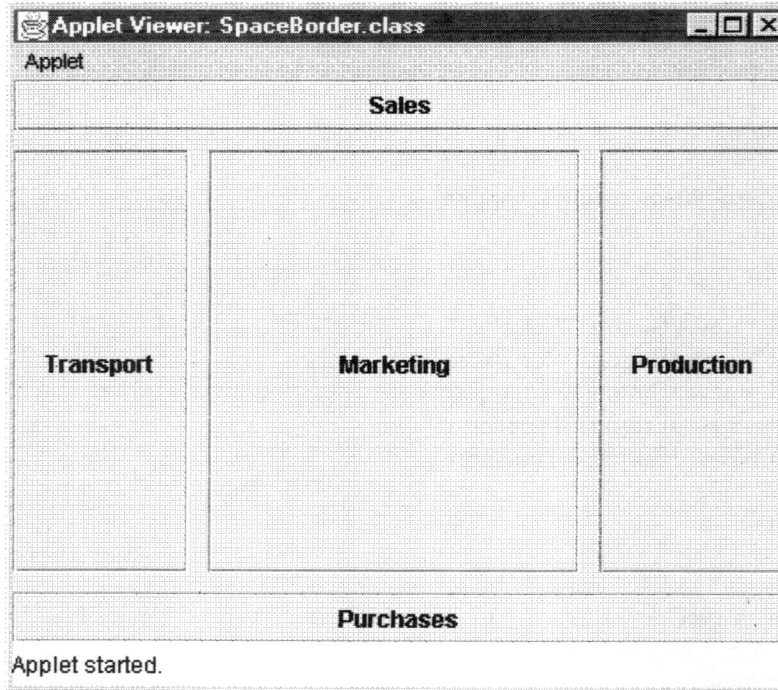

Diagram 24

. Is it possible to add gaps to a flow layout?

Yes, you can do so. You have to include the horizontal and vertical gaps in pixels in the constructor. You should amend at least one of the above programs in this chapter to experiment and learn by attempting it for yourself.

Grid Layout Manager

This manager gives you more control over the arrangement of components inside a panel. It places the components in rows and columns. Its arrangement looks like a spread sheet grid. The cells of this grid are organised, for displaying components, starting in the top row, continuing along the row from left to right, progressing to the next row in the same way, until the last cell of the last row. You have to specify the number of rows and columns. If you do not specify the number of row and columns in your program, the grid layout manager will still arrange the components. The size of display area for each component is the same size. The size of the grid is stated in terms of number of rows and columns.

Grid . Java

This program creates seven buttons called Apples, Bananas, Pears, Grapes, Peaches, Strawberries and Melons. These buttons are displayed by the GridLayout manager in the applet pane in the order given. The size of the grid is 3 rows and 3 columns. The program is listed in diagram 25.

Explanation

The structure of this programs is pretty much the same as the other programs you have studied in this chapter.

• In the following constructor of the grid layout **object**, you must specify the size in terms of how many rows and columns the grid should have.

pane. setLayout (new GridLayout (3, 3));

↓

These two integers specify 3rows and 3 columns - grid size

This is another format of the constructor, which you have not met before.

Grid .html document

It is shown in diagram 26. You should use it to test the applet with the appletviewer Java tool.

Grid .html

```
<Object code = "Grid.class", height = 300 width  = 400>
</Object>
```

Diagram 26

In diagram 27, you can see the gaps between each component. These components are arranged in the same order as are listed in the code. The size of each component is the same. Unlike, the FlowLayout manager, the GridLayout manager does not increase the size of components in order to fill the whole area. Instead, it leaves the remaining area empty, if there are not enough components to occupy the whole space. In this example, I declared the size as 3 rows and 3 columns. In response to this requirement, the GridLayout manger divided the area into 9 equal places, and the first 7 are filled with the 7 components given in 7 constructors as parameters. See the code in diagram 27.

Grid .java

```
import java.awt.*;
import javax.swing.*;
public class Grid extends JApplet
{
 JButton Button1 = new JButton ("Apples");
JButton Button2 = new JButton ("Bananas");
JButton Button3 = new JButton ("Pears");
JButton Button4 = new JButton ("Grapes");
JButton Button5 = new JButton ("Peaches");
JButton Button6 = new JButton ("Strawberries");
JButton Button7 = new JButton ("Melons");
public void init ( )
{
 Container pane = getContentPane (   );
 pane. setLayout ( new GridLayout (3,3));          // constructor
 pane.add (Button1);
  pane.add (Button2);
  pane.add (Button3);
  pane.add (Button4);
  pane.add (Button5);
  pane.add (Button6);
  pane.add (Button7);
 }
 }
```

Diagram 25

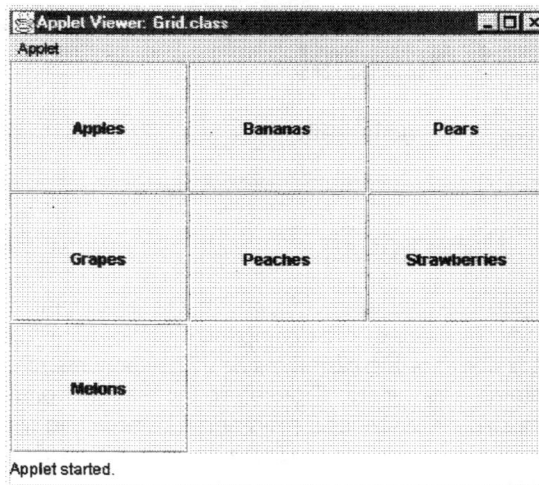

Diagram 27- Applet Grid

•Is it possible to specify the vertical and horizontal gaps between the components with the GridLayout manager?

Yes, like the FlowLayout manager, the GridLayout manager allows you to specify vertical and horizontal gaps. The following constructor shows how to include these gaps as parameters in the constructor code: **pane. setLayout (new GridLayout (3, 3,   20, 30)) ;**

$$\qquad\qquad\qquad\qquad\qquad \begin{array}{cc} ----- & ---- \\ \downarrow & \downarrow \\ \text{vertical} & \text{horizontal} \\ \text{gap} & \text{gap} \end{array}$$

Remember that in this constructor (3, 3) represent rows and columns. In program Grid .java, I made the following changes:

. **public class Grid extends JApplet** replaced by: **public class Grid1 extends Japplet**

. **pane. setLayout (new GridLayout (3,3));**   replaced by: **pane. setLayout (new GridLayout (3, 3, 20, 30));**

Having made these two amendments, I saved the program as **Grid1. java** and compiled it successfully.

• The Grid.html document was also altered to: "Grid1 . Class", and then saved as Grid1. Html.

• I then tested my applet with the **appletviewer** Java tool. It worked well, as you can see it in diagram 28. Here, you can see both vertical and horizontal gaps between the components. Once more, it is suggested that you should run this set on your machine to gain some more experience and improve your practical programming skills.

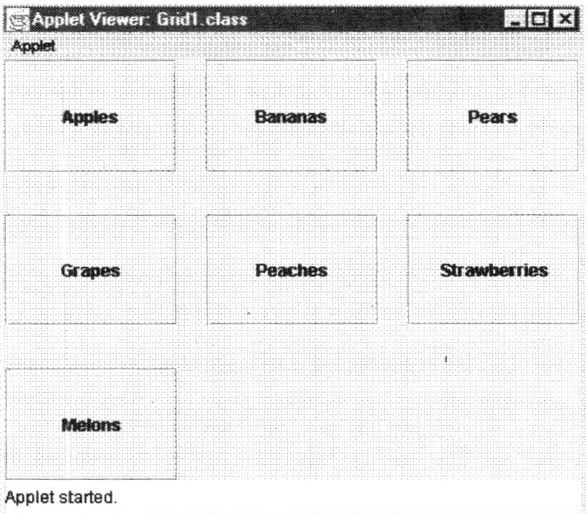

Diagram 28 - Applet Grid1

Panels

Now you have seen the application of some layout managers. Of course, these play an important role in arranging components in an applet. Similar to these organising classes, Java also has the **panel class**.

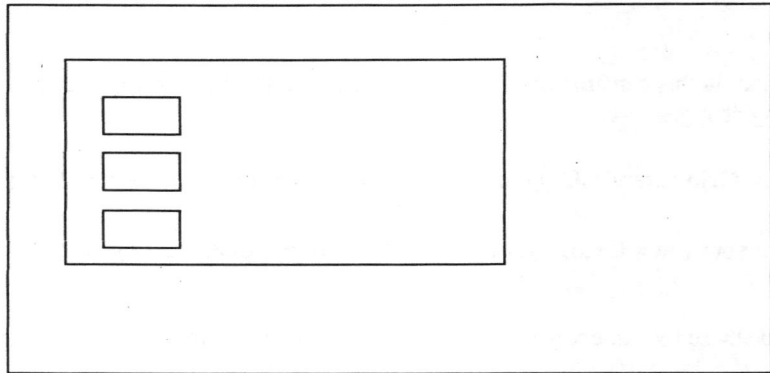

Figure 5: A panel with three Check Boxes in an applet

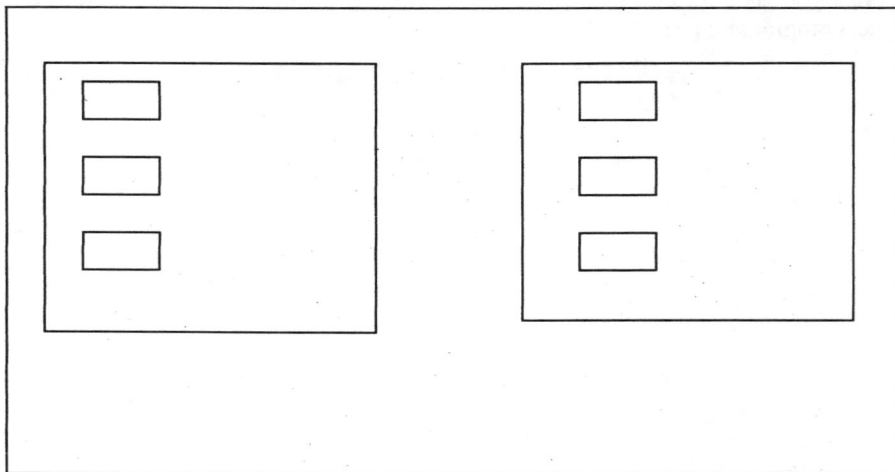

Figure 6: Two panels with three controls in each panel in an applet

Earlier on in this chapter, I briefly outlined what we meant by a panel. A panel is in fact, just a rectangular region that can contain some controls/components. Panels are invisible, but an essential part of organising controls in an applet. The figure 5 illustrates the idea of having a panel with three check boxes in an applet.

The same idea is taken further in figure 6 to demonstrate that you can have more than one panel in an applet, and that each panel can hold a number of controls. In this figure, there are two panels, each with three check boxes. You might have rightly guessed by now that panels are a helpful and perfect method for organising groups of controls. As shown in diagram 6, that panels sub-divide the display are into different groups. In this illustration, the display area is divided into two separate groups of different. Panels are containers, and you can place a panel into a larger container, i.e. panel. You can use panels with border layouts, flow layouts, and other components. By mixing panels with layouts, you can arrange some components in almost every desirable position in an interface.

• How do you create a panel and display components in an applet?

The method is best explained by constructing the example shown in figure 6 below.

Summer . java

The purpose of this program is to demonstrate how to create a **JPanel object**, add a group of three check boxes and display these in an applet. The program is listed in diagram 29.

Explanation

• This program has one special feature. What is this feature?

This program involves the creation of a panel class called **SeasonPanel**. The class SeasonPanel is used to create a panel with three check boxes called June, July and August. These check boxes are then displayed in the applet. Since, Java Swing is being implemented in this chapter, the SeasonPanel extends the superclass **JPanel**. In this program, SeasonPanel class supports the JApplet class. When you compile **Summer . java**, the compilation generates two separate **class** files (.class). These are:

       . **SeasonPanel . class**   and   . **Summer . class**.

The panel class does not support an init ( ) method.

• Is there any advantage of saving the Summer . class as a separate class?

Yes, there is one big advantage. You can use this panel class in another applet. It means you can add your components to another user interface.

• During the execution of the **Summer . java**, the **SeasonPanel** class will be loaded as well.

• You have to create an instance of JPanel class. This is done as follows:

JPanel year = new SeasonPanel (   );

            ↓
an instance/object of JPanel class

• The FlowLayout is the default layout manager for the JPanel class. Thus, you can make use of the setLayout method. The creation of an **object** of JPanel class, and adding it to the applet is achieved by the following segment of the code:

```
JPanel year = new SeasonPanel (   );
FlowLayout flow = new FlowLayout (   );
Container pane = getContentPane (   );
pane.setLayout (flow);
pane.add (year);
```

• The panel is designed to display 3 check boxes. Therefore, these 3 check boxes have to be created as instances of the **JCheckBox class**. You have already leant how to create these check boxes.

• In order to add these check boxes to this panel, you have to implement its constructor method. A constructor method of the panel class must have the same name as the panel class itself. Thus, it has to be called: **SeasonPanel (   )**.

• Can you add these check boxes in the init (   ) method?

No. The panel class does not support an **init (   )** method currently. Remember that the individual check boxes are added to the panel by using the **add** method.

• The positioning of these check boxes is under the control of the FlowLayout manger. The code for the constructor method for adding these check boxes and displaying them in the panel is as follows:

```
SeasonPanel (   )
  {
     FlowLayout flow = new FlowLayout (   );
     setLayout ( flow);
     add (season1);
     add (season2);
     add (season3);
  }
```

Summer . html file

I made use of this file to test the applet with the appletviewer. It is in diagram 31.

Summer . java

```java
import java.awt .*;
import javax.swing .*;
public class Summer extends JApplet
{
    JPanel year = new SeasonPanel(  );     // constructor to create JPanel instance year
    public void init (  )
{

  FlowLayout flow = new FlowLayout (  );
  Container pane = getContentPane (  );
  pane.setLayout (flow);
  pane.add (year);
  setContentPane( pane);
  }
}

  class SeasonPanel extends JPanel
  {
    JCheckBox season1 = new JCheckBox ("June");
    JCheckBox season2 = new JCheckBox ("July");
    JCheckBox season3 = new JCheckBox ("August");

    SeasonPanel (  )
   {
    FlowLayout flow = new FlowLayout (  );
    setLayout ( flow);
    add (season1);
    add (season2);
    add (season3);
    }
}
```

Diagram 29

Summer . html

```html
<Object code = "Summer.class", height = 300 width = 400>
</Object>
```

Diagram 30

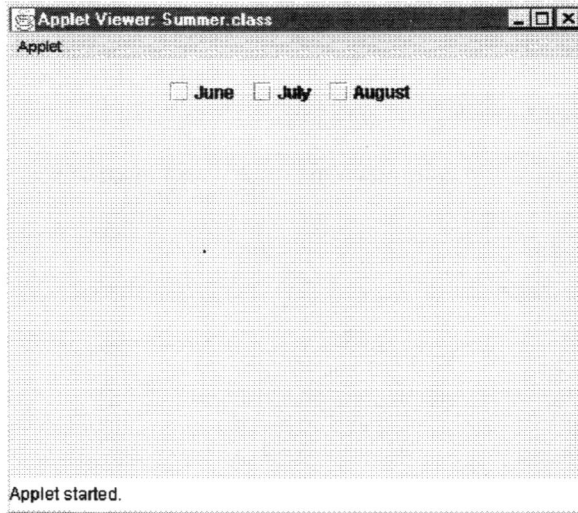

Diagram 31

A layout manager arranges all components in a container. Thus, check boxes are managed by the flow layout manager. It is the default manager for the Panel class. The default manager places the components in the centre of the row, as shown above.

Exercises

1. List at least six graphical user interface components.

2. It is said that an applet is a panel and also a container. Discuss this statement.

3. What is the purpose of a layout manager? What is the name of the default layout manager?

4. With your GUI you have to use a container. Which of the following should you specify first?

    . add components   . establish a layout manager.

5. Layout managers have their own names. Name the layout manager which enables you to place components where you want? Also, name positions for placing components by this layout manager.

6. Panel and pane are used with GUI. Make a distinction between these two words.

7. Write and test an applet called **"Cities . class"** in order to display user components called New York, London, Paris, Berlin, Rome and Moscow. Create these cites as instances of JButton class. Use Grid Layout Manager to position these components in the applet pane. The background colour for this applet should be green. Also, create and save an html document so that you can load your applet into a Web page using appletviewer, and test it.

Chapter 10

Event Handling

When you click a button, type text, press a key, use a mouse, or do any thing which is associated with the interface in an applet, then an event occurs. Mouse click, mouse pointer movements, key pressed and released, buttons clicked, scroll bars scrolled up and down, are all examples of events. With a graphical user interface, it is important to understand how program reacts to user events. The way the program responds to user events is termed as event handling. You will learn some of the basics of event handling in this chapter.

Events in Java

An operating system such as Windows is constantly monitoring the hardware environment. So, when you click the mouse, the operating system registers this click, and communicates this action to the program that is being run. In response to this communication, the program takes an appropriate action. For instance, when you click the arrow in your applet, which is in diagram 18 in the last chapter, the operating system Windows instantly informs the applet, and the applet takes the action immediately, by displaying the drop-down list of surnames in this applet. Thus, like the operating system Windows, the program you write for GUI responds to user events in this way.

The event delegation model

In Java 2, the event delegation model is used for event handling. This model is based on the concept of **eventListener**. An eventListener is an **object** of a class that receives a notification from the **event source**, such as button, when a GUI event takes place. In Java, event handling is object oriented. It means that all events descend from the **EventObject** class. This class is in the **java . util** package, which is a sub-package of the AWT : **java . awt. event package**.

• The super class is the EventObject class. Its sub-class is the AWTEvent class.

• In the inheritance hierarchy structure, the following classes are derived from the **AWTEvent** class:

　. ActionEvent　　. AdjustmentEvent　　. ItemEvent　　. TextEvent　　. Component Event

. In this class hierarchy, the **Component Event class** is the parent class for the following classes:

. ContainerEvent   . FocusEvent   . InputEvent   . PointEvent   . WindowEvent

. **KeyEvent** and **MouseEvent** classs are derived from the InputEvent class.

The **EventObject** superclass is supposed to be the superclass of all imaginable event types. The event delegation model was released with Java 1.1 version, and it is now part and parcel of Java.

How does the event delegation model work?

The following special terms are associated with this model. You must understand these terms prior to using them.

. **event Source** - In the GUI an event source means a component. This component may be a button, label or scrollbars or any other component. It is an **object**.

. **eventListener object** - When an event occurs (say a mouse click), it is passed on from the **event source**, such as buttons, to the **eventListener object**. Any object can be designated as an event listener object for a certain type of event, providing it must implement a special interface called listener interface. In your program, you can have a number of **Listener** objects to handle different events.

. **registered listener objects** - When an event occurs at the source, e.g. a button receives a click from the mouse, the source communicates this to the listener object. In order to receive this communication from the source object, the listener object has to be registered.

Register with whom and how? The source objects have methods for registering the listener objects with them. Event source registers listener objects and send them event objects.

. **listener interface** - This interface corresponds to the event type. An **interface** is a set of methods, which must be defined by the class that implements it. There are a number of methods for event handling in a Java program.

. **ActionListener interface** - Was it mouse movement or button click or whatever? The action Listener interface is used to find out which event has taken place. You can create a new class to implement the ActionListener interface.

Interface types

There are 11 listener interface types, and corresponding interface methods and add methods. Some are listed below.

Some Java Listener Interfaces

Interface	Interface Method	Add Method
. ActionListener	actionPerformed(ActionEvent)	addActionListener (ActionListener)
. MouseListener	for different mouse movements (MouseEvent)	addMouseListener (MouseListener)
. ComponentListener	for different forms(ComponentEvent)	addComponentListener (ComponentListener)
. TextListener	textValueChanged (TextEvent)	addTextListener

- **The following figures demonstrate responses to user events**

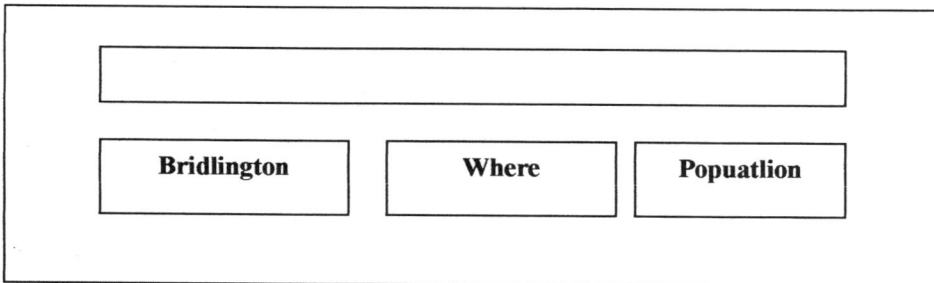

Figure1: The applet showing three buttons and no user event

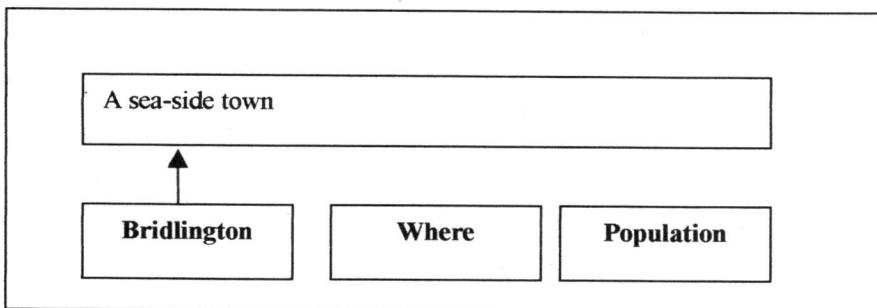

Figure 2: The applet with three buttons showing a response of a button **Bridlington** when clicked - a user event took place

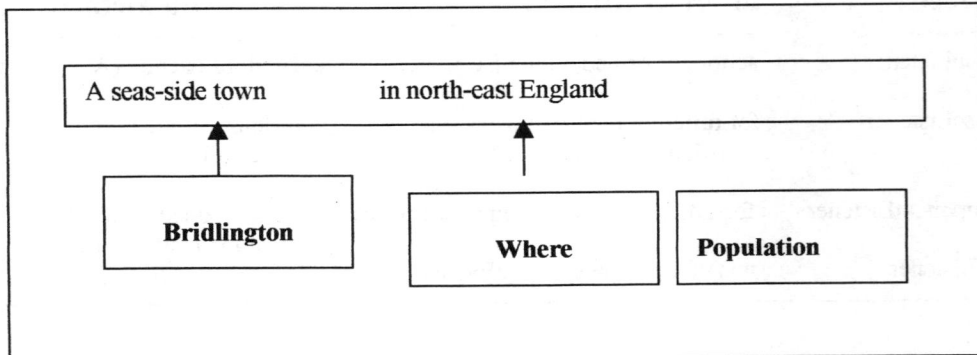

Figure 3: The applet with three buttons showing two responses of two buttons
Bridlington and **Where** when clicked - two user events took place

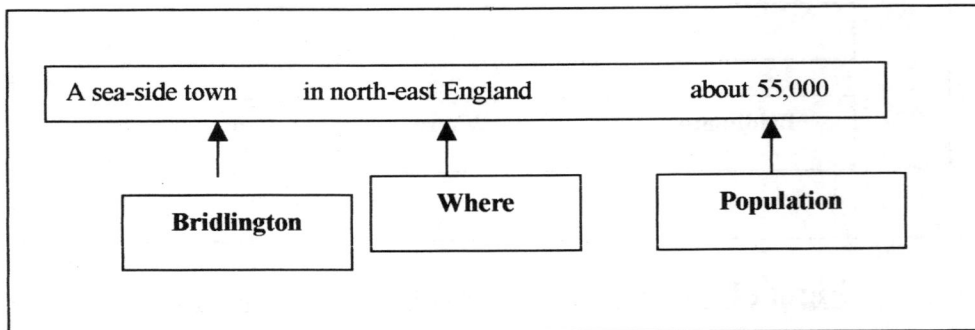

Figure 4: The applet with three buttons showing three responses of all three buttons
when clicked - three user events took place

• In the last chapter, you have seen that an applet containing a simple graphical user interface can be run on its own. For instance, you can click a button. The fact of the matter is that users do not just want to click a button or any other component, but the graphical user interface that leads to things happening in response to user action, say a mouse click. This is where events handling comes in, that is the interface responding to user events.

The program **Bridlington . java** is designed to set up an applet, which has three buttons namely, Bridlington, Where and Population. The following 4 figures are drawn to depict the state of the applet in accordance with user events. When a user clicks:

- button called **Bridlington** - it responds to this event (**click**) by displaying information: a sea-side town

- button called **Where** - it responds to this event (**click**) by displaying information: in North-east England

- button called **population** - it responds to this event (**click**) by displaying information: about 55,000

Bridlington . java

The program is designed to demonstrate how to handle user events described above. The program also illustrates how to know which component (**button**) clicked. The program is listed in diagrams 1 and 2, and the applet is in diagram 3.

Explanation

- This program begins with the following three import statements:

        import java. awt.*;
        import java.applet.Applet   // **Use it first time to demonstrate its application**
        import java . awt. event.*;

import java . applet . Applet - It means you can extend the Applet class, without calling it by its full name: java . applet . Applet. It is not in the Swing package. You can implement Swing, if you wish. Our applet class is **Brid** and we implement ActionListener. The declaration begins as follows:

        public class Brid extends Applet
        implements ActionListener

- We need to implement the **Button class** as button1, buttone2, and button3. We also do the same for **Textfield class** as text1, text2, and text3. These buttons are used to create a group of three buttons called Bridlington, Where and Population. On the other hand, text fields are used for holding texts which will be displayed in response to each separate event and when it occurs.

- Three following constructor statements create the required buttons:

```
            button1 = new Button ( "Bridlington" );
            button2 = new Button ( "Where" );
            button3 = new Button ( "Population" );
```

- Use three **add ( )** methods for adding these buttons to the applet.
                     add (button1);
                     add (button2);
                     add (button3);

• In addition, you must create three text fields to hold the text which will be displayed when an event occurs. The following segment of the code is for creating textfileds.

```
text1 = new TextField ( 20 );      // the parameter is the size of this text filed in characters
text2 = new TextField ( 20 );
text3 = new TextField ( 20 );
```

• Apply three **add ( )** methods for adding these text fields to the applet. The following code is for this purpose:

```
add ( text1 );
add ( text2 );
add ( text3 );
```

• A further requirement is to apply **actionListener add ( )** methods. This way, you are registering these buttons as **eventListener objects**. ActionListener send button events to the applet when each individual button event occurs.

```
button1 . addActionListener ( this );      // keyword this means here this object
button2 . addActionListener ( this );
button3 . addActionListener ( this );
```

• Having set up buttons as evenListener objects, the next thing is to ask yourself: How do we make use of the button events? You have to include a block of code for actionPerformed ( ) method.

```
public void actionPerformed (ActionEvent event)
{
  String b = new String ( "A sea-side town" );      // constructor for creating the text
  If ( e . getSource ( ) == button1 )              // checks which button is clicked. If it is button1
  {
  text1.setText ( b );                             // text string is displayed
  }
                                                   // code for checking other two buttons is written here
        .                                          // code for the other two strings goes here
        .
        .
}
}
```

• This code lets you check which button was clicked with the **ActionEvent** class's **getSource ( )**. If it is button1, the code within the { } following the **if statement** is executed. Why? Because of the equality operator "== " which compares the control returned by **e. getSource ( )** and buttonl.

This is how the system knows which button was clicked.

$$\text{text1. setText (b);}$$

↑	↑	↑
text field for Bridlington	method	actual information to be displayed in response the event took place that is button1 clicked

Now you should examine the whole structure of this program for yourself.

Program output

In order to run this program, obviously, you require a Web page. In diagram3 is **Brid. html** file for this purpose. I used this file for testing this applet with appletviewer. The test proved successful. Now, you can see the result of this test in diagrams 4 and 5.

The diagram 4 shows the applet displaying the user buttons unchecked. These buttons are waiting to be clicked/ checked whenever a user wants them to respond individually. In diagram 5, you can see that I have experimented with this applet, and it responded the way it should do, that is to display the appropriate information. You can reload the applet and repeat the process.

Brid . java

```
import java. awt.*;
import java.applet.Applet;
import java . awt. event.*;

public class Brid extends Applet
implements ActionListener
{
Button button1, button2, button3;
TextField text1, text2, text3;

public void init (  )
{
  text1 = new TextField ( 20 );
  add (text1);
  button1 = new Button ( "Bridlington" );
  add ( button1 );
  button1.addActionListener ( this );
```

Diagram 1

Brid. java continued

```
text2 = new TextField ( 20 );
add ( text2 );
button2 = new Button ( "Where" );
add ( button2 );
button2.addActionListener ( this );

text3 = new TextField ( 20 );
add ( text3 );
button3 = new Button ( "Population" );
add ( button3 );
button3.addActionListener ( this );

}
public void actionPerformed ( ActionEvent e )
{

String b = new String ( "A sea-side town" );
If ( e.getSource (   ) == button1 )
{
text1.setText ( b );
}


String b1 = new String ( "in north-east England" );
if ( e.getSource (   ) == button2 )
{
 text2.setText ( b1 );
}

 String b2 = new String ( " about 55,000" );
 if (e.getSource (   ) == button3 )
{
  text3.setText ( b2 );
}
}
}
```

Diagram 2

See diagram 3 on page 206

Diagram 4

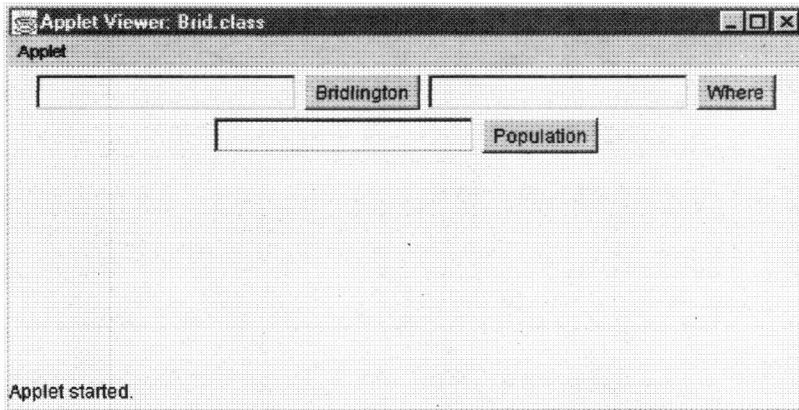

Applet Brid displaying three unchecked user components

Diagram 4

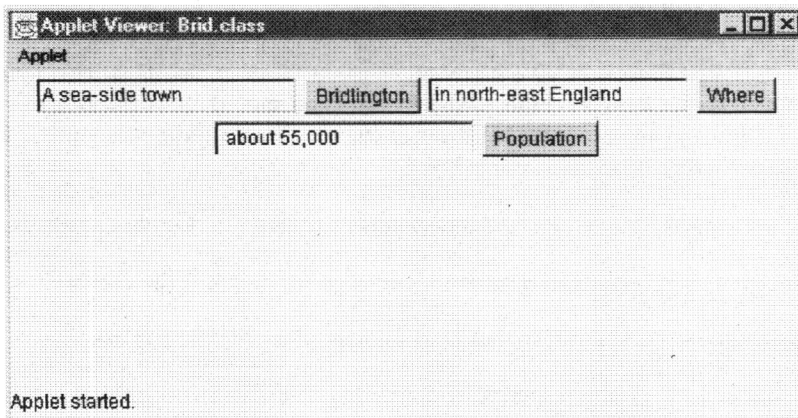

**Applet Brid displaying three user checked buttons with
and their responses to user actions**

Diagram 5

Brid . html

```
</html>
<head>
<title>
        Event Handling
</title>
</head>
<body>
<applet code= "Brid.class" width  = 500 height  = 200>
</applet>
</body>
</html>
```

Diagram 3

Exercise

The following task must be completed:

. Write an applet class called Europe or give it any other name. Your applet must have four user buttons namely United Kingdom, Germany, France, and Russia. You should allow the user of your applet to click any of these buttons in any order so that the user can get an appropriate response from the button clicked/checked. These responses are given below.

    . When Button United Kingdom is checked it responds by displaying: **London is the capital**

    . When Button Germany is checked it responds by displaying: **Berlin is the capital**

    . When Button France is checked it responds by displaying: **Paris is the capital**

    . When Button Russia is checked it responds by displaying: **Moscow is the capital**

    . The background colour for this applet must be yellow or any other colour of your choice.

    . Use the GridLasyout manager in order to place controls (buttons or user components) in the applet.

. write the html file for testing the applet with the appletviewer. Or if you have the facility, test it with a browser.

Chapter 11

Drawing Shapes

Drawing shapes in a Java applet are facilitated by the graphics methods, which are defined in the Graphics class in the AWT package. The purpose of this chapter is to show you how to make use of the Graphics class by creating some shapes.

Lines

FirstLinedraw . java

The program listed in diagram 1 is designed to demonstrate how to draw a straight line and display it in the applet.

Explanation

• The program starts with two import statements. The first statement refers to the Java awt Graphics package. It is needed because the straight line is drawn by using the **Graphics.drawLine ( )** method. The other import statement must be included, because the following code:

public class FirstLinedraw extends JApplet

extends the class FirstLinedraw class as a sub-class of the superclass JApplet.

• You have to supply four arguments to the drawLine ( ) method within the ( ) as shown below.

drawLine (30, 30, 70, 70)

              ↑   ↑

         a pair of **int**   a pair of **int** values for ending point of a line

values for the starting point x and y co-ordinated of the end/last point of a line

of a line. X and y co-ordinates

of the starting point of a line

- Why is it necessary to declare a pair of integer values for start and end points of a straight line?

There are two reasons for it. These are:

     1 . Java co-ordinate system begins at (0, 0) which is the top-left corner of the window. You have met this system earlier on in this book.

     2 . Pixels values are always in inter, as there is no fractional points to measure pixels.

In this example, the starting point of the required line is at (30,30). It means that the line starts from the top left corner at 30, 30 pixels to a point 70 pixels from the left, and 70 pixels down.

-             **g . drawLine (30, 30, 70, 70);**

                $\uparrow$

 Graphics class object. This graphics class object represents the graphics environment, in which the line will be drawn and displayed. This code associates the line with the graphics object **g**.

- the **paint ( )** method inside my class called **FirstLinedraw** draws the line.

FirstLineDraw . html

The document is shown in diagram 2. I used this document with the appletviewer to test the applet. The applet is shown in diagram 3. The applet displayed the straight line as required. Now, it is your turn to experiment with it.

FirstLinedraw . java

```
import java .awt. Graphics;
import javax.swing.*;

public class FirstLinedraw extends JApplet
{
public void paint (Graphics g)          // the graphics class object
{
   super.paint (g);
 g. drawLine ( 30, 30, 70, 70);
}
}
```

Diagram 1

• The straight line shown in the applet is rather thin. **Is it possible to draw a thicker line?**

Yes, you can draw a line as thick as you wish. If you draw two lines, the thickness of the line will be twice as much as that of the thin line. The program **FirstLinedraw2 . java** is shown in diagram 4 is designed to demonstrate to you:

. how to draw a thin line from the top left corner at (0, 0) to the point (100, 100)
. how to draw a thick line. The thickness of the line is three times as thick as a thin line.
. to display these two lines in the applet by means of the graphics environment.

FirstLineDraw . html

```
<html>
<head>
<title>
      Line Drawing
</title>
</head>
<body>
<applet code= "FirstLinedraw.class" width = 500 height = 300>
</applet>
</body>
</html>
```

Diagram 2

Explanation

• The structure of this program is very similar to the structure of the last program. The distinction between this program and **FirstLinedraw . java** is that this program draws two lines, one of them is thick. The code for drawing a line, which is three times thicker is shown below.

```
g.drawLine ( 150, 150, 220, 220 );
g.drawLine ( 150, 151,220, 221 );     // note the difference in int values - it is for thickness
g.drawLine (150, 152, 220, 222 );     // note the difference in int values - it is for thickness
```

If you wish to make it much thicker it would be better to do it with a **for** loop. I have included an exercise for you to apply a **for** loop to achieve this aim of drawing a thicker line. Try to solve the problem yourself. If you cannot succeed then see the solution.

• The HTML document for testing the applet is in diagram 5, and the applet itself is in diagram 6.

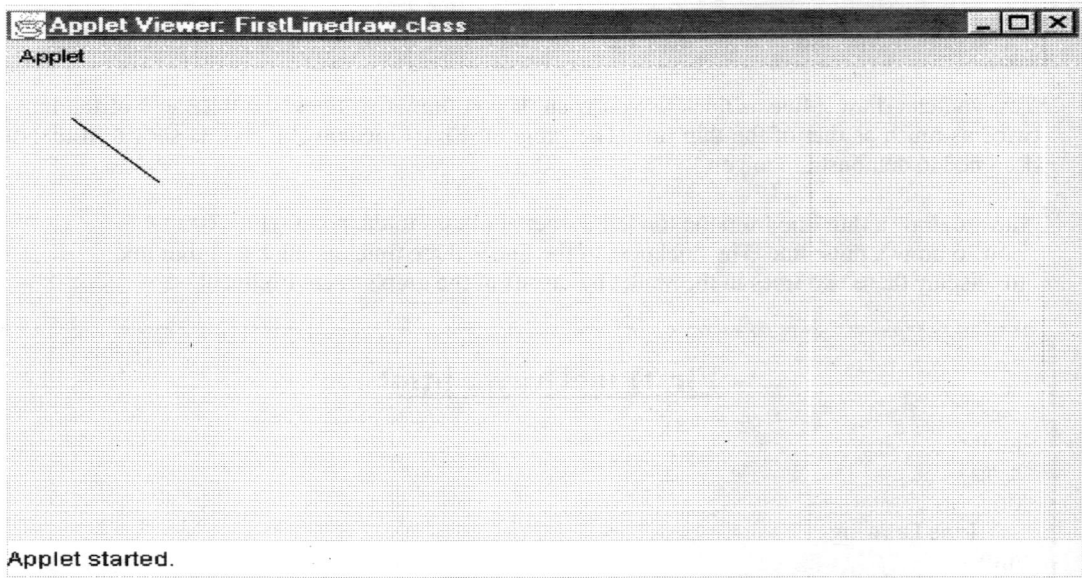

Diagram 3: AppletFirstLinedraw

FirstLinedraw2.java

```
import java .awt. Graphics;
import javax.swing.*;

public  class FirstLinedraw2 extends JApplet
{
public void paint (Graphics g)
{
   super.paint ( g );
  g.drawLine ( 0,0, 100, 100 );                // thin line

  g.drawLine ( 150, 150, 220, 220 );        // thick line - 3 times thicker
  g.drawLine ( 150, 151,220, 221 );
  g.drawLine (150, 152, 220, 222 );


}
}
```

Diagram 4

FirstLineDraw2 . html

```
<html>
<head>
<title>
     Line Drawing
</title>
</head>
<body>
<applet code= "FirstLinedraw2.class" width = 500 height = 300>
</applet>
</body>
</html>
```

Diagram 5

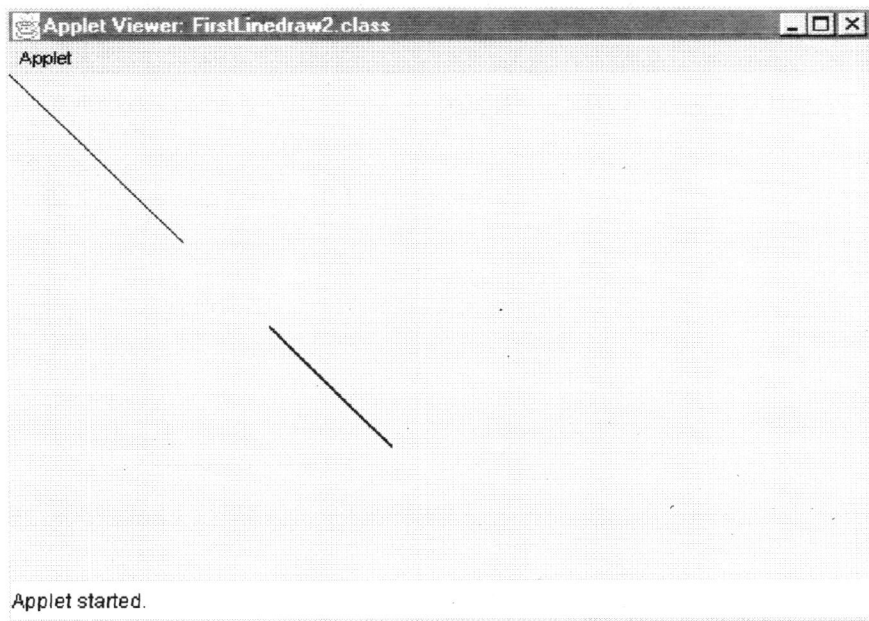

Applet FirstLinedraw displaying both thin & thick straight lines

Diagram 6

Rectangles

What are these shapes? A rectangle shape can be:

1 . a plain shape - it has 4 corners. It is drawn by calling **g.drawRect ( )** method. It takes 4 parameters as shown below by the following code:

.

g . drawRect (x , y,   width, height);

        ↑   ↑   ↑

    starting position width   height of the shape
    from the top left   of the
    corner   shape

. The method **g. FillRect (x , y, width , height);**

It will fill the rectangle to look like a block. This method also takes 4 parameters. You can call any one of these methods or both of them in a program.

2. rounded corners rectangle shape

a corner has both width & height

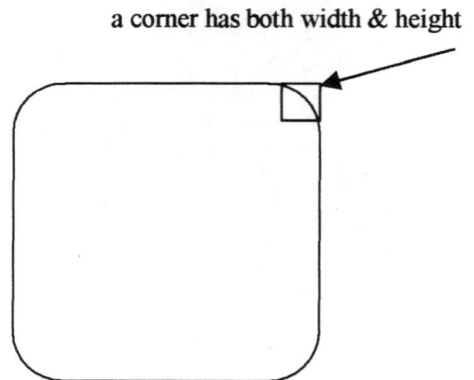

Figure 1 showing the rectangle with its corner pointed out

. Since the corner has its own width and height, both following methods take 6 parameters:

. drawRoundRect (x, y,   W, H,   w, h)

       ↑   ↑   ↑

    starting point **corner**   width & height of the shape
    co-ordinates width & height integer values
    co-ordinates integer values
    integer values

. The other method is fillRoundRect (x, y, W, H, w, h). It takes 6 parameters like the above method.

MyRectangle . java

```
import java .awt. Graphics;
import javax.swing.*;

public  class MyRectangle extends JApplet
{
public void paint (Graphics g)
{
  g . drawRect ( 130,30,80, 80);
}
}
```

Diagram 7

MyRectangle . html

```
<html>
<head>
<title>
        Drawing Rectangle
</title>
</head>
<body>
<applet code= "MyRectangle.class" width = 500 height = 300>
</applet>
</body>
</html>
```

Diagram 8

3. three-dimensional rectangle shape

it is a shape with a border/frame around it. The following two methods can be called for drawing this kind of rectangle shape.

. **draw3DRect (x, y, width, height, true /false)**

. **fill3DRect (x, y, width, height, true /false)**

. **What do true and false indicate in these two methods?**

The 3D rectangle uses boolean true and false values in order to indicate:

     . true $\rightarrow$ raised rectangle   . false $\rightarrow$ sunken rectangle

MyRectangle . java

The program is listed in diagram 7. The purpose of this diagram is to illustrate how to create a plain rectangle shape, and to display it on the applet.

Explanation

. In order to draw this plain rectangle, I have used the drawRect ( ) method. The paint ( ) method inside my class called **MyRectangle** draws the required rectangle in accordance with the values given as arguments within the ( ). The program was compiled and run successfully.

. The diagram 8 contains the html document for testing this applet with the appletviewer java tool. I tested this program successfully. The rectangle shape is displayed on the applet in diagram 9. Once again, it is your turn to experiment with this exercise.

Applet MyRectangle

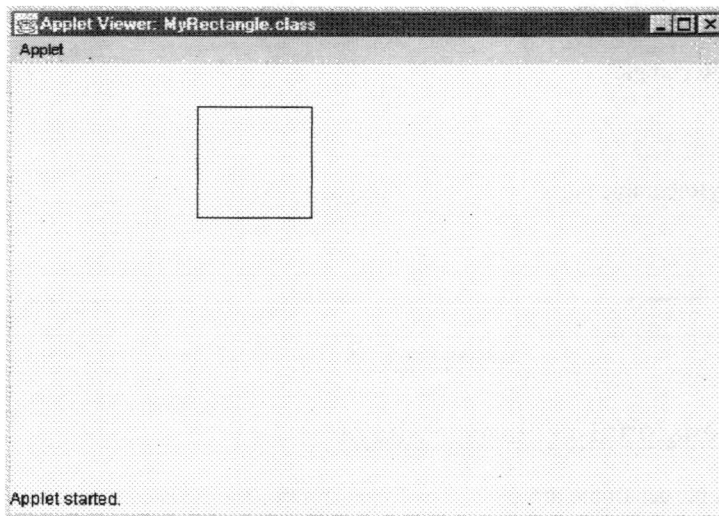

Diagram 9

MyRectangle2 .java

```
import java .awt. Graphics;
import javax.swing.*;

public  class MyRectangle2 extends JApplet
{
public void paint ( Graphics g )
{
  g . drawRect ( 130, 30, 80, 80 );        // plain rectangle
  g. fillRect ( 200,200, 100, 100);        // solid block rectangle
}
}
```

Diagram 10

MyRectangle2.html

```
<html>
<head>
<title>
        Drawing plain and block/filled rectangles
</title>
</head>
<body>
<applet code = "MyRectangle2.class" width = 500 height = 350>
</applet>
</body>
</html>
```

Diagram 11

MyRectangle2 . java

The main purpose of this program is to demonstrate how to display in the same applet two rectangles. One of them is a block (filled) rectangle.

Explanation

• The structure of this program is the same as the previous program. Although it does differ in the following two ways:

. the class that extends the parent class JApplet is called MyRectangle2.

. the code for this block rectangle is given below. This is an additional statement.

g. fillRect (200, 200, 100, 100);

This code is inside the paint ( ) method of the class MyRectangle2. The program is in diagram 10.

. In order to provide you with a full set of documents for each example, the html document is also listed in diagram 11. Of course, you are right in thinking that MyRectangle2.html differs slightly from the document used to test the applet MyRectangle.class. This is to emphasise that you cannot test successfully the applet MyRectangle2.class, by using the document shown in diagram 8. The applet MyRectangle2 is in diagram 12.

Applet MyRectangle2 displaying both plain and block/filled rectangles

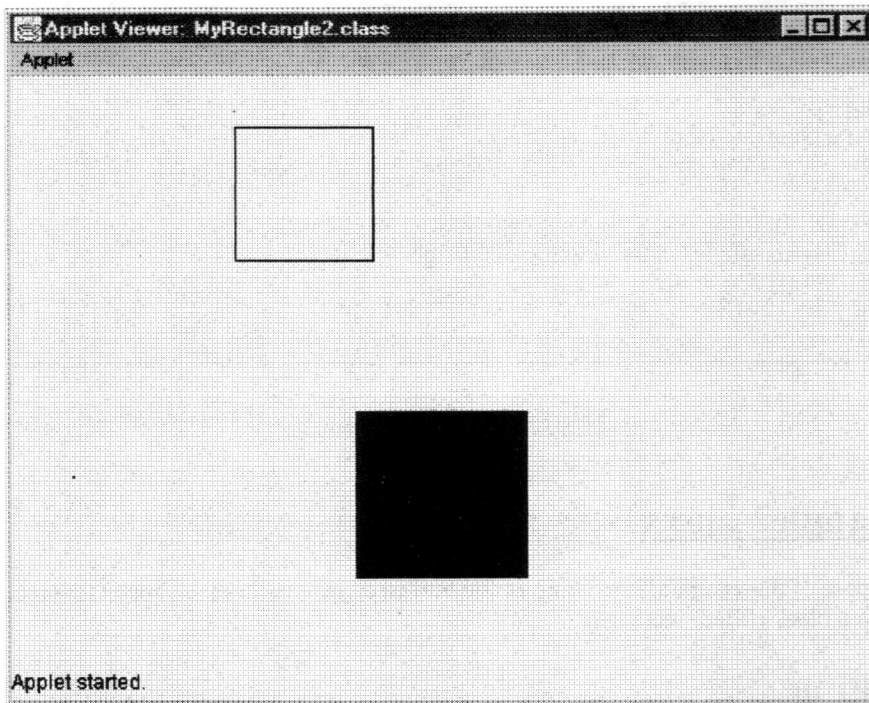

Diagram 12

MyRectangle4 . java

This program is aimed to show you how to draw:

> 1 . a rectangle with a frame (border) around , and filled with a dark grey colour,
> 2 . a rectangle with a 3D border around it, and filled with a yellow colour, and
> 3. display these in the applet: MyRectangle4.class.

The program is listed in diagram 13.

Explanation

• This program starts with " import java . awt.*; ". This package is required as it includes both java . awt. Graphics and java .awt . Color classes. The other import statement is also needed as once again, the user class called MyRectangle4 extends the JApplet parent class.

• In the paint (   ) method, the segment of the following code:

> **g.setColor (Color.darkGray);**
> **g . drawRect (30, 30, 100, 60);**
> **g. fillRect (35, 35, 90, 50);**

generates an instruction to the system to draw the rectangle within the frame. I have already outlined in this section, the nature of arguments given within the pair of (   ). The rectangle shape is filled with a dark grey colour.

• The following segment of the code creates a rectangle, and places it within the frame. It uses 3D ( ) methods. For this rectangle, the colour is yellow, which you cannot see in this book. Of course, when you run this applet in the appletviewer, you should be able to see both colours in this applet.

```
g.fill3DRect ( 200, 200, 100, 130, true );
g.setColor ( Color.yellow );
g.fill3DRect ( 202, 202, 96, 126, false );
```

• The HTML document is in diagram 14 for testing the applet in the appletviewer. The applet is shown in diagram 15.

• What should you do to learn more about this segment of the code?

It is suggested that you change the integer values in these methods to see what sort of shape the system generates. Run this program without the following two statements to see the effect on the applet's display.

```
        g.setColor (Color.yellow);
        g.fill3DRect ( 202,202, 96,126, false);
```

• **Have they affected the display of the rectangle drawn by the 3D method?**

 The answer is yes. Now, think in terms of true , false, raised or sunken in order to analyse what has happened.

• The border of the 3D frame is too thin. You can thicken it by drawing several rectangles using the following **for loop**.

```
 int thickness = 3;
 for (int i =0; i <thickness; i++)
  g.fill3DRect( 200+ 3*i, 200+3*i,100+3*i, 130+3*i, true);
```

This code will generate a much thicker border which you may or may not prefer. In this statement, the factor **3*i** gives thickness. You can use any number of your choice.

• The applet shown in diagram 15A shows the same two rectangles that are in diagram 15 but the rectangle with the 3D frame has a much thicker border.

MyRectangle4 . java

```
import java . awt.*;
import javax . swing.*;

public  class MyRectangle4 extends JApplet
{
public void paint ( Graphics g )
{
 g.setColor ( Color.darkGray );
 g . drawRect ( 30, 30, 100, 60 );
 g. fillRect ( 35, 35, 90, 50);
 g.setColor(Color.gray);
 g.fill3DRect ( 200, 200, 100, 130, true );
 g.setColor ( Color.yellow );
 g.fill3DRect ( 202, 202, 96, 126, false );
 }
}
```

Diagram 13

MyRectangle4.html

```
<html>
<head>
<title>
        Rectangles with frame and with 3D
</title>
</head>
<body>
<applet code = "MyRectangle4.class" width = 500 height = 350>
</applet>
</body>
</html>
```

Diagram 14

Applet MyRectangle4 displaying two rectangles drawn within frame and 3Dborder

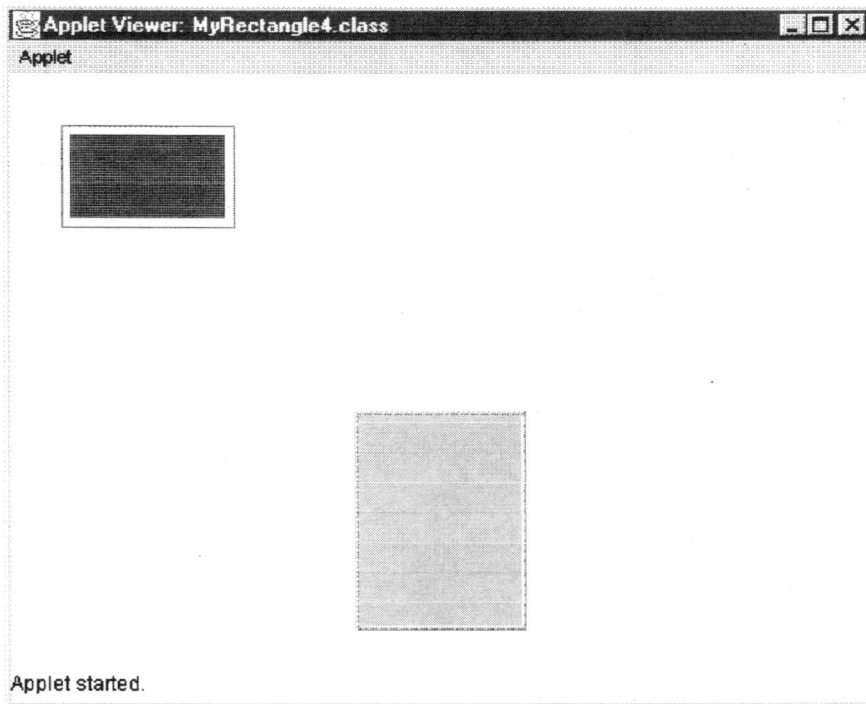

Diagram 15

Applet MyRectangle5 displaying two rectangles drawn within frame and 3D thick border

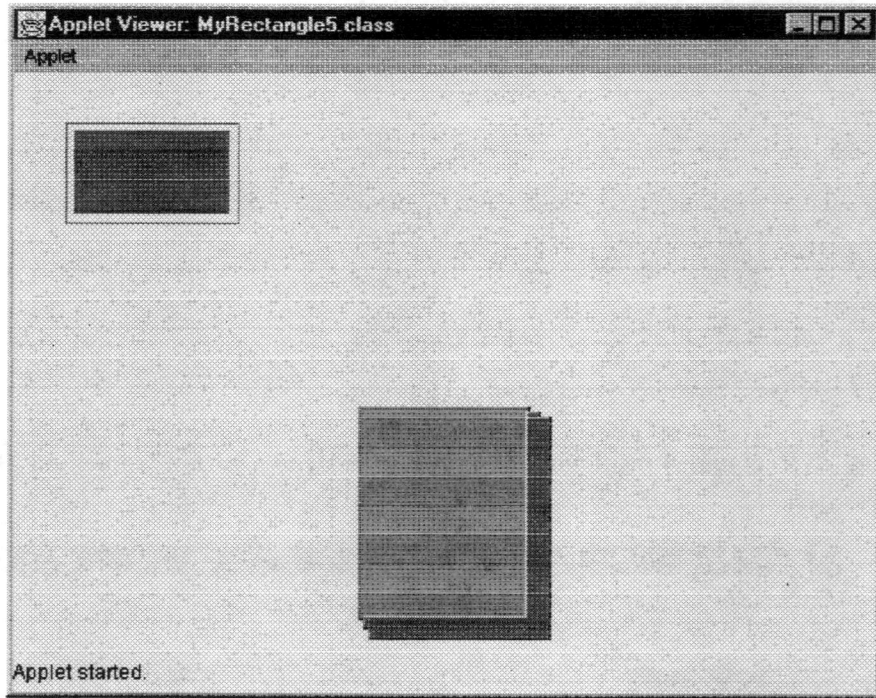

Diagram 15A

Roundedshape . java

```
import java .awt.*;
import javax.swing.*;

public class Roundedshape extends JApplet
{
public void paint ( Graphics g )
{
  setBackground ( Color. gray );
  g.setColor ( Color. black );
  g . drawRoundRect ( 130, 130, 150, 150, 80, 90 );
}
}
```

Diagram 16

Roundedshape . java

The program listed in diagram 16 demonstrates how to create a rounded rectangle shape, and display it in the applet. The program is identical to the programs in this chapter, but it gives you the opportunity to learn how to put theory into practice. The html file for testing this applet is in diagram 17, and the applet is shown displaying the rounded rectangle.

Roundedshape . html

```
<html>
<head>
<title>
        Rounded shape
</title>
</head>
<body>
<applet code= "Roundedshape.class" width = 500 height = 300>
</applet>
</body>
</html>
```

Diagram 17

Applet Rounded displaying the rounded rectangle

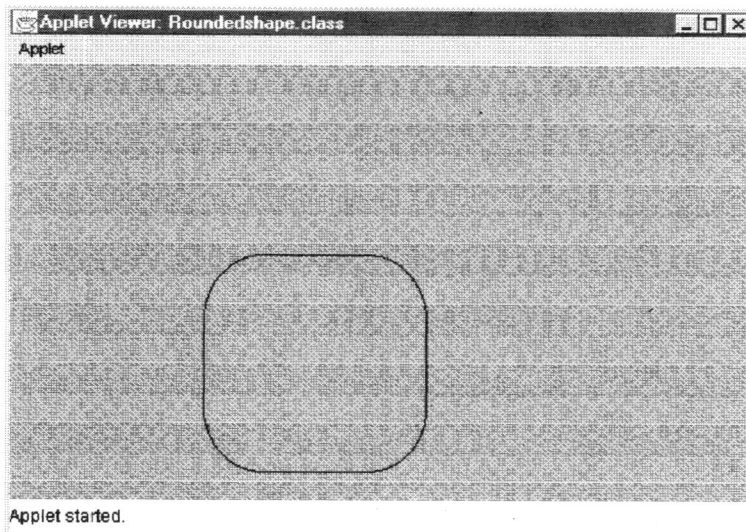

Diagram 18

Polygons

Polygons can have many sides. Thus, you are free to use your unlimited imagination to draw shapes of unlimited sides. You can think of a polygon as a straight line drawing, using several straight lines. These lines are drawn from the first point to the second, from the second to the third, from the third to the fourth point, until the last point.

You can draw either a plain or filled polygon. The first thing you have to decide is how you are going to declare the list of co-ordinates needed for drawing the polygon. Here, I will make use of the array technique to list the co-ordinates for drawing a polygon. This is illustrated below.

MyPolygon. Java

The program shown in diagram 19 is designed to show you how to draw and display in the applet a polygon which has 10 sides.

Explanation

• Although the structure of this program is identical to the structure of the last program, yet it applies the following specific technique which must be understood. In order to specify the values of **x co-ordinates** of a polygon which has 10 sides, the array method is implemented in the following statement:

int Xval [ ] = { 40, 67, 50, 70, 20, 100, 50, 34, 75, 20 } ;

integer x values	nothing here	curly bracket is essential to start the list	list of 10 integer numbers array elements	curly bracket is necessary to mark the end of the list

• The **y co-ordinates** are also declared as a list in this manner. The number of elements in the y co-ordinates must be equal to the number of elements in **x** co-ordinates. See the program.

• the computer should know the total number of points to complete the drawing. The code for it is given below:

int total = Xval . length;

It must be an integer.

• The polygon is drawn by calling the method drawPolygon ( ) , and it is filled by using the fillPolygon ( ) method.

• The html document is in diagram 20. The applet: **MyPolygon. Class** is shown in diagram 21.

MyPolygon. java

```java
import java .awt. Graphics;
import javax.swing.*;

public  class MyPolygon extends JApplet
{
public void paint (Graphics g)
{
  int Xval  [ ]  = { 40,  67,  50,  70,  20, 100,  50,  34,  75, 20 };
  int YVal [ ] = { 50, 100,  78, 89,  90,  66,  100,  80,  58, 60 };

   int total = Xval .length;                // number of points

  g . drawPolygon ( XVal, YVal, total);

  g . fillPolygon ( XVal, YVal, total);
}
}
```

Diagram 19

MyPolygon .html

```html
<html>
<head>
<title>
        Drawing Polygon
</title>
</head>
<body>
<applet code= "MyPolygon.class" width = 500 height = 300>
</applet>
</body>
</html>
```

Diagram 20

Applet MyPolygon displaying the polygon

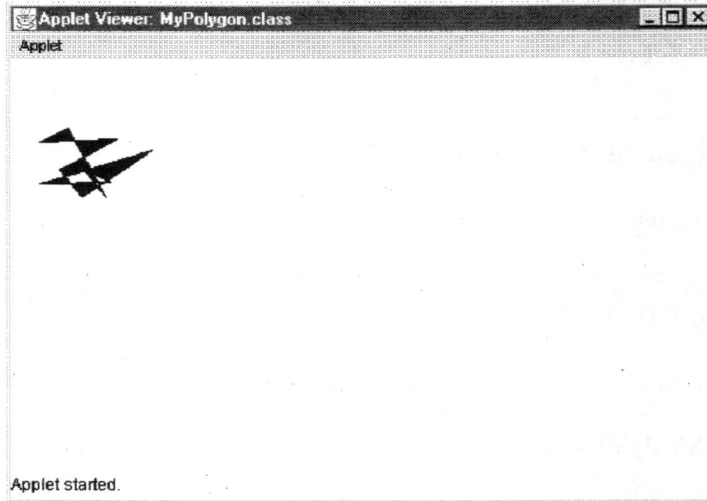

Diagram 21

MyPolygon1.java

This is another program designed to display a polygon in the applet MyPolygon1.class. The program is listed in diagram 22.

Explanation

• For this polygon the background colour is grey, and that the polygon is filled with a red colour. You will be able to see these colours on your screen if you test it with the appletviewer.

• Since the Colour class is implemented here, the import statement **import java .awt. Graphics;** is now **import java .awt.*;**

•The x, y co-ordinates have different values to draw entirely a different polygon shape so that you can compare it with the polygon shown in diagram 21.

• Now, you can appreciate that the Java AWT package enables you to use a number of graphics primitives to create many different types of shape.

. The **html** document is in diagram 23 so that you can use it with the appletviewer to test this applet. The applet is in diagram 24, showing the required polygon shape. It works well!

MyPolygon1.java

```java
import java . awt.*;
import javax . swing.*;

public  class MyPolygon1 extends JApplet
{
public void paint ( Graphics g )
{
  setBackground ( Color.darkGray );

  int Xval  [ ] = {140, 167, 50,   170, 120,  100, 250, 234, 275, 120};
  int YVal [ ] = {150,  100, 178, 189,  290, 266, 200, 180, 158, 160};
  int total = Xval . length;
  g . drawPolygon (  XVal, YVal, total );
  g. setColor( Color. red );
  g. fillPolygon (  XVal, YVal, total );
}
}
```

Diagram 22

MyPolygon1.html

```html
<html>
<head>
<title>
        Drawing Polygon
</title>
</head>
<body>
<applet code= "MyPolygon1.class" width = 500 height = 300>
</applet>
</body>
</html>
```

Diagram 23

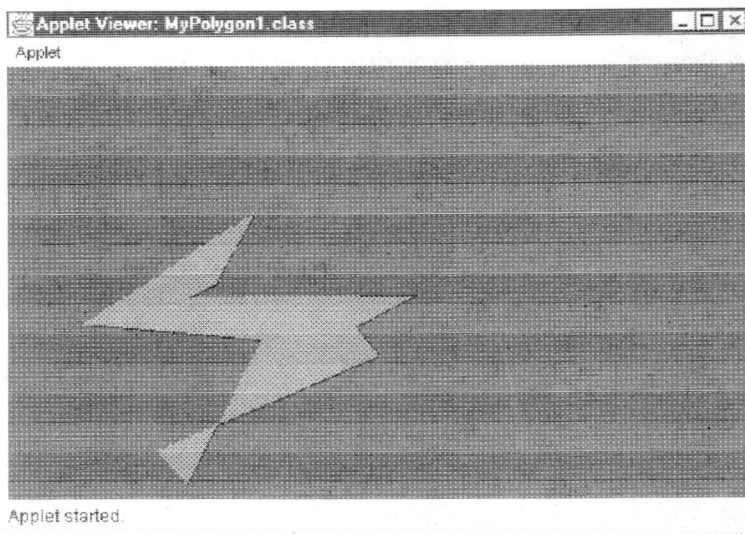

Applet MyPolygon1 displaying a polygon

Diagram 24

Ovals

Ovals are another type of rectangles. Ovals have **overly** rounded corners. How can you draw an oval?

You have to provide the drawOval ( ) method with 4 parameters. These parameters are highlighted in the following general drawOval format;

DrawOval (x, y, w, h)

```
------------  -----  ---  ---
     ↑          ↑     ↑    ↑
```

Method to draw oval   x,y   width height   - width and height set the size of an oval.
for plain or   co-ordinates
outline oval   for the top left corner

The parameters are whole numbers. Ovals are used to draw circles and ellipses. The general format of the filled oval is identical, except that **fillOval ( )** method is called to draw it.

MyOval . Java

This program is designed to show you four different oval shapes. These are in different colours and sizes, and are displayed in the applet. The program is listed in diagram 27. The program is identical to the other programs in this chapter. The html file is in diagram 26. The applet MyOval is in diagram 25 below. It has 4 ovals of different sizes and shapes. Now, it is your turn to experiment with ovals. What are circles and ellipses? Circles and ellipses are regular ovals.

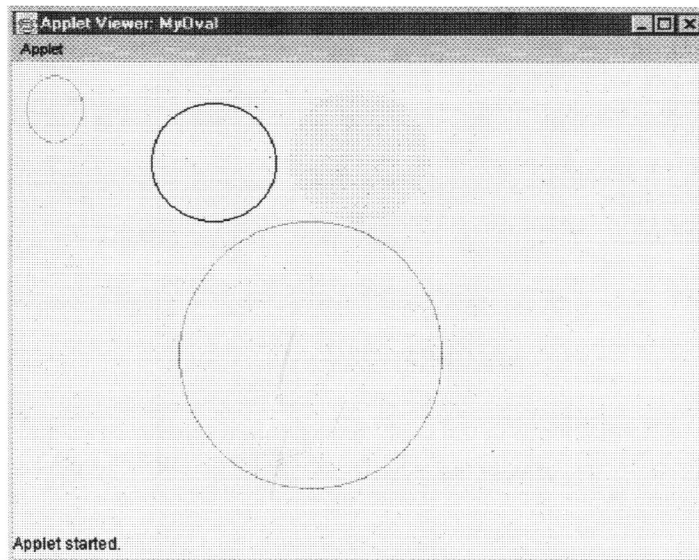

Diagram 25 - Applet MyOval displaying 4 oval shapes (red & yellow faint in black & white)

MyOval . html

```
</html>
<head>
<title>
        Drawing  oval of different shapes
</title>
</head>
<body>
<applet code= "MyOval" width = 500 height = 350>
</applet>
</body>
</html>
```

Diagram 26

MyOval.java

```
import java . awt . *;
import javax.swing.*;

public  class MyOval extends JApplet
{
public void paint (Graphics g)
{
  g.drawOval (100,30,90,90);
  g.setColor(Color.yellow);
  g.fillOval (200,20,100,100);
  g.setColor (Color.red);
  g.drawOval (10,10, 40,50);
  g.setColor(Color.blue);
  g.drawOval (120,120,190,200);
}
}
```

Diagram 27

Note There is no difference in terms of stating parameters for ovals and rectangles. Thus, when you draw a circle or ellipse, you do not state the centre of the ellipse or circle. The (x, y) co-ordinates are not for the centre, but for the top-left corner as described earlier on.

Arcs

The arc is a segment of an ellipse or a circle. The arc methods are also in the AWT Graphics class. The drawing methods for arcs have been developed from the oval methods. In order to draw an arc, you have to provide 6 integer values as parameters to the drawArc ( ) method. The general format of the drawArc ( ) method is as follows:

.

DrwaArc (x, y, w, h, a)
        ↑ ↑   ↑   ↑   ↑
        x y width height angles at which arc starts and angle at
        -----   which arc stops drawing - 2 values
          ↑
(x , y) co-ordinates for the top left corner stated as integer values

• Angles are stated in degrees. The size of an angle may be negative, if you wish to state it as clock-wise; otherwise the direction of the angle is counter-clockwise. Thus, **0** (zero) degree is at 3 o'clock, 180 degrees at 9 o'clock, 90 degrees at 12 o'clock, and 270 at 6 o'clock. The positive direction is clockwise. When planning to draw an arc, it may help you to visualise it as a slice of a circle.

• In order to fill an arc, you can call the **fillArc ( )** method. This method also takes 6 arguments as shown above.

<u>Applet MyArc displaying three arcs started at a different angle</u>
<u>with different width and height, and ended at a different angle</u>

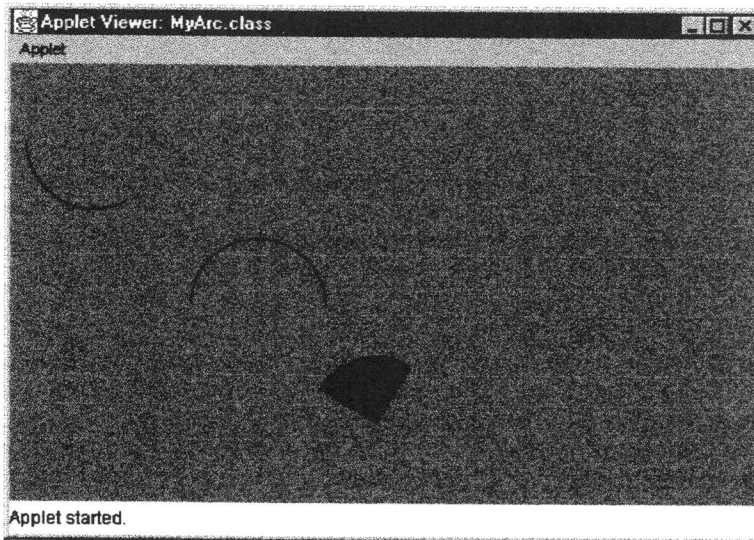

Diagram 28

<u>MyArc . java</u>

```
import java.awt.*;
import javax.swing.*;
public  class MyArc extends JApplet
{
public void paint (Graphics g)
{
 setBackground (Color.gray);
 g.drawArc ( 120, 120, 90, 90, 0,180 );      // starting at 3 o'clock  - counter-clockwise
 g.fillArc ( 200, 200, 90, 90, 60,90 );       // starting at 60 degrees - counter-clockwise
 g.drawArc ( 10, 10, 90, 90,-180, 120);      // staring at 9 0'clock clockwise
 }
 }
```

Diagram 29

MyArc1 . html

```
<html>
<head>
<title>
        Drawing arcs
</title>
</head>
<body>
<applet code = "MyArc1.class" width = 500 height = 300>
</applet>
</body>
</html>
```

Diagram 30

MyArc.java

The program shown in diagram 29 is designed to demonstrate how to create three different arcs and display these in an applet. The applet MyArc is in diagram 28. MyArc. html is in diagram 30 above.

Explanation

• The structure of the program is identical to the structure of the last program. The arcs are drawn by calling the **drawArc ( )** method, The filled arc is drawn by calling the **fillArc ( )** method.

• The following code results in drawing an arc starting at 3 o'clock (0 degree) , and ending at 9 o'clock0 (180 degrees).

g. drawArc (120, 120, 90, 90, 0, 180);

↑   ↑

start   end
angle angle

• When deciding the shape of the arc, think in terms of degrees around a circle. In this case, the zero degree gives the starting point at 3 o'clock. How far should the arc sweep? You have to decide. Here, it sweeps in the counter-clockwise direction, and ends at 180 degrees. This way, you can analyse the other statements.

• The filled arc looks like a portion of a pie since both ends of the arc are joined to the centre of the arc. This is how a filled arc is drawn. **Try it on your machine!**

Exercises

1. By applying the Java graphics primitives as illustrated in this chapter, write an applet class which will extend the **JApplet** parent class (a Swing class). The applet's background colour should be **light grey**. In this applet, you should display the following shapes created by using the Java graphics techniques as illustrated in this chapter.

. Draw a straight line. Use any colour of your choice.

. Where this straight line ends, start another straight line, joining the first straight line. The joining line should be in any different colour of your choice so that it can be distinguished from the first straight line.

. Use the **for loop** in order to draw another line which should be thicker than any of the straight lines drawn by using the drawLine ( ) method alone.

. draw a circle using the rounded rectangle method. You can use any colour for this circle.

. Draw an arc which starts at 270 degrees in a clockwise direction and ends at 12 o' clock. Use any colour to fill it.

. Write the html document, using the applet tag for testing the applet with the appletviewer Java tool.

. Test the applet to ensure all the above tasks are completed successfully.

2. Write an applet class DemoTC (or call it by another name) which will extend the JApplet superclass. In this applet, you should display a pie chart using different colours for each portion or slice of the pie.

. Use the following figures called sum for each size of the pie.

    1500,1500, 2000, 1200, 1900, 2500, 1800, 2400, 3000, 900.

. call the **Color class** for filling each portion/slice with different colours for each portion. For instance, red colour for the portion sum 1500, blue colour for the next portion sum 1500, and some other colours of your choice.

Hints

. Think in terms of arrays for 10 sum values.

. Extend arrays idea for filling each portion with a different colour.

. The pie is a circle. This pie is divided into ten different portions. The circle has 360 degrees.

. Use for statements.

. A portion/slice of this pie is just like an arc. Think! Think! Think!

Chapter 12

Drawing Shapes using 2D Graphics

Most graphics operations are methods defined in the Graphics class in the AWT package as demonstrated in the last chapter. It is possible, because the Graphics class has methods which you have already met. You have also learnt that a particular shape can only be drawn by calling the relevant method from the Graphics class. In JDK 2 version, the AWT Graphics class has been extended. The new class is called **java. awt . Graphics 2D**. The 2D enables you to draw more shapes. You can also define your own shapes. The purpose of this chapter is to discuss how to use the Graphics 2D class, that is Graphics two-dimensional Graphics.

. How do you use the Graphics 2D class ?

In the last chapter, you saw that the graphics class stores information about whatever has to be displayed in the applet. The class object **screen** is used to represent the applet window. In the paint ( ) method of the applet, the method's argument is declared to be an instance of Graphics as follows:

```
Public void paint ( Graphics screen )
{
   //  code
}
```

.The first step for a 2D drawing is to create a Graphics 2D object.

To use the new Graphics class 2D, inside the paint ( ) method, you have to create a 2D object by casting method argument to Graphics 2D as follows:

Graphics2D screen2D = (Graphics 2D) screen ;

| Graphics 2D class | Graphics 2D object | Graphics 2D class | Screen -applet's window/ drawing surface |

This creates a Graphics2D object.

• Having created the Graphics2D object, you can call Graphics2D methods for drawing the required graphical shape. This is the second step for a 2D drawing process. It draws the required thing.

In fact, Graphics 2D is a cub-class of Java Graphics in the AWT package, and therefore, it inherits methods from the Graphics class. A set of new classes have been introduced by the Graphics 2D. Some of these new classes reside inside the AWT package, and the rest of them are in the new package called **java . awt. geom**. When you use any of these classes, you have to include in your program the **import java . geom.***; statement. This new package includes the following classes:

1. Arc2D   2. Ellipse2D   3. Line2D   4. Rectangle2D

5. RoundRectangle2D   6. QuadCurve2D   7 . CubicCurve2D   8 . GeneralPath

Classes 1-7 are abstract classes, and each of them has two inner classes namely, **float** and **double**. Thus, you have to instantiate either float or double class. You are now allowed to instantiate the abstract class itself.

• <u>**Why is it necessary to have precision levels when declaring arguments with a 2D class?**</u>

For the graphics, the unit of measurement is in pixels. In the JDK 1.2, which is now re-named as JDK 2, you can rotate, translate, and scale the (**x, y)** co-ordinates system, involving + and 1 pixels. For this reason , it is required to declare arguments with floating -point precision.

Drawing Operations

You can perform three major operations on a graphics shape. These operations are known as drawing, filling, and clipping. The first two operations, you have already seen in the last chapter. The 2D class, provides a variety of ways to draw and fill a shape, or use a shape as a stencil - clipping. Another important feature of 2D class is shape transformation. The shape transformation process involves, rotation, translation and scaling. These operations will be discussed in this chapter. Now, it is time to put theory into practice, so that it makes more sense. It is likely that you will use the above listed classes. Therefore, the following practical examples are presented to demonstrate how to implement some of these classes.

Line2D class

The Line2D shape is simple enough to draw. You have already learnt to draw a line shape in the last chapter. The technical requirements for drawing line shapes also apply to Line2D shapes, though the code differs in some respects. This is demonstrated by the program called **DLine . java**, which is in diagram 3. This program is designed to draw a straight line and display it on an applet.

Explanation

• Like any other program, it starts with the required import statements. Since this program implements Line2D class, it is essential to include the import statement: **import java . awt . geom.*;**

As mentioned above, you cannot instantiate an abstract class. Graphics 2D is an abstract class. You can can instantiate any of its two inner classes. In this example, Float class is implemented in the constructor:

Line2D . Float Lin = new Line2D . Float (40, 200, 250, 300);

```
        ↑                     ↑                                      ↑
Float sub-class      line object              Parameters for the line object Lin
of Line2D class      to be created            these are points - start and end of the line
```

This constructor creates the required line from the point (40, 200) to the point (250,300).

• In order to draw the line on the surface or window of the applet, you must call the relevant Graphics 2D class method, and insert the object to be drawn in the (   ). It is done as shown below:

screen2D.draw (Lin);

```
              ↑              ↑         ↑
        screen.window   method's   object/line to be displayed
        for drawing the   name
        line called Lin
```

• The rest of the code is identical to the code you have met on numerous occasions in this book. The html document is in diagram 2. I used this document with the appletviewer in order to test this applet. The test proved successful. **The applet DLine is shown below in diagram 1.**

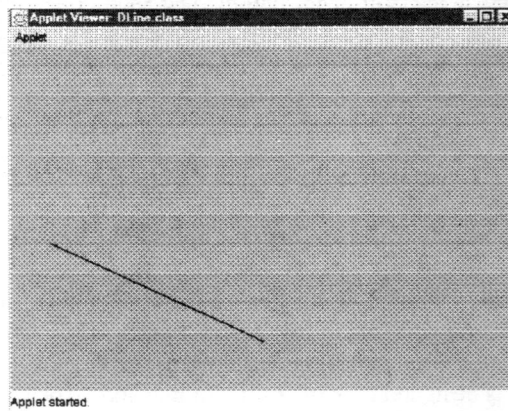

DLine . html

```
</html>
<head>
<title>
          2D straight line
</title>
</head>
<body>
<applet code= "DLine.class" width = 500 height = 350>
</applet>
</body>
</html>
```

Diagram 2

DLine . java

```
import java.awt.*;
import java.awt.geom.*;
import javax.swing.*;

public class DLine extends JApplet
{
  public void init ( )
{
  setBackground ( Color.red );
}
public void paint ( Graphics screen )
{

  Graphics2D  screen2D = ( Graphics2D ) screen;
  Line2D.Float Lin = new Line2D.Float ( 40, 200, 250, 300 );
  screen2D.setColor ( Color.black );
  screen2D.draw ( Lin );
  }
}
```

Diagram 3

Ellipse2D class

In Chapter 11, you learnt how to draw an oval. An ellipse is a regular oval. It is a flat shape, shaped like an egg. You can draw an ellipse by implementing Ellipse2D class, as demonstrated by the programming example below.

Ellipse . java

The program shown in diagram 4 is designed to draw two ellipses of two different sizes and colours, and display these in the applet window. The background colour of the applet is light grey.

Explanation

• I have chosen a background colour of light grey for this applet. This has be declared in the **init ( )** method as: setBackground (Color.lightGray);

• In the **paint ( )** method, you have created the graphics 2D object called screen 2D first. The code for it: Graphics2D screen2D = (Graphics2D) screen;

• At the time of creating an instance of the Ellipse2D.Float class, you have to specify the shape of the ellipse by providing the x, y co-ordinates for the top left corner, width and height values for the shape. The following constructor creates an instance called **large**:

Ellipse2D.Float large = new Ellipse2D.Float (85F, 157F, 13F, 50F);

                                ↑   ↑

               ellipse name   parameters for drawing shape

The capital **F** with each value of the argument stands for float. There is no need to include F with your values. The code is valid without F with each parameter. I have included it here, merely to show you this method of supplying parameters. In the same way, the other ellipse called **small** is created by the following statement:

Ellipse2D.Float small = new Ellipse2D.Float (85F, 87F, 130F, 50F);

• Having created the graphics2D.Float instances **large** and **small**, the next thing is to call the appropriate methods to draw these shapes on the screen. The method for drawing an ellipse is:

screen2D.draw (   );

                            ↑

Here, you must write the name of the instance/ellipse to be drawn

• The html document is in diagram 5. I have used this document to test the applet with the applet-viewer. The applet is shown in diagram 6, which displays two ellipses as required. Test it on your system.

Ellipse . java

```java
import java.awt.*;
import java.awt.geom.*;
import javax.swing.*;
public class Ellipse extends JApplet
{
  public void init ( )
{
  setBackground ( Color.lightGray );
}
public void paint ( Graphics screen )
{
  Graphics2D  screen2D = ( Graphics2D ) screen;
  Ellipse2D.Float large = new Ellipse2D.Float ( 85F, 157F, 13F, 50F );
  Ellipse2D.Float small = new Ellipse2D.Float ( 85F, 87F, 130F, 50F );
  screen2D.setColor ( Color.black );
  screen2D.draw ( large );
  screen2D.setColor ( Color.blue );
  screen2D.draw ( small );
 }
}
```

Diagram 4

Ellipse . html

```html
</html>
<head>
<title>
     Drawing 2DEllipse
</title>
</head>
<body>
<applet code= "Ellipse.class" width = 500 height = 350>
</applet>
</body>
</html>
```

Diagram 5

Diagram 6 - Applet Ellipse displaying two ellipses

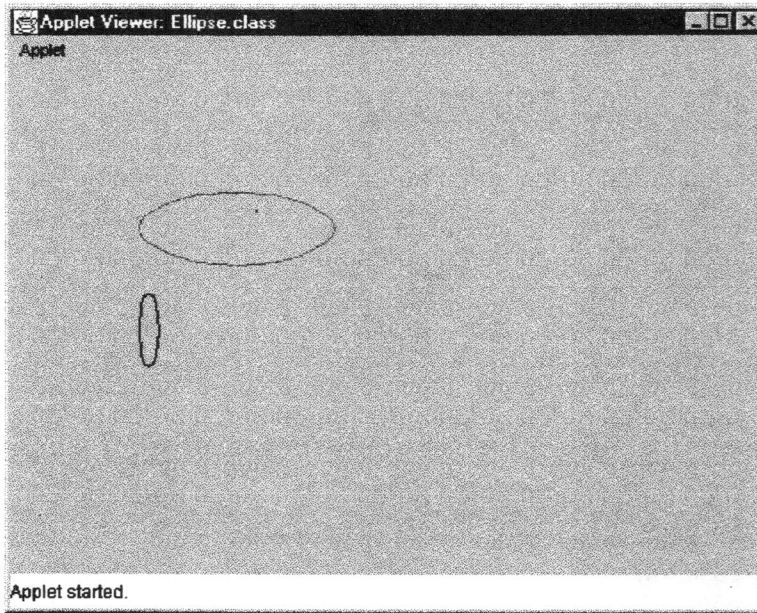

RoundRectangle2D class

This is another sub-class for drawing rectangular shapes with rounded corners. You have already met rounded rectangles in the last chapter. The basic technique for drawing rounded rectangle shapes is the same, which is in the last chapter, but the coding differs. This is demonstrated by the program shown in diagram 7 called Droundrect . java.

Droundrect . java

The program is designed to illustrate the method of drawing rounded rectangular shapes by implementing the inner class **Float** of the Graphics 2D class. The code will result in two rounded rectangles displayed in the applet window in different colours. Th background colour for the screen is yellow.

Explanation

The program is identical to the last program. In this program, you have to provide the constructor with six parameters. The first two parameters are for x, y co-ordinates, the next two for width and height, and the last two for the width and height of the rounded part of corners.

• The constructor for one of the rounded shapes called big is given below:

    RoundRectangle2D big = new RoundRectangle2D . Float (50, 50, 100, 150, 30, 20);

In this case, the rounded rectangle shape is 100 pixels wide, and 150 pixels high. The rounded part of each corner is 30 pixels wide and 20 pixels high.

• The html document is in diagram 8. This document was used to test the applet with the appletviewer. The appletL Droundrect .class is in diagram 9. It was tested successfully.

Droundrect . java

```
import java.awt.*;
import java.awt.geom.*;
import javax.swing.*;

public class DRoundRect extends JApplet
{
  public void init (   )
{
  setBackground ( Color.yellow );
}
public void paint ( Graphics screen )
{

  Graphics2D  screen2D = ( Graphics2D ) screen;

RoundRectangle2D big = new RoundRectangle2D . Float ( 50, 50, 100, 150, 30, 20 );
RoundRectangle2D small = new RoundRectangle2D. Float (170, 170, 100, 100, 40, 30 );

  screen2D.setColor ( Color . black );
  screen2D.draw ( big );
  screen2D.setColor ( Color . blue );
  screen2D.draw ( small );
 }
}
```

Diagram 7

DroundRect . html

```
</html>
<head>
<title>
        D Round Rectangular shapes
</title>
</head>
<body>
<applet code= "DRoundRect.class" width = 500 height = 350>
</applet>
</body>
</html>
```

Diagram 8

Applet DroundRect
displaying two rounded rectangle shapes

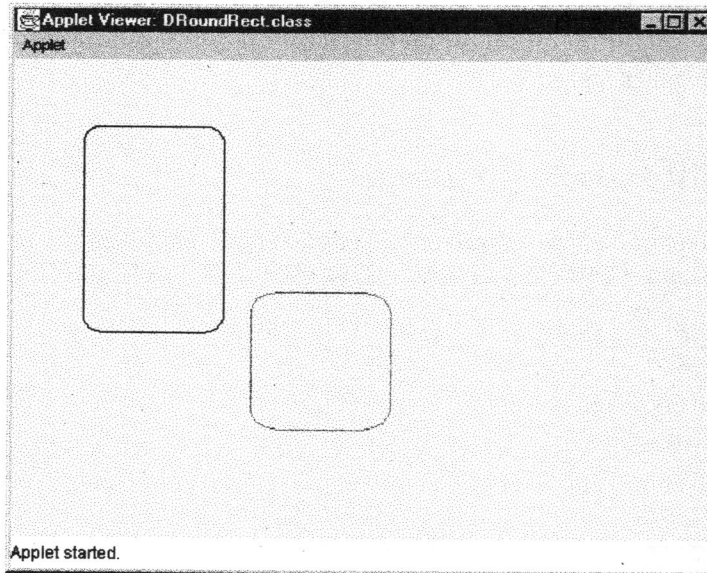

Diagram 9

Arc2D class

How to draw an arc by using AWT Graphics class methods is covered in the last chapter. You can also implement Arc2D class to draw an arc. In Graphics2D, the arc can be any one of the following three types:

Arc types in Graphics2D

Arc2D. CHORD	Arc2D . ARC	Arc2D . PIE
--------------------------	--------------------	---------------------
A closed arc. It has a straight line, which joins the arc's end points	It is an open arc. The end points not joined	It looks like a portion of a pie. Two straight lines drawn from each end of the arc/circle meet at its centre, creating a pie shape

DShapes . java

The program is designed to demonstrate how to draw these three different types of arcs, and display these in the applet. The program is listed in diagram 10.

Explanation

The structure of this program is identical to the structure of the previous program. However, there is a major difference between the constructor statements of this program and all other constructor statements in other programs discussed so far in this chapter.

• There are three constructor statements for creating three instances (arcs) namely a1, a2, and a3. Since the **Float class** is instantiated, the constructor for **a1** is:

Arc2D a1 = new Arc2D.Float (150, 70, 80, 60, 0, 90, Arc2D . CHORD) ;

```
            float   float  float  float  float float        type of arc
             x       y    width  height  arc   arc
                                        start  extent in degrees
                                      in degrees
```

The arc starts at 0 degree, which is 3o'clock, and extends counter-clockwise to 90 degrees that is 12 o'clock. (remember x, y co-ordinates values for the starting corner from the top left to position the arc on the screen). The width and height values of the arc give its size. This way, you can analyse the other two constructor statements. The rest of the program is similar to the code of the last program.

. The html document for running this program with the appletviewer is in diagram 11. I used this document to test this applet. The test proved successful as the result shows in diagram 12.

DShapes. java

```
import java . awt . * ;
import java . awt . geom .* ;
import javax .swing .*;

public class DShapes extends JApplet
{

 public void init ( )
{
 setBackground ( Color . pink ) ;

}
   public void paint ( Graphics screen )
{

 Graphics2D  screen2D = ( Graphics2D ) screen;

Arc2D a1 = new Arc2D.Float ( 150, 70, 80, 60, 0, 90, Arc2D . CHORD ) ;
Arc2D a2 = new Arc2D.Float ( 150, 150, 100, 50, 0,180, Arc2D . PIE ) ;
Arc2D a3 = new Arc2D.Float (250, 220, 100, 50, 0, 90, Arc2D . OPEN ) ;

 screen2D. setColor ( Color . black ) ;
 screen2D. draw ( a1 ) ;
 screen2D. setColor ( Color . blue ) ;
 screen2D. draw ( a2 ) ;
 screen2D. setColor ( Color . darkGray);
 screen2D. draw ( a3 ) ;
}
}
```

Diagram 10

DShapes . html

```
</html>
<head>
<title>
        2D arc Shapes drawings

</title>
</head>
<body>
<applet code = "DShapes.class" width = 500 height = 350>
</applet>
</body>
</html>
```

Diagram 11

Applet DShapes

displaying three different shapes

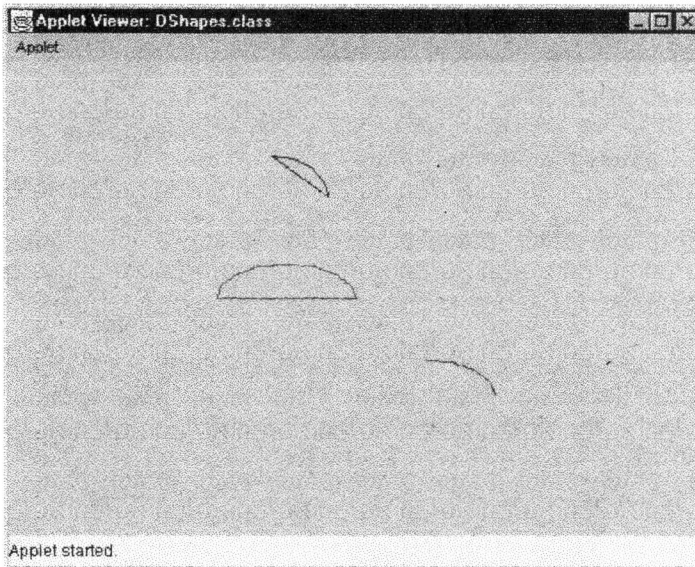

Diagram 12

The CubicCurve2D

The CubicCurve2D is a smooth curve. This curve has points at each two ends, and two other control points. These control points direct the curve how to curve. There is another curve type called **Quad-Curve2D**, which has one control point to control how it curves. The program **Dshapes . java** is designed to demonstrate how to construct it and displays it in the applet window.

CubicCurve2D class

This class is in the package called **java . awt . geom**. In order to draw the cubic curve 2D, you have to implement this class. The following program illustrates how to draw this curve. The idea of Cubic-Curve2D class shapes is to support smooth curve shapes. The general format of the constructor for this curve is shown below.

- **CubicCurve2D. Float**

(Float x0, Float y0, Float ctrl X0, Float ctrl Y0, Float ctrl X1, Float ctrl Y1, Float X1, Float Y1) ;
--------------------   ----------------------------   ------------------------------   ------------------------
        ↑   ↑   ↑   ↑

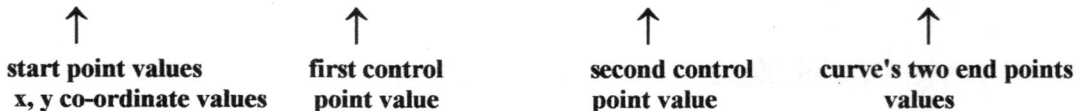

start point values   **first control**   **second control**   **curve's two end points**
x, y co-ordinate values   **point value**   **point value**   **values**

- Two control points are required as shown above. These points are drawn by calling the fill Oval method: The control points will be filled with blue colour.

                    screen2D.fillOval (   );

This method takes 4 arguments. See the program in diagram 13.

DShapes2 . java

The program Dshapes2 . java illustrates how to construct Rectangle2D and CubicCurve2D shapes by implementing Rectangle2D and CubicCurve2D classes. These shapes are displayed in the applet. Three different colours are added to the applet, so that the background of the applet and both shapes are displayed in different colours.

Explanation

- There are two 2D shapes to be drawn. One is Rectangle2D, and the other is CubicCurve2D. For drawing the Rectangular shape, you need 4 integer values for x, y co-ordinates of the top left corner of the rectangle 2D, width and height of the shape to be drawn.

. The constructor statement for the instance of the Float class is:

Rectangle2D R = new Rectangle2D.Float (20, 20, 80, 100);

In fact, you have drawn rectangular shapes in the last chapter as well. However, here you are using the inner class Float of the Graphics2D class to instantiate it. The following block of code sets the colour black for this rectangular shape, and draws it on the screen surface(applet window). It will be displayed on the screen.

screen2D . setColor (Color . black);   // color ( ) method of Graphics2D class
screen2D.draw (R);   // draw ( ) method of Graphics2D class

. For drawing the CubicCurve2D, you need to create an instance of the Float class in the paint ( ) method. The constructor for this task is:

CubicCurve2D c = new CubicCurve2D.Float (150, 100, 200, 300, 320, 300, 310, 340);

. The following code is for filling the two control points

```
screen2D.fillOval ( 148, 98, 4, 4 );
screen2D.fillOval ( 198, 298,4, 4 );
screen2D.fillOval (318, 298, 4, 4 );
screen2D.fillOval (308, 338, 4, 4 );
```

. The method **screen2D.draw (R);** displayed (drawn) the rectangular shape on the screen.

. The method **screen2D.draw (c);** will display the Cubic Curve 2D on the screen

The html document is in diagram 13. This was used to test the applet with the appletviewer. It worked well. The applet is shown in diagram 14. The program DShapes2 is in diagram 15.

DShapes2. html

```
</html>
<head>
<title>
      2D Shapes drawing
</title>
</head>
<body>
<applet code = "DShapes2.class" Width =450 height =350>
</applet>
</body>
</html>
```

Diagram 13

Applet DShapes2 - Displaying CubicCurve2D and Rectangle2D

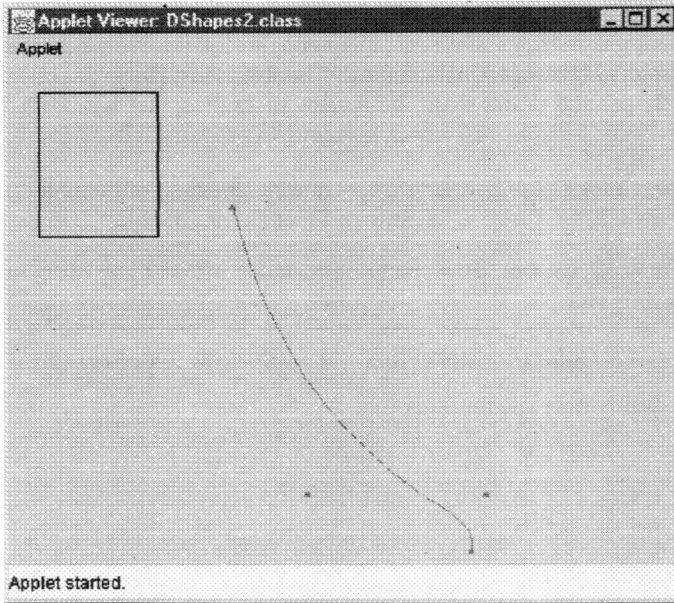

Diagram 14

QuadCurve2D

The Quad Curve is similar to the Cubic Curve, except that it has one control point.

QuadCurveA . java

The program is listed in diagram 16. Upon careful study of the code, you will find out that it's method of drawing is identical to the method of CubicCurve2D. The only difference, which is minimum, lies in the constructor statement. The constructor statement for this curve has six values instead of eight values as arguments. It is due to the fact that this has only one control point whilst its sister curve, CubicCurve2D has two control points.

QuadCurve2D c = new QuadCurve2D.Float (50, 100, 420, 250, 310, 320);

‒‒‒‒‒‒‒‒‒
↑
These are the values for the control point

Dshapes2 . java

```java
import java.awt.*;
import java.awt.geom.*;
import javax.swing.*;

public class DShapes2 extends JApplet
{
 public void init ( )
{
 setBackground ( Color.lightGray );
}
public void paint (Graphics screen )
{
 Graphics2D  screen2D = ( Graphics2D ) screen;

 Rectangle2D R = new Rectangle2D.Float ( 20, 20, 80, 100 );
 CubicCurve2D c = new CubicCurve2D.Float ( 150, 100, 200, 300, 320, 300, 310, 340 );
 screen2D.setColor ( Color.black );
 screen2D.draw ( R );
 screen2D.setColor ( Color.blue );
 screen2D.fillOval ( 148, 98, 4, 4 );
 screen2D.fillOval ( 198, 298,4, 4 );
 screen2D.fillOval (318, 298, 4, 4 );
 screen2D.fillOval (308, 338, 4, 4 );
 screen2D.draw ( c );
 }
}
```

Diagram 15

QuadCurveA . html

```html
<html>
<head>
<title>
        Drawing Quad Curve 2D
</title>
</head>
<body>
<applet code= "QuadCurveA.class" width = 500 height = 350>
</applet>
</body>
</html>
```

Diagram 16 - I used this document to test the applet. The test was successful.

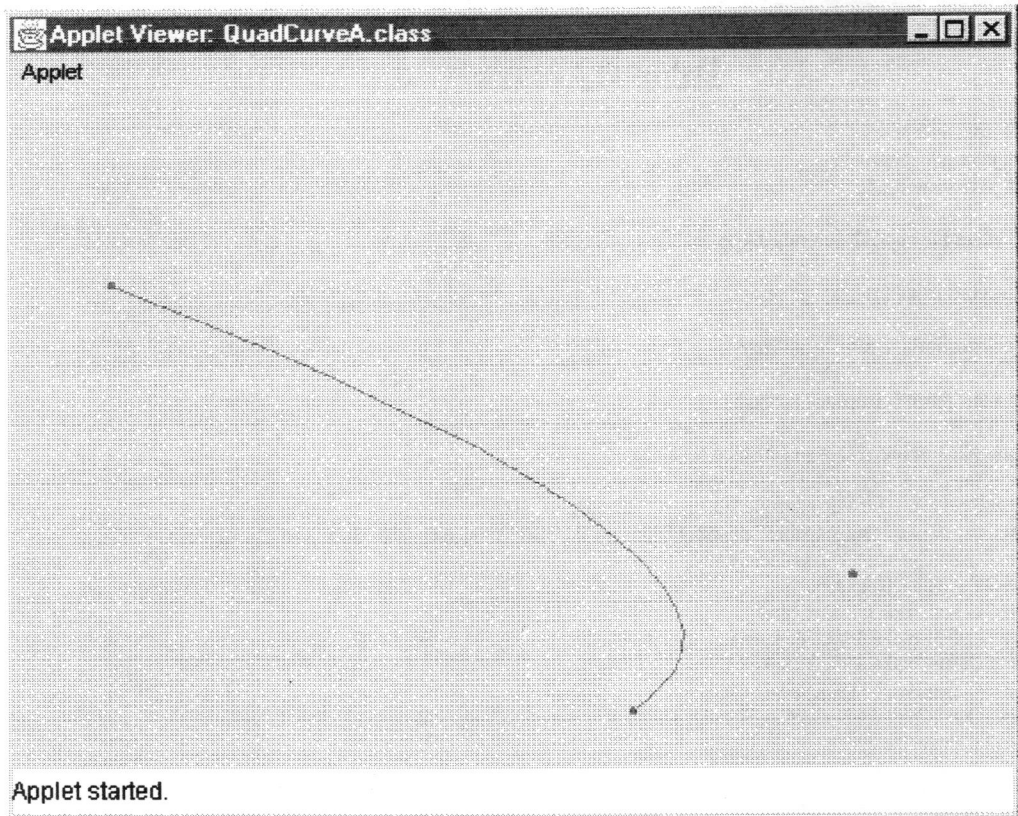

Diagram 17 - **Applet QuadCurveA Displaying the QuadCuve2D**

QuadCurveA . java

```
import java.awt.*;
import java.awt.geom.*;
import javax.swing.*;

public class QuadCurveA extends JApplet
```

Diagram 18 - **due to lack of space continued in diagram 18 A below**

```
{
  public void init ( )
  {
  setBackground ( Color.lightGray );
  }
  public void paint (Graphics screen )
  {
  Graphics2D  screen2D = ( Graphics2D) screen;
  QuadCurve2D c = new QuadCurve2D.Float ( 50, 100, 420, 250, 310, 320 );
  screen2D.setColor( Color.black );
   screen2D.setColor ( Color.blue );
   screen2D.fillOval ( 48, 98, 4, 4 );
   screen2D.fillOval ( 418, 248, 4, 4 );
   screen2D.fillOval ( 308, 318,4, 4 );
   screen2D.draw (c );
  }
}
```

Diagram 18 A - Please read diagrams 18 & 18A together

Clipping

Clipping is a new operation. The program **ClipShape . java** is designed to demonstrate how to create a clipping shape and display it in the applet. The program is listed in diagram 21.

ClipShape . java

The program is aimed at drawing an ellipse2D . This ellipse is then to be turned into the clipping rectangle red shape as a stencil for displaying it in an applet. The back ground colour of the applet is green.

Explanation

• The program is identical to some programs you have worked with in this chapter. Even so, this program equips you with a further Graphics 2D technique of performing a clipping operation on a shape. In this case, the shape is 'ellipse' form.

• It is ,therefore, required to create an ellipse first by instantiating the Float class, as:

Ellipse2D el = new Ellipse2D.Float (20, 20, 170, 170);

This code creates **el** object (instance) of ellipse2D, whose shape is determined by the parameters in it.

• This shape has to be specified. This is done by calling the **Clip ( ) method** of the Graphics2D class.

The code for it: **screen2D.clip (el);** **el** - the shape of the ellipse.

- The **fillRect ( )** method of the Graphics2D is called to fill the rectangular shape with the colour red. The code for this operation is **screen2D.fillRect (30, 40, 300, 300);** The parameters in this method filled the rectangular with a circular clip region.

- The html document used for testing this applet with the appletviewer is shown in figure 19, and the applet is in diagram 20. It displays a clipping rectangle. The test proved successful.

ClipShape . class

```
</html>
<head>
<title>
            2D Clipping
</title>
</head>
<body>
<applet code= "ClipShape.class" width = 400 height = 350>
</applet>
</body>
</html>
```

Diagram 19

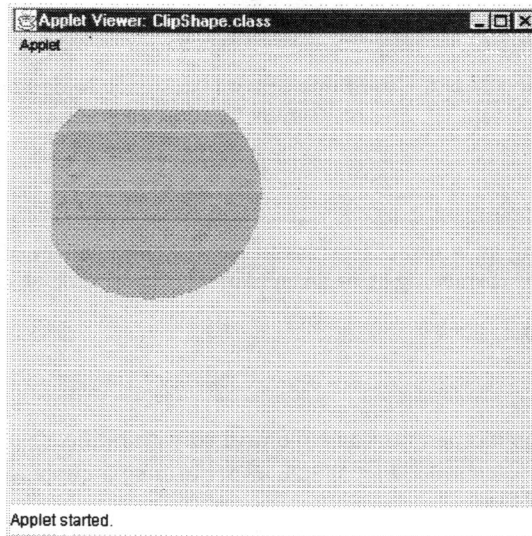

Diagram 20 Applet ClipShape . class displaying rectangular clip region

The 2D Graphics (or Graphics 2D) is a subject in its own right. It is not possible to discuss it in some depth, or demonstrate some of its topics mentioned in this chapter, due to limited space in this book. If you visit a major bookshop specialising in computer books, you may find a number of books recently published on this subject. If you are in the UK, you can ask your local librarian to search for new titles on 2D Graphics. It is highly likely that the British Library catalogue has some new 2D Graphics or Graphics 2D titles listed.

ClipShape . java

```java
import java.awt.*;
import java.awt.geom.*;
import javax.swing.*;

public class ClipShape extends JApplet
{
  public void init (  )
{
  setBackground ( Color.green );
  }
    public void paint ( Graphics screen )
{
  Graphics2D  screen2D = ( Graphics2D ) screen;

 Ellipse2D el = new Ellipse2D.Float ( 20,  20, 170, 170 );
  screen2D.setColor ( Color. red );
  screen2D.clip ( el );
  screen2D.fillRect (30, 40, 300,300);
}
}
}
```

Diagram 21

Exercises

1. Write a program called **ClipShape1 . java** (or give another name) in order to perform the following tasks:

> . create a RoundRectangle2D in the colour red.
>
> . perform a clipping operation on this round rectangle shape, and
>
> . display this clipping rectangle shape in a frame, whose background colour is yellow

2. Is it true to say that circles and ellipses do not have any corners?

> . Give an example of a constructor method/statement for creating an ellipse or a circle, and identify its arguments.
>
> . Which two methods will you call for drawing one filled ellipse or circle filled and the other circle or ellipse as an outline? (filled means colour inside, making it solid.)

3. How will you change the current colour before drawing something in the applet window?

Chapter 13

Animation and Threads

The purpose of this chapter is to introduce you to animation and threads in Java.

Creating an animation

Complex images can be produced by using pixels. You can also generate photographic images by using a scanner or by means of image software. You have already learnt to draw simple images by means of lines and shapes. Thus, you can create simple animation by using Java methods for fonts, colours, line, and shapes. On the other hand, if you want to create some exciting images for animation, you have to provide your own images. The process of creating an animation involves the following steps.

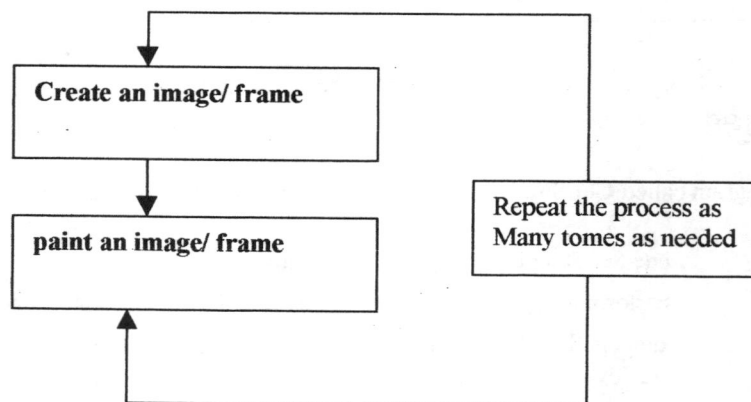

```
        ┌─────────────────────────────┐
        │  Create an image/ frame      │
        └─────────────────────────────┘

        ┌─────────────────────────────┐        ┌──────────────────────┐
        │  paint an image/ frame       │        │ Repeat the process as│
        └─────────────────────────────┘        │ Many tomes as needed │
                                                └──────────────────────┘
```

Figure 1

How does this process work?

The above method involves painting and re-painting of the applet. This way, the paint method ( ) is called more than once. In the first instance, you create an applet. It is in a window initially. You decide to move the window containing the applet. Thus, the paint method is called to repaint it.

In your applet code, you can have a segment of the code that can repaint the applet and it can do so as many times as required. You can also include a code that can repaint when it is needed. The image you create in your applet can be repainted as many times as required and as fast as you wish. Since an animation means changes of image faster and a number of times, you can create an animation by this process of changing the image by paining and repainting faster and doing it several times. The animation program, like play music programs, can only be written with **multiple threads**.

Threads

An applet without threading is limited to just one task at a time but threads can enable it to do a number of things at once. Threads and multithreading is a big topic in Java. So far, I have discussed programs which have a single thread. What does it mean?

It means that all previous programs have a single line of execution. In a single threaded program which you have designed until now it started executing the code in accordance with the program's structure and the method of completing the task for which the program was designed. The program continued running until the task was completed and exited. Thus, the program not only performed one task at a time, but also ran in a **single thread** - execution of a single job.

Today's operating systems are capable of allowing you to run multiple programs concurrently. Each program can be doing multiple tasks at the same time within a single program. Thus, a number of different parts of the same program can run at the same time. These different parts, or **threads,** of the same program are doing their own things, at the same time, in parallel, without interfering with each other. Similarly, a number of programs can run simultaneously. This technique is called **multithreading** - execution of a number of jobs simultaneously. Each task that a computer handles is a thread.

Figure:2 Stages in a thread life

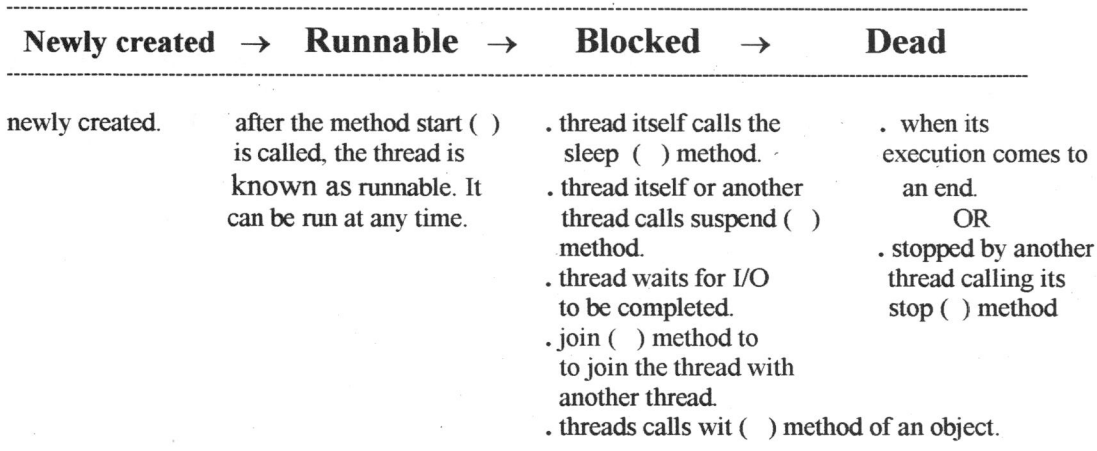

Newly created	→	Runnable	→	Blocked	→	Dead
newly created.		after the method start ( ) is called, the thread is known as runnable. It can be run at any time.		. thread itself calls the sleep ( ) method. . thread itself or another thread calls suspend ( ) method. . thread waits for I/O to be completed. . join ( ) method to to join the thread with another thread. . threads calls wit ( ) method of an object.		. when its execution comes to an end. OR . stopped by another thread calling its stop ( ) method

The advantage of using threads is that you can create not only applets but also applications which run in their own threads without interfering with each other. Java was designed for multithreading. However, if you run too many threads, the system will slow down, but even so all threads will run independently. In a multithreading environment, better use of resources is made. A thread has the following 4 stages in its life. A thread is a class, which is in java . lang, and thus you do not have to import it.

Applets using threads

In order to create applets using threads, you must first know how to create an applet. In fact, you can make the following four modifications to your existing applet to convert it into the applet that uses threads. Or when you write an applet, you must include the following requirements in your code, so that it uses threads.

1.   Add the Runnable to your applet's class definition (signature/declaration). As you have seen in figure 2, Runnable is one of the 4 stages in a thread life cycle. The runnable is an interface which defines the state of your applet. It signals that a run (   ) method can be called.

2.   Include a thread object called runner. The thread object runner starts when the start (   ) method is handled. It stops when the stop (   ) method is handled. You can give it another name, as long as it is of the Thread type.   **Example**

```
    public class anim1 extends JApplet
         implements Runnable              // class definition
    {
       Thread runner;                    // thread object
      public void init (   )
      {
      setBackground (color.red);
      }
```

3. Include a **start (   ) method**. Your applet must have a start   (   ) method for the following two reasons:
       . After the initial start of the applet, if you stop the applet, and re-start it again, the start (   ) method is handled whenever you repeat the process of starting-stopping the applet.
       . User switched from the applet page to another Web page. If the user returns to the applet page then, the applet re-starts, and thus the start (   ) method is handled. The following is an example of start (   ) method.
                              Example

```
              public void start (   )
              {
                  if ( runner == null )
                  {
                  runner = new Thread ( this );
                  runner. Start ( ) ;
                  }
              }
```

4. Include a **run ( ) method** for controlling the applet. It is the heart of the applet with threads. This method has the code for controlling the applet. <u>The animation occurs inside this method.</u> The following example is used to illustrate its working.

```
public void run ( )
 {
 Thread thisThread = Thread.currentThread ( );
 while ( runner == thisThread )
 {
 repaint ( );
  try                                    // exceptions handling
  {
      Thread.sleep ( 1000 );
 }
 catch
      ( InterruptedException e ) {  }
}
}
```

. You must create a thread object called **thisThread**. This object is

$$\textbf{Thread} \quad \textbf{thisThread} = \textbf{Thread} \cdot \textbf{currentThread ( );}$$

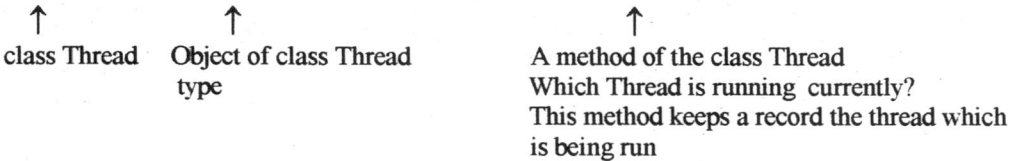

    ↑   ↑   ↑

class Thread   Object of class Thread   A method of the class Thread
              type   Which Thread is running currently?
                                      This method keeps a record the thread which
                                        is being run

. A while loop is required in order to compare the runner object with the **thisThread** object. Runner object and **thisThread** object are two threads.

. The While (runner == thisThread) loop continues as long as both runner and **thisThread** objects return the same value (both have the same value). This loop never exits. Why? It is because of no interference within the loop, which can stop the loop.

. In this loop, the first statement, to be called, is the **repaint ( )** statement. This statement causes the paint ( ) method to be handled. The paint ( ) method has the code for the creation of the applet. Thus within the While loop, a single animation frame is constructed (see also page 9 - flickering).

. Then the control is passed on to the **try ------ catch** block of statements

The **Thread . sleep (10000);** statement is within the try---catch block of statements. What is the purpose of it? This block is also within the While loop. The **sleep method** is one of the methods of the thread class. It controls the speed of the applet.

Thread . sleep (1000);

---------------------   ----------

↑   ↑

Method of Thread class   1000 milliseconds = 1 second time duration.
                          Long enough for the user to see the animation

. **What will happen without the sleep method ?** There is nothing else in this segment of the code to control the applet's running speed. Thus it will run as fast as it can.

. The idea of having **try-catch** block in the run ( ) method is to handle any InterruptedExceptions, which may occur. This type of exception can happen during the execution of the thread sleep statement. For instance, if there is an interference when the tread is trying to sleep.

. What else can be coded in the run ( ) method?

It should be noted that the run ( ) method is similar to the main ( ) method of a Java application. Therefore, it can have any other items that are required to run each separate thread. For instance, it can have other if statements, initialisation values, etc.

5. Include a **stop ( ) method** - it must be added to the code for the following reasons:

. whenever the user moves on to another Web page, the stop method is handled and the execution of the applet stops. In this case, there is no need to keep running the thread. Of course, when the user returns to the same applet, then the start method creates a new thread to start the applet once again. Now, examine the following example of the stop ( ) method:

```
public void stop ( )
    {
       if ( runner != null )
       {
       runner = null;
       }
    }
```

. Here, the purpose of the **if statement** is to test the runner object, whether the value of the runner object is **null or not**. If it is null, it means that the applet is not **active**, but **dead**. It is dead simply because the thread has finished its execution. If its value is not equal to null, and the thread has stopped, then the statement sets the thread's runner object to null. Can it be dead due to any other reason? The answer to this question is in figure 2 above.

. What is the effect of setting the runner object to a null value?

When the runner object is set to null, it does not have the value **thisThread**, which is given in the **while loop** of the run ( ) method. This means that the runner object has some other value. If this is the case, then the while loop of the run ( ) method stops running.

Anim1.java

The program listed in diagrams 1& 1A is designed to demonstrate the application of all the methods discussed earlier, together with the design of an applet. The applet uses the basic applet animation methods to display the following message: The applet's background colour is red. It is drawn by using **TimesNewRoman** font bold , size 30. The message is enclosed within the two lines (blue colour) as shown in the above required format.

```
*******************************
         Contact me at
      WWW. NOBODY. COM

*******************************
```

Explanation

The idea is to demonstrate how to write an applet which applies the basic animation techniques in order to animate. The above examples of basic animation techniques are incorporated into the code of this applet and thus there is no need to repeat them again. The applet itself is simple. You have written identical code before. Diagram 1 is on page 258. Diagrams 1A and 3 are on page 259.

Ani1.html

In order to test this animated applet, you must prepare an html page. This is shown in diagram 2. I used anim1. html in order to test applet: Anim1.class with the applet viewer. The test proved successful. The applet is shown in diagram 3.

Flickering

When you run this applet on your machine, it is likely that you will experience some flickering. It has nothing to do with the code itself. You can write a code that will eliminate flickering, and improve the appearance of the animation. It will be discussed soon.

Anim1.html

```
<HTML>
<HEAD>
<TITLE> < First Trial>
</TITLE>
</HEAD>
<BODY>
<Applet CODE = "Anim1.class" width = 600 height = 250>
</Applet>
</BODY>
</HTML>
```

Diagram 2

Anim1 .java

```java
import java . awt.*;
import javax. swing.*;

public class Anim1 extends JApplet
implements Runnable
{

 Thread runner;                    // Thread object runner

public void init (  )
{
  setBackground (Color.red);
}

public void start (  )
{
   if ( runner  ==  null )
  {

  runner = new Thread ( this );
   runner.start (   );
   }
 }

public void run (  )
 {

 Thread thisThread  =  Thread.currentThread (  );
 while ( runner ==  thisThread  )
 {

  repaint (  );

  try                                // exceptions handling
   {

    Thread.sleep ( 1000 );
  }
  catch
       ( InterruptedException e ) {   }
}
}
```

Diagram 1

```
                    Anim1. Java    ( continued)
public void stop  (  )
   {
     if ( runner != null )
  {
    runner =  null;
 }
 }

 public void paint ( Graphics g )
{
 super. paint ( g );

Font f = new Font ( "TimesNewRoman",  Font.BOLD, 30 );
g.setFont (f);

g.setColor ( Color.black );
g.drawString ( "***************************", 140, 80 );
g.setColor ( Color.blue );
g.drawString  ( "Contact me at ", 195, 100 );
g.drawString   ( " ", 150, 115 );                    // space between two lines
g.drawString   ( "WWW.NOBODY.COM", 150, 130 );
g.setColor (Color.black);
g.drawString ( "***************************", 140, 160 );
 }
 }
```

Diagram 1A

Diagram 3 - Anim1 animated applet on a Web page loaded by appletviewer

. How can you prevent animation flickering ?

If you examine the code in diagram 1, you can see that the first statement in the While loop is the re-paint method. This method calls two other methods namely the **update** method and **paint** method. In the While loop, there is no statement for the update method but it is a default method which is called automatically whenever the repaint method is called. The **default update ( )** method is in the **Component class**, which is in the AWT package.

. What does this default update (   ) method do?

The task of the default update ( ) method is to clear the screen, and fill the screen with the background colour. In fact, it gets the screen ready for the paint (   ) method, so that the paint (   ) method can draw the applet again. Any time the animation loop goes around once again, a different image should appear but between any two different things appearing on the screen. The update ( ) method is trying to clear the screen, so that there is nothing on the screen from the image just shown on the screen. This task of clearing the screen between animation loop causes flickering.

In order to avoid this flickering, you should override the default update ( ) method. This means that you must include the following code in your program. This should come at the end of your paint method.

```
public void update (Graphics g)
   {
     paint ( g);
   }
 }
```

Anim 6A. java

Computer animation is complex. However, at the basic level, your program should be able to draw an image at a particular place, move it from its original place to several places, bring it back to its starting point, and repeat this process as long as the applet is being displayed on the screen.

This program is designed to illustrate how to create an animated applet. It has an image which the program draws in a white colour in a particular place, moves it along the x-co-ordinate to some places, and then takes it back to its original position. All these movements take place on a yellow rectangular shape. The program is listed in diagrams 4 & 4A.

Explanation

All drawings in our program **Anim1. Java** are based on the Graphics class, which is apart of **java . awt** package. Now-a-days, in Java 2, applets are constructed by implementing Graphics2D object which represents the applet window.

• The mobile applet is an animated applet. It is threaded. Its basic structure is identical to the structure of the last program. Since the oval shape has to move along the x-co-ordinate, an instance variable called **xPosition** is declared. This variable keeps a record of the current starting position of the moving oval shape. It has to move along the x, therefore, there is no need to change y values.

• Like the previous program, the applet has start ( ) and stop ( ) methods to start and stop the applet. It also has the run ( ) method to control the operation of the thread.

• In the Run ( ) method, the x - value changes in accordance with the for statement. The waiting time between each movement along the x is **1000 milliseconds**, that is **1 second**. The oval shape moves from the left to the right on the yellow rectangle. When it reaches the end of the rectangle it returns to its starting position.

• In the paint ( ), the background rectangle is drawn in yellow colour, then on it the oval shape is drawn, at its current position.

• In order to avoid flickering, this program includes the update ( ) method. There is still some flickering. It happens when the oval shape moves to its starting position. The reason for this unwanted flickering is that the background is painted first and then on it, the oval shape is drawn. This program is re-written with the double-buffering technique in attempt to make this animation smoother on your screen.

• In diagram 5 is Anim6A.html Web page to test this applet with the appletviewer. The applet is in diagram 6. The applet ran successfully. It is your ran to experiment with it.

Double buffering

Double-buffering technique allows you to create a second surface on which you can do all your painting. This surface is called **offscreen**. With this technique, you draw your applet first to an **offscreen bufffer** (storage area). This buffer is as big as your applet's display area. Therefore, once you have drawn your applet on it, you can copy the whole thing at once to your display area.

In double-buffering, you have to create two Graphics2D objects. One is for the offscreen image to draw on, and the other object is for the graphics context for the graphics object. A further requirement is to create an image. This image holds the drawings which are done in the offscreen bufffer (hidden area). Finally, at the end of the paint ( ) method, copy from the offscreen to the applet's display area.

This method works better than just to override the update ( ) method. It greatly reduces flickering from the animation. It makes your applet smoother, as it eliminates things which are visible while the paint ( ) method is drawing. It does not mean that with this technique all your animations will be displayed smoothly. On the other hand, it does generate a better animation.

You can see that in double-buffering, there are two buffers. On one buffer you draw offscreen. On the other buffer, you copy. Your program switches between these two buffers. Duble-bufffering takes more memory space.

Anim6A . java

```java
import java . awt.*;
import javax. swing.*;

public class Anim6A extends JApplet
implements Runnable
{
 Thread runner;
 int xPosition;
public void init (  )

{
setBackground ( Color.white );

}

public void start (  )
{
 if ( runner == null )
  {
   runner = new Thread ( this );
   runner.start (  );
  }
 }

 public void run (  )
 {
 Thread thisThread  = Thread.currentThread (  );
 while ( runner ==  thisThread )
  {
 for ( xPosition = 50; xPosition <=300; xPosition+=49 )
{
   repaint (  );

 try
  {
    Thread.sleep ( 1000 );
  }
  catch
  ( InterruptedException e ) {  }
 }
  xPosition = 50;
 }
 }
```

Diagram 4

Anim6. Java (continued)

```
public void stop  (   )
  {
  if ( runner != null )
  {
  runner = null;
  }
  }
  public void paint (Graphics screen)
{

Graphics2D screen2D  = ( Graphics2D ) screen;
                                        // Background rectangle
screen2D.setColor ( Color.yellow );
screen2D.fillRect ( 0, 0, 600, 300 );

                        // Rolling shape
screen2D.setColor ( Color.blue );
screen2D.fillOval( xPosition, 50, 200, 200 );

}

public void update (Graphics screen)
{
  paint(screen);
}
}
```

Diagram 4A

Anim6A . html

```
<HTML>
<HEAD>
<TITLE> <    Animated applet with2D Graphics>
</TITLE>
</HEAD>
<BODY>
<Applet CODE = "Anim6A.class" width = 600  height = 330>
</Applet>
</BODY>
</HTML>
```

Diagram 5

<u>**Applet Anim6A**</u>
<u>An animated oval shape running on a Web page loaded by appletviewer</u>

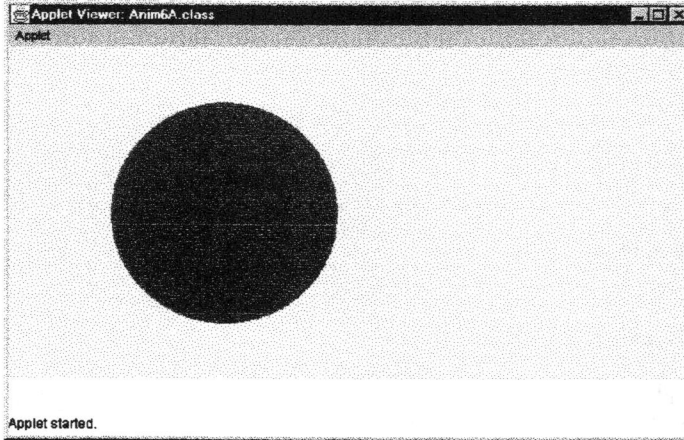

<u>**Diagram 6**</u>

Anim 7. Java

This program **Anim 7. java** is designed to incorporate the double-buffering technique in order to reduce animation flickering. The program is listed in diagrams 7 & 7A. The Anim7.html for testing the applet is in diagram 8, and the applet is shown in diagram 9. It amends and extends the previous program in the following ways:

int xPosition;	// variable for x values, where the oval shape will be drawn
Image mobile;	// image object called mobile
Graphics offscreen;	// Graphics object called offscreen

These statements are declared in the class definition.

In the init ( ) method the following objects are created:

> **. mobile = createImage (getSize ( ).width,getSize ( ).height);**

This statement calls the creatImage ( ) method in order to set up an instance (object) called mobile. It is an empty image whose size and width are equal to the size and height of the applet.

> **. offscreen = mobile.getGraphics ( );**

By calling the getGraphics ( ) method of the Image class this code associates the offscreen object with the mobile image.

- Usually, drawing work is done in the paint ( ) method. In double-buffering, all drawings are completed in the offscreen area within the paint ( ) method.

- Since you draw offscreen you must use the offscreen object for displaying methods. In this example, the followings are the display methods:

```
offscreen.setColor (Color.yellow);        // background colour of surface on which the image moves
offscreen.fillRect(0,0,600,300);          //  rectangular background  """"""""""""""""""""""""""""""""""""
offscreen.setColor (Color.blue);             // blue colour for the image
offscreen.fillOval(xPosition,50,200,200);    // image oval shape
```

- At the end of the paint ( ) method you must add a statements which will draw the offscreen bufffer to the applet's real bufffer (applet's window). Here, the following statement is added to the paint ( ) method:

screen2D.drawImage (mobile, 0, 0, this);

This statement draws an image called mobile at position 0,0. This fills the display area of the applet.

- This program also overrides the default update ( ) method.

- The mobile oval shape animated applet is shown in diagram 9. It runs smoother than the previous applet.

The writing of the code for animated applet is not so hard as controlling the image. For instance in the **for** statement the increment is 49 pixels. If you are trying to control the movement of a mobile object along the x co-ordinate you have to experiment. It may be that the **sleep** timing is not matching with that of the **distance**. You may have to alter the sleep time. It does not have to be 1000 milliseconds (1 second). You can choose any suitable number. You can create a simple animation by calling the Java's lines, fonts and colours methods. They are good enough for learning.

<hr>

<u>Anim7 . html</u>

```
<HTML>
<HEAD>
<TITLE> < second animation>
</TITLE>
</HEAD>
<BODY>
<Applet CODE = "Anim7.class" width = 500 height = 330>
</Applet>
</BODY>
</HTML>
```

Diagram 8

Anim7 . java

```java
import java . awt.*;
import javax. swing.*;

public class Anim7 extends JApplet
implements Runnable
{
 Thread runner;
 int xPosition;
 Image mobile;
 Graphics offscreen;

public void init ( )
{
mobile = createImage (getSize ( ).width,getSize ( ).height);
offscreen = mobile.getGraphics ( );
}
public void start ( )
{
 if (runner == null)
  {
   runner = new Thread (this);
   runner.start ( );
  }
 }
    public void run ( )
{
 Thread thisThread = Thread.currentThread ( );
 while (runner == thisThread )
  {
  for (xPosition = 50; xPosition <= 300; xPosition+=49 )
{
   repaint ( );
 try
  {
    Thread.sleep (1000);
  }
 catch
  ( InterruptedException e) { }
 }
 xPosition =50;
 }
 }
```

Diagram 7

Anim7. java (cont)

```java
public void stop  ( )
{
 if ( runner != null )
{
 runner = null;
}
}
 public void paint (Graphics screen)
{
 Graphics2D screen2D =(Graphics2D) screen;


                                        //rectangular background
offscreen.setColor (Color.yellow);
offscreen.fillRect(0,0,600,300);


                                        // mobile shape/oval
offscreen.setColor (Color.blue);
offscreen.fillOval(xPosition,50,200,200);
screen2D.drawImage (mobile, 0, 0, this);
}
public void update (Graphics screen)
{
  paint(screen);
}
}
```

Diagram 7A

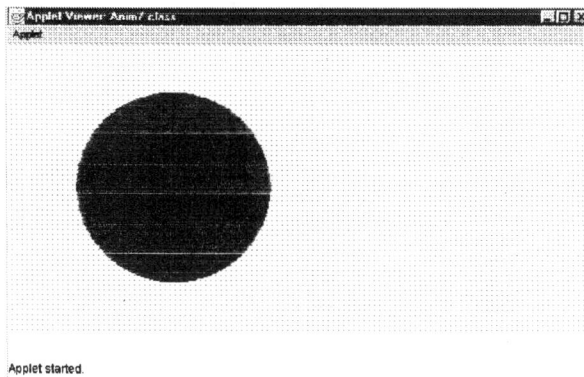

Diagram 9 - the mobile oval shape running on a Web page by appletviewer

Images

Images are stored in two places other than the applet itself. These are local files and Net (Internet). You can read images, but to do so, first you must know the location of the required image file. An image file may be stored as **. GIF or . JPEG.**

GIF stands for Graphics Interchange Format. **JPEG** for Joint Photographic Experts Group, the group that created it. Java can handle graphics files of these types. Most browsers also support animated and GIF images, which are also known as GIF89a format. You have already learnt how to load graphics into applets. At this stage, you must also learn the basics of creating animation, and how to display images in the **.GIF** and **. JPG** format in your applet. GIF files are comparatively much smaller than JPEG files. The difference in size is due to the difference in ranges of colour palettes. JPEG files have palettes of 16.7 million colours. On the other hand, GIF files have 256 colour palettes. GIF format is more popular. The prime reason for this popularity is that huge number of users still view applets in 256 or even less colour screen. Thus you are on the safe side with the GIF format.

There is not any more space in this chapter to demonstrate how to read an image file. You need special code for each type of file to locate it and make use of it.

Exercise

Write an animated applet: **BlueMan . java**. It should display the image shown below. Use update ( ) method to avoid flickering and design it with Graphics2D. You must also write BlueMan.html in order to test your animated applet.

Chapter 14

Exception Handling

Your program may be compiled successfully but it may not run satisfactorily due to a variety of exceptional situations. Exceptions are such occurrences as the class file that you want to load may be missing, bad data input, the file you wish to open is in the wrong format, or any other situation that leads to incorrect working of the program, or the abrupt abortion of the program during the program execution. In Java, like other programming languages, there are methods for handling such exceptional situations. These methods are termed as exception handling. If such exceptional conditions are not handled correctly, these will cause further abnormal conditions which become more difficult to eliminate and make the program workable. In this chapter, the basic idea of exception handling is discussed.

Exceptions

In Java, an exception is an instance of a class derived from **Throwable**. A skelton sketch of the exception hierarchy is shown in figure1.

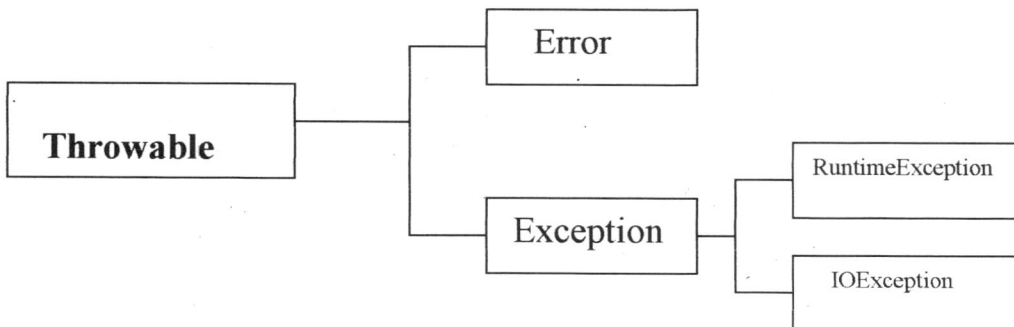

Figure 1 - A skeleton sketch of the exception hierarchy

Runtime exception subclass has its own subclasses. Similarly, IO exception has its own subclasses. A **RuntimeException** is caused by a programming error. Some examples of runtimeExceptions are given below:

. ArrayIndexOutOfBoundsException - occurs when trying to access an array element that does not exist within its defined boundaries.
. ArithmeticException - occurs when an arithmetic rule is violated. For instance, if you try to divide an integer by zero.

On the other hand, IOExceptions are the result of things which are out of control.

. EOFException occurs when a file is read and it comes to end before end is expected.
. FileNotFoundException - occurs when you try to open a file which does not exist.

These and other subclasses are arranged in class hierarchy of which a tiny portion is shown in figure 1 above. The superclass is the **Throwable.** Most exception classes are in the **java . lang** package. There are some other exception classes which are available by referring to Java library classes. For instance, the **java . io** package for both input and output exceptions.

In order to handle exceptions, in your program you can have a method that can indicate the types of errors it can **throw**. The method will throw errors if the method is unable to handle the situation it has encountered. For instance, during the program execution. a block of statements is being executed, and an exceptional condition has been encountered. The method will **throw** an exception (reporting error) that you can **catch**. Once you have caught it, it can be dealt with by the **handler** code. The handler is a segment of code (see figure 2). It is, indeed, jargon, and probably does not make much sense at this stage but eventually, you will understand it. Be patient!

How do you throw exceptions?

Assume that your program is trying to read a file, which does not exist. Your program also has a method that can throw some kind of **IOException**. If it does, the system starts searching for an exceptional handler. An exceptional handler can deal with IOException objects. Thus, there is no need to terminate the program. You should know that the Java language also has some default exceptions. When Java finds any of its default exceptions during the run it reports it as a message shown below.

java.lang.ArrayIndexOutOfBoundsException

• The inclusion of a **throw clause** in a method declaration means that when its code meets an exception it throws it. The general format of a method for a single throw is given below.

```
public void ThrowMethod ( ) throws TypeOfExceptionFound     // method declaration
   {
      //  relevant segment of code
   }
```

• The following general format is for throwing two exceptions. The same format can be extended for throwing more than two exceptions.

It should be noted that the inclusion of the keyowrd **throws** in a method declaration does not mean that it will certainly throw an exception. It will only do so, if it meets any exception.

```
public void ThrowMethod (  ) throws   ExceptionType1, ExceptionType2
   {
      //  relevant segment of code

   }
```

. How do you catch exceptions?

Throwing an exception is just not enough. You must catch it. In order to catch an exception, you must include a block of statements for try-catch construct. The following is a general format for a single try-catch construct.

```
try
   {
       block of statements          // catch block - to test and catch an exception
   }
   catch ( ExceptionType exception variable)                    // types of errors to catch
   {
       code for this type of exception          // handler code
   }
```

Figure 2: The general format for a single try-catch construct

• The above general format of try-catch construct shows a single **catch**, but there can be a number of **catch clauses**. Figure 3 shows a general format for two catch blocks. It illustrates how you can construct try-catch for a number of exceptions which your method may throw.

• The keyword **try** signals the beginning of a block of statements. This segment of code may throw exceptions (report exceptions) to catch, which is another keyword. The catch

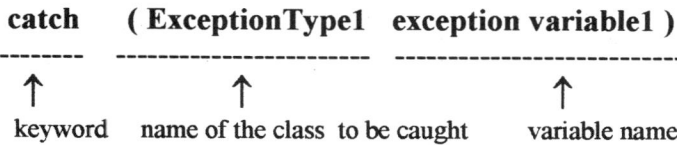

catch   (ExceptionType1   exception variable1)
--------   ------------------------   ---------------------------
↑   ↑   ↑
keyword   name of the class to be caught   variable name

• The keyword **Finally** - irrespective of whether an exception has occurred or not, there must be a segment of your program that must be executed. For instance, you must close the current file. Therefore, you can include an optional clause called Finally to the try-catch construct, as shown above.

```
    try
    {
       block of statements   }                              // catch block

    catch ( ExceptionType1 exception variable1 )            //  types of errors to catch
    {
        code for handling  exception type1  }               // handler code
    catch ( ExceptionType2 exception variable2 )
    {
        code for handling exception type2  }                // handler code
    finally
    {
        code ....      // Finally clause  - irrespective of  exception caught or not finally is executed.
    }
```

Figure 3: The general format for a multiple try-catch construct

. Is it possible to use Finally without a catch clause?

Yes, you can do so. This is illustrated below:

```
        try
        {
            code                   // it may or may not throw an exception
        }
        Finally
        {
            code                   // to be exececuted irrespective of  an exception occurrence
        }
```

If there is no return statement in the catch-finally segment of your program, execution continues with the code following the finally block.

TestTC . java

The program shown in diagram 1 illustrates how to catch an exception and deal with it. The program works out the sum of 5 **int** values. It stores the answer in the variable called calculation and divides the value of calculation by int e. It is also designed to display the result **div** as **answer**, as well as the word **End** to mark the end of this program. The program will display an error message if an exception of arithmetic type is found.

Explanation

The computation in this program is simple enough to follow. You have met this type of code before. The segment of the code which is try-catch-finally has been added to this simple computational code. In order to demonstrate how exceptions are dealt with, I have attempted to divide **div** by **zero,** which is not allowed. This data item **0** is included in the declaration of data items and then used to divide the calculation. It is a deliberate mistake so that it can be picked up by the Java system for reporting it as an exceptional error.

Program output

You can examine program output in diagram 1A. The try-catch-finally code has pointed out my arithmetic error. You can also see that the finally clause has also worked. The word required **End** is displayed. Finally clause is always executed irrespective of an exception is caught or not.

TestTC . java

```
class TestTC
{
 public static void main ( String [  ] args )

 {
  try
  {
   int a = 20,  b = 30,  c = 50,  d = 10,  e = 0,  cal,  div ;
   cal = ( a +  b +  c +  d + e );
   div = cal/e;

   System.out.println ( " Answer  = " + div  );
  }
  catch ( RuntimeException e )
  {
   System . out . println ( "\n\t Caught arithmetic error: " +e );
   }

finally
{
 System . out . println ( "\n\tEnd" );
}
}
}
```

Diagram 1

```
===========================Program Output=======================
C:\Examples>javac TestTC.java

C:\Examples>java TestTC

    Caught arithmetic error: java.lang.ArithmeticException: / by zero

    End
```

Diagram 1A

TestTC1 . java

```
class TestTC1
{
 public static void main (String [ ] args)

 {
  try
  {
   int a = 20, b = 30, c = 50, d = 10, e = 0, sum,  average;
   sum = ( a+ b+ c+ d+ e );
   average = sum/5;

   System.out.println ( "\n\tThe average value =  " + average );
   System.out.println ( "\t.........................………………….." );
   }
   catch ( RuntimeException e )
    {
    System.out. println ( "\n\t Cought arithmetic error: " +e );
      }
 finally
 {
  System.out.println ( "\tEnd" );
  System.out.println ( "\t……" );
  }
  }
  }
```

Diagram 2

```
=========================== Program Output =======================
C:\Examples>javac TestTC1.java

C:\Examples>java TestTC1

    The average value =  22
    ............................................
    End
    .....
```

Diagram 2A

TestTC1 . java

The purpose of this program is to work out the average of 5 numbers and display it on your screen. If it finds any exceptional error, it should display it. It will also print the word **End** to mark the end of this program end.

Explanation

The program shown in diagram 2, is identical to the last program, except that it has no deliberate mistake. Since there were no exceptions to report, the program was executed successfully. The output of the program is also listed in diagram 2A. There were no exceptions to report.

Exercise

Make a strict distinction between exceptions, errors, and run time exceptions?

Chapter 15

Suggested Solutions

Chapter 1

Suggested answer

Justification should include:

Personal development

. Becoming familiar with modern programming skills.
. getting ready to enter the programming profession.
. Better job prospects due to the increasing demand for Java programmers world-wide.

Languages capabilitie

. A Java program is in bytecode. This makes the program independent of any platform, because the bytecode can be executed on any system that is running the JVM. It makes Java programs portable and machine independent.

. You can write Java applets for commercial and other purposes for a wide audience over the Internet. This can give software development businesses a considerable commercial advantage, and thus more job opportunities for Java programmers.

. Java is a programming language which has extensive libraries. These libraries contain pre-defined classes which greatly help the programmer in developing software, saving considerable programming time and effort.

. Larger organisations in both the public and the private sectors throughout the world are increasing using the Internet. Java language is flexible and powerful to enable the software expert to integrate relational databases into the Web browser for the dissemination of information.

. Java Bean is a re-usable software component Java Bean technology enables software developers to design their own components.

. Java language is big and flexible. It has the capability and suitability for programming tasks.

Chapter 2

1. The correct statement is given below.

$$\text{System . out . println (" This is my book") ;}$$

↑   ↑   ↑

begins with capital S   point is needed   semicolon is essential

2. There is no difference between data, argument/s and parameter/s. From a practical point of view, all three words mean the same thing. What goes inside (   ) is called parameters or arguments or data. Data is not often used for this purpose.

3. **Class Book** means a class called book. On the other hand, **Book . java** indicates the name of a Java program called Book. It is your source program.

4. The **javac tool** is the compiler. It is **javac.exe** in the JKD file. This converts your source program into **bytecode**. Thus, you use it when compiling your source code into Java bytecode.

5.

• HTLM stands for the **Hypertext Markup Language**. It is the language of the World Wide Web. A document on the Web is written in HTML The Java applets are viewed in the html document with a browser.

• a logical error is usually caused by poor program design.

6. **int a (30*450)/5** is incomplete and incorrect for the following reasons

     a) the equal sign operator is missing , and

     b) to mark the end of a statement, you must have a semicolon, which is also missing.

The correct expression or statement is: **int a = (30*450)/5 ;**

7. • Javac MyFirstProgram . java

This command refers to MyFirstProgram source file in order to compile it into the bytecode. If this command is correct, the Javac will convert the source code into the bytecode, and then the cursor flashes, indicating the user to enter on the next line:

          • java MyFirstProgram to execute the program.

8. WordPad is used to prepare a source file (program) and save it. If the **Javac** finds errors in the source file, you use the WordPad again, to open your source file in order to edit it accordingly and save it again.

Chapter 3

1.

Joint . Java

```
class  Joint
{
 public static void main ( String [ ] args)
 {

    String  Learn  = ( " I am learning Java.");
    String  Help =("You are good at it.  Please help me to understand it.");
    String  Learning  = ( Learn + Help );
    System.out.println ( "  ");
    System.out.println ("\n" + Learning );

     int n = Learning.length (  );
     System.out.println("\nThe length of String Learning is " + n + " characters.");
 }
 }
```

Program output

```
C:\Examples>javac  Joint . java

C:\Examples>java Joint


 I am learning Java. You are good at it.  Please help me to understand it.

The length of String Learning is 72 characters.
```

2.

MeanValue . java

```
class MeanValue
{
 public static void main ( String args [ ] )

  {
  int a = 156;  int b = 184;  int c = 200;  int d = 210; int e = 222;
  int f = 215; int g = 255;
  float h = 199.90f;   float i = 175.55f;
  float j = 167.90f;    float sum = 0.00f;    float average = 0.0f;

  System.out.println ( " ");
  System.out.println("The Average Weekly Wages Computation");
  System.out.println("-------------------------------------------------");

  sum = ( a + b + c + d + e + f + g + h + I + j );
  average = sum/10;
  System.out.println ( "\nThe average weekly wages = " + average);
  System.out.println (" -------------------------------------------");
 }
}
```

Program Output

```
C:\Examples>javac MeanValue.java

C:\Examples>java MeanValue

The Average Weekly Wages Computation
-------------------------------------------------

The average weekly wages = 198.535
 -------------------------------------------
```

3.

Drink . java

```
class Drink          // compares two strings for equality

{
 public static void main ( String args [ ] )
  {
  System.out.println("\nThis program performs equality test");
  System.out.println("---------------------------------\r");
  String early  = ("tea");
  String late =  ("coffee");
  System.out.println ( "\n John Do you always drink tea in mornings and evenings?");
  System.out.println("\n It is "+ early.equals (late)+ ".");

  String morning  = ("I drink tea");
  String evening =  ("I drink tea");
  System.out.println ( "\n Anne Do you always drink tea in mornings and evenings?");
  System.out.println("\n It is "+ morning.equals (evening)+ ".");
  }
}
```

Program Output

```
C:\Examples>java Drink

This program performs equality test
-----------------------------------

 John Do you always drink tea in mornings and evenings?

It is false.

 Anne Do you always drink tea in mornings and evenings?

It is true.
```

Chapter 4

Program Part A

Commission .java

```java
class Commission
{
  public static void main ( String [  ] args )
   {
    int [  ] [  ]com;
    com = new int [ 3 ] [ 3 ];
    com [ 0 ] [ 0 ] =  45000;
    com [ 0 ] [ 1 ] =  42580;
    com [ 0 ] [ 2 ] =  35060;
    com [ 1 ] [ 0 ] =  44000;
    com [ 1 ] [ 1 ] =  25678;
    com [ 1 ] [ 2 ] =  28005;
    com [ 2 ] [ 0 ] =  39000;
    com [ 2 ] [ 1 ] =  29008;
    com [ 2 ] [ 2 ] =  34006;
    System.out.println (   );
    System.out.println  ( "Friendly Insurance PLC Commission paid 1997-1999" );
    System.out.println   ( " ...............................................\n" );
    System.out.println ( "Year " + "\t\t" + "Asia" + "\t\t" + "Europe" + "\t\t" + "USA"  );
    System.out.println ( "......." + "\t\t" +"......." + "\t\t" + ".........." + "\t\t" +".......\n" );
    System.out.println ( "1997" + "\t\t"  + com [ 0 ] [ 0 ] + "\t\t" + com [ 0 ] [ 1 ] +"\t\t" + com [ 0 ] [ 2 ]
);
    System.out.println ( "1998" +"\t\t"   + com [ 1 ] [ 0 ] + "\t\t" + com [ 1 ] [ 1 ] +"\t\t" + com [ 1 ] [ 2
] );
    System.out.println  ( "1999" +"\t\t"   + com [ 2 ] [ 0 ] + "\t\t" + com [ 2 ] [ 1 ] +"\t\t" + com [ 2 ] [ 2
]  );
    System.out.println ( " ..............................................");
    System.out.println ( "Sum " +"\t\t" + (com [ 0 ] [ 0 ] + com [ 1 ] [ 0 ] + com [ 2 ] [ 0 ] )
                + "\t\t" + ( com [ 0 ] [ 1 ] + com [ 1 ] [ 1 ] + com [ 2 ] [ 1 ] )
                + "\t\t" + ( com [ 0 ] [ 2 ] + com [ 1 ] [ 2 ] + com [ 2 ] [ 2 ] ) );
   System.out.println ( "Average " + "\t\t" + ( com [ 0 ] [ 0 ]   + com [ 1 ] [ 0 ] + com [ 2 ] [ 0 ] )/3
                + "\t\t" + ( com [ 0 ] [ 1 ] + com [ 1 ] [ 1 ]  + com [ 2 ] [ 1 ] )/3
                + "\t\t" + ( com [ 0 ] [ 2 ] + com [ 1 ] [ 2 ]  + com [ 2 ] [ 2 ] )/3 );

    System.out.println (" ....................................................");
```

Program Part B

```
 System.out.println (  );
System.out.println   ( "\t\t" + "Friendly Insurance PLC"  );
System.out.println ("\t\t" + "...................................\n" );
System.out.println ("Commission paid to sales representatives 1997-1999" );
System.out.println  ( "..............................................................\n" );
System.out.println  ( "Average Commission =  " + ( com [ 0 ] [ 0 ] + com [ 0 ] [ 1 ]
               + com [ 0 ] [ 2 ] + com [ 1 ] [ 0 ] + com [ 1 ] [ 1 ] + com [ 1 ] [ 2 ] + com [ 2 ] [ 0]
               + com [ 2 ] [ 1 ] + com [ 2 ] [ 2 ])/9 );
 int subsc = com [ 1 ] [ 2 ];
 System.out.println ( "\nCommission earned by American sales representatives in 1998 =  " + subsc );
}
}
```

Program Output

```
Friendly Insurance PLC Commission paid 1997-1999
..........................................................................

Year        Asia        Europe       USA
......       ......       ..........    ......

1997        45000        42580        35060
1998        44000        25678        28005
1999        39000        29008        34006
.......................................................................
Sum         128000       97266        97071
Average     42666        32422        32357
......................................................................

         Friendly Insurance PLC
         ..................................

Commission paid to sales representatives 1997-1999
.........................................................................

Average Commission = 35815

Commission earned by American sales representatives in 1998 = 28005
```

Chapter 5

1.

Program ExitLoop.java

```
class ExitLoop
{
  public static void main ( String [ ] args )
  {
  System.out.println ( "\n\t\t How to exit a loop" );
  System.out.println ( "\t\t .........................\n" );
  System. out.println( "\t\tNumber" + " \t(Repeat*3/2)" );
  System.out.println ( "\t\t ........." + "\t..............\n" );
  int Repeat = 10;
  while ( Repeat <= 200 )
    {
    Repeat ++;
     System.out. println ( "\t\t"+ Repeat  + "\t\t" + (Repeat *3/2));
   if
    ( Repeat = = 16 )
     break;                // exit
    }
System.out.println ( "\t..............................................................\n" );
System.out.println ( "\tThe Required end has reached which is  " + Repeat );
System.out.println ( "\t..................................................." );
}
}
```

Program Output

C:\Examples>javac ExitLoop.java

C:\Examples>java ExitLoop

```
        How to exit a loop
        .........................

        Number     (Repeat*3/2)
        ..........    .................

        11         16
        12         18
        13         19
        14         21
        15         22
        16         24
        .................................................

        The Required end has reached which is 16
        .................................................
```

Chapter 6

1.

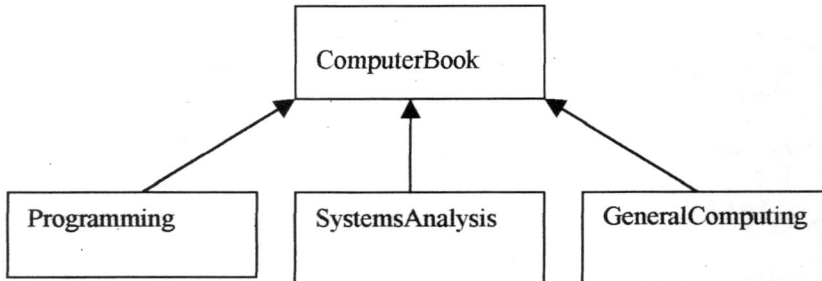

ComputerBook class is an abstract class because, as you move up the inheritance hierarchy, classes contain less and less information. In this case, the class ComputerBook has so little information that it should be considered as an abstract class. As opposed to ComputerBook class(parent class) class, **Sy-** **sytemAnalysis** is a sub-class of ComputerBook. It contains all relevant information on systems analysis books kept in this library.

2. The given code: **Student   JavaEveningProg = new Student (   ) ;**

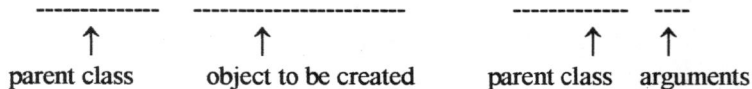

```
            ↑              ↑                        ↑        ↑
      parent class   object to be created     parent class  arguments
```

The purpose of this statement is to create an instance (or object, if it is easier for you to understand). This instance of the class Student is called **JavaEveningProg**.

3. The given code:

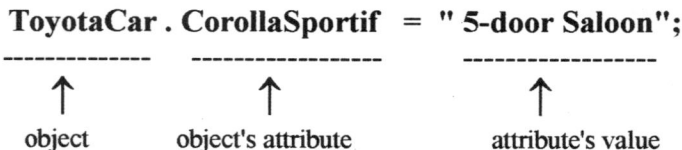

ToyotaCar . CorollaSportif = " 5-door Saloon";

```
       ↑              ↑                      ↑
    object     object's attribute      attribute's value
```

Note that **. (dot)** is essential here for association.

4. Cast takes place within an inheritance hierarchy. Thus, it is essential that a class is a subclass of the other class. Casting an object from the subclass to its immediate superclass is shown below.

```
Miminsters MinisterA;
CentralGovernmet Minister;
MinisterA = new Ministers ( );
CentralGovernment Minister  = ( CentralGovernment ) MinisterA;
```

5. The following is the code for deriving the **Java** class from the existing class **Programming**

```
class Java extends Programming
    {
       your code ---
    }
```

6.   Yes indeed, it is true to say that the difference between an object and a class is often blurred.

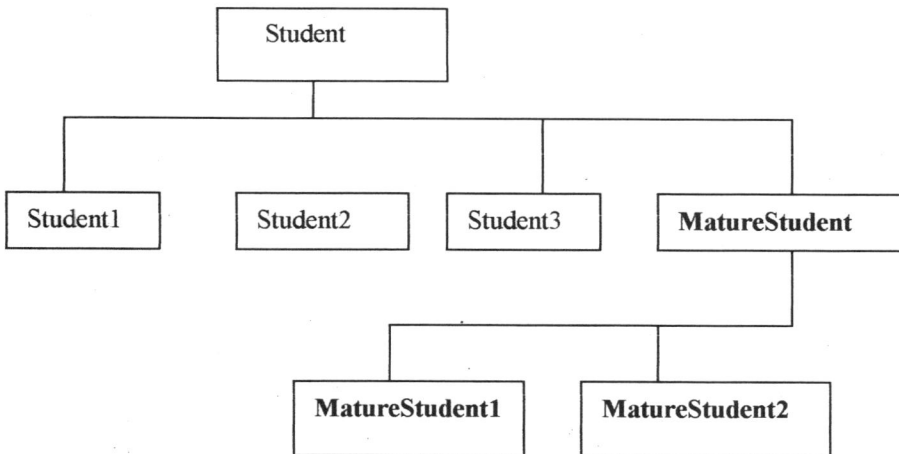

Let's assume that you wish to develop a database system for students registered with your university Students' Union. You wish to devise a record structure which will store the name, courseCode, and age for each student, together with methods of handling the database.

The superclass is **Student**. You can use this class to create objects namely, **Student1**, **Student2**…..**Student3000**. Suppose that it is desirable to keep a record of matureStudents. In this case, there is no need to create another data structure, as you can add a new object called **MatureStudent**. This way, in fact, you are creating a new class called **MatureStudent**. Now, you can see that the difference between an object and a class has disappeared. This is what I mean when I say that the difference between an object and a class is often blurred.

 It should also be noted that MatureStudent2 is a subclass of the superclass called Student. MatureStuden1, and MatureStudent2 are objects. You can also add more subclasses and objects to this data structure.

7. import java . awt; - it contains the basic classes which provide you with the facility for user interface (GUI components such as buttons, menus …). If you are using a number of classes, which are in the java . awt package, in this case, you must include in your program: import java . awt .*;

This import statement will let you use any or all classes in your program, as it imports all classes which are in the Java AWT package.

8. It is rather confusing jargon. It means methods. If you can understand the meaning of method I congratulate you as it means you know what the behaviour implies. Methods give information on different components of a class, so does the behaviour. Both words, behaviour and method, mean practically the same .

9. In my view, again the jargon can be confusing. An object is said to be an instance of a class. A class has to be instantiated to create an object variable. From our practical point of view, an object and an instance have the same meaning, that is an object of a class. There is no shortage of confusing jargon in Object Oriented Language. For example:

Class Employee. We can declare three instance variables: manager, supervisor, clerk. At the same time, I can say, the class Employee has three subclasses. I can also say that the class employee has three objects namely manager, supervisor and clerk.

10. a) The code is a constructor method. It will be called when the following statement is met in your program during the program execution:

```
        Temeperature  Temp = new Temeperature (   );    // constructor.
```

10. b) To make a method into a class method, start with static as below:

```
     Static int Cal ( int a, int b, int c)       // it can be without parameters within  (   )
   {
       int d = ( a + b + c)/3;
       System . out . println (" The average value =  " + d );
   }
```

Chapter 7

HTML Document: Attempt1 . html

```
<HTML>
<HEAD>
<TITLE> < First Trial>
</HEAD>
<BODY>
<Applet CODE = "Attempt1 .class" width = 400 height = 320>
</Applet>
</BODY>
</HTML>
```

<u>Chapter 7 Program</u>   <u>**Attempt1 . java**</u>

```
import java . awt.*;
import javax. swing.*;
public class Attempt1 extends JApplet
{

  public void paint (Graphics g)
{
 super. paint ( g);
g. drawString  ("Contact me at ", 165, 100);
g. drawString   ( " ", 150, 115);       // space between two lines
g. drawString   ("WWW.NOBODY.COM", 150, 130);
}
}
```

Applet Attepmt1

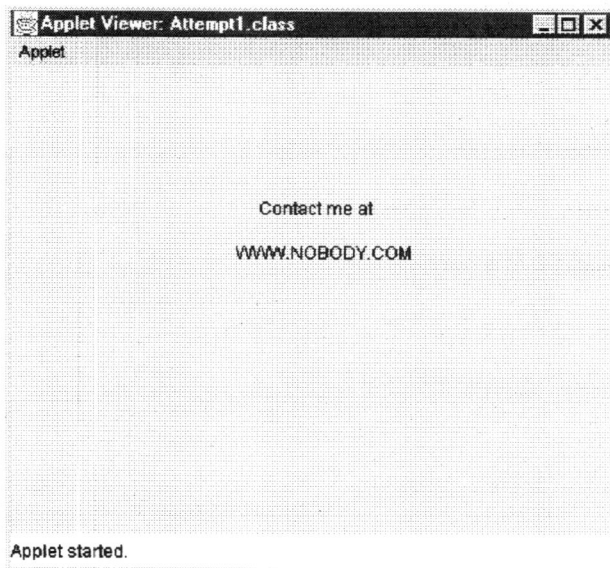

Applet Viewer: Attempt1.class

Applet

Contact me at

WWW.NOBODY.COM

Applet started.

Chapter 8

Program

Exercise8. java

```
import java . awt.*;
import javax . swing.*;

public  class Exercise8 extentds JApplet
{
public void init (  )
{
 setBackground (SystemColor.window);          // applet's background
}

public void paint (Graphics g)
{

super. paint ( g);
                                                    // create fonts objects
Font f1 = new Font ( " Helvetica", Font.BOLD, 20);
Font f2 = new Font (" Monospaced", Font.BOLD, 20);
Font f3 = new Font ( "SansSerif",Font.BOLD,25);
                                                // draws fist line
g.setFont (f3);
g.setColor ( Color. blue);
g.drawString ("*****************************************", 48, 80);
                                                // first text line
g.setFont ( f1);
g.setColor ( SystemColor.windowText);
g.drawString (" Text Colour inside  Windows - this one ",50, 120);
                                                // second text line
g.setFont (f2);
g.setColor ( SystemColor.text);
g.drawString ( " Background colour for text - this one ", 50, 150);
                                                // third text line
g.setFont (f3);
 g.setColor ( SystemColor.textHighlightText);
g.drawString (" Text colour for selected text this one ", 50, 180);
                                                // draws last line
g.setColor ( Color. blue);
g.drawString ("*****************************************", 48, 220);

}
}
```

Chapter 8

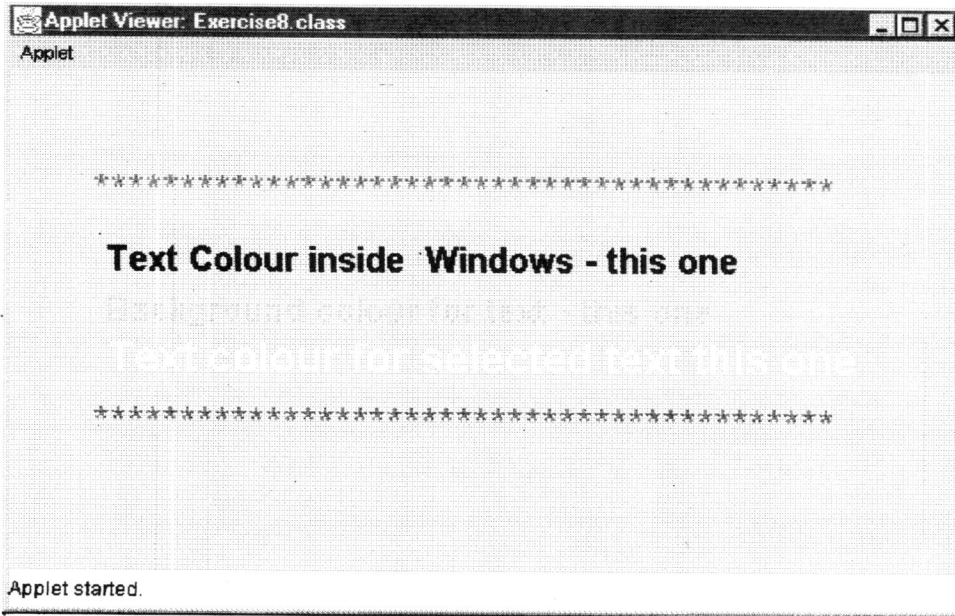

Applet: Exercise8.class

Colours are not so visible in black and white. However, you can test your applet if you load it into a Web page using appletviewer. You don't have to be on the Internet to use the applet viewer Java tool.

Exercise8 . html

```
<html>
<head>
<title> Fonts and Colours
</title>
<head>
<body>
<applet CODE= "Exercise8.class" width = 550 height = 300>
</applet>
</body>
</html>
```

Chapter 9

1. Buttons, check boxes, combo boxes, text areas and labels are commonly used. There are some more components. In your own interest find out .....

2. An applet (JApplet) is an extension of both Panel and Container classes. The following skeleton sketch of class inheritance hierarchy illustrates this relationship:

Object ← Component ← Container ← Panel ← Applet ← **JApplet**

This class inheritance hierarchy enables us to take advantage of many of the properties of classes in this inheritance chain. This chain is just a small portion of Java complex class hierarchy. This way, for instance, an applet provides an area upon which you can draw. Further more, like Container or Panel, an applet holds components.

3. The positioning of components in an applet or any other kind of container or frame is organised by a layout manager. So, when you see something displayed on screen, it is placed in this particular place by the layout manager. The default layout manger is called FlowLayout manager.

4. You must first specify the layout manager. The components are added to the container by the layout manager. Thus, the code for the layout manager must come first, and then in the correct place in your program the code for add components can be listed.

5. The **BorderLayout** manager can let you place user components in five areas namely: NORTH, SOUTH, EAST, WEST, and CENTER. In the question, it say, "where you want". Of course, the choice is still limited, but you can place your component anywhere within its five area.

6. A panel is a container. On the other hand, there are four panes of a **JFrame**. One of them is the **content pane**. The content pane is implemented with Java Swing.

7.
Applet Cities

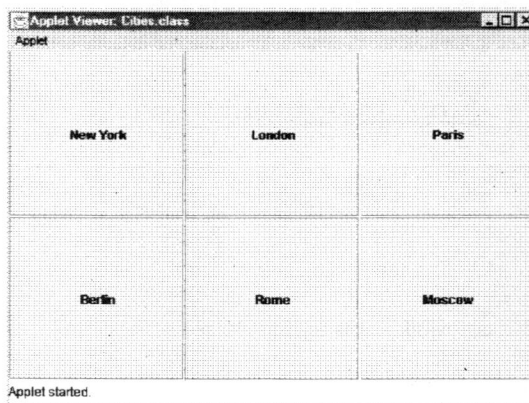

7. continued

Cities . java

```java
import java. awt.*;
import javax. swing.*;

public class Cities extends JApplet

{

JButton city1  =  new  JButton  ( " New York"  );
JButton city2  =  new  JButton  ( " London"  );
JButton city3  =  new  JButton  ( " Paris"  );
JButton city4  =  new  JButton  ( " Berlin");
JButton city5  =  new  JButton  ( " Rome"  );
JButton city6  =  new  JButton  (" Moscow"  );

public void init (    )

{
  setBackground (Color.green);
  Container  pane = getContentPane (   );
  pane .setLayout ( new GridLayout ( 2, 3 ));
  pane.add ( city1 );
  pane.add ( city2 );
  pane.add ( city3 );
  pane.add ( city4 );
  pane.add ( city5 );
  pane.add ( city6 );
}
}
```

Cities.Html

```html
<Object code = "Cities.class", height = 320 width = 500>
</Object>
```

Chapter 10

Europe . html

```
</html>
<head>
<title>
        Event Handling
</title>
</head>
<body>
<applet code= "Europe.class" width = 600 height = 320>
</applet>
</body>
</html>
```

Applet Europe with buttons checked

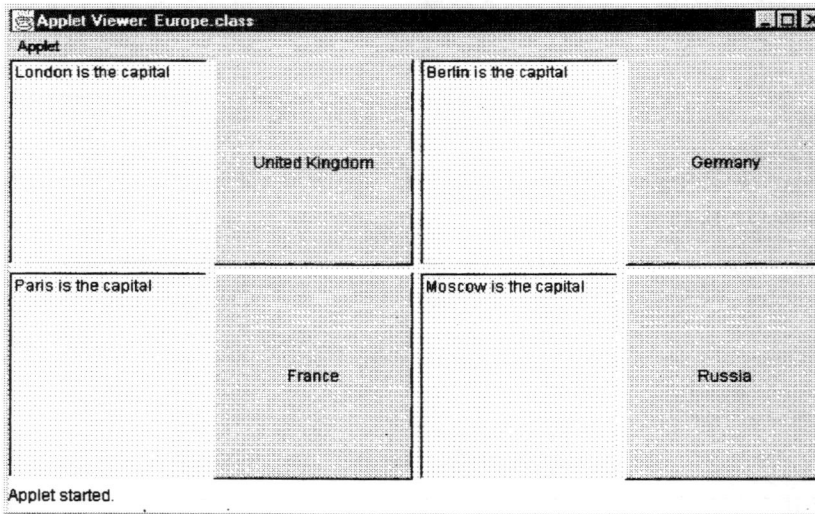

```
┌─────────────────────────────────────────────────────────────────┐
│ Applet Viewer: Europe.class                              _ □ X   │
│ Applet                                                            │
│ ┌──────────────────────┬────────────────────────────────────┐   │
│ │ London is the capital │        Berlin is the capital       │   │
│ │                       │                                    │   │
│ │            United Kingdom │                Germany         │   │
│ │                       │                                    │   │
│ ├──────────────────────┼────────────────────────────────────┤   │
│ │ Paris is the capital  │        Moscow is the capital       │   │
│ │                       │                                    │   │
│ │            France     │                Russia              │   │
│ └──────────────────────┴────────────────────────────────────┘   │
│ Applet started.                                                   │
└─────────────────────────────────────────────────────────────────┘
```

Europe. Java   continued on page 293

```
import java. awt.*;
import  java.applet.Applet;
import java . awt. event.*;

public class Europe extends Applet
implements ActionListener
```

Program Europe.java continued on page 294

```
{
Button button1, button2, button3, button4;
TextField text1, text2, text3, text4;

 public void init ( )
{
  setBackground ( Color.yellow );
  setLayout ( new GridLayout ( 2,4,5,5 ));
  text1 = new TextField ( 40 );
  add ( text1 );
  button1 = new Button ( "United Kingdom" );
  add ( button1 );
  button1.addActionListener ( this );

  text2 = new TextField ( 40 );
  add ( text2 );
  button2 = new Button ( "Germany" );
  add( button2 );
  button2.addActionListener ( this );

  text3 = new TextField ( 40 );
  add ( text3 );
  button3 = new Button ( "France" );
  add( button3 );
  button3.addActionListener ( this );

  text4 = new TextField ( 40 ) ;
  add ( text4 );
  button4 = new Button ( "Russia" );
  add( button4 );
  button4.addActionListener ( this );
}
public void actionPerformed ( ActionEvent e )
{
String s1 = new String ( "London is the capital" );
if( e.getSource ( ) == button1 )
{
text1.setText ( s1 );
}
 String s2 = new String ("Berlin is the capital ");
if (e.getSource ( ) == button2)
{
text2.setText ( s2  );
}
```

Program Europe.java from page 293 continued

```
String s3 = new String ( "Paris is the capital" );
if (e.getSource ( ) == button3)
{
 text3.setText ( s3 );
}
String s4 = new String ("Moscow is the capital");
if (e.getSource ( ) == button4)
{
text4.setText ( s4 );
}
}
}
```

Chapter 11

1.

Exercise12 . java

```
import java.awt.*;
import javax.swing.*;

public  class Exercise12 extends JApplet
{
public void paint (Graphics g)
{
 super.paint ( g);
 setBackground (Color.lightGray);

 g.setColor (Color.blue);
 g.drawLine (10,10,70, 70);
 g.setColor (Color.black);
 g.drawLine ( 70,70, 150,150);
 for ( int y1 = 160; y1< 170; y1++)
 g.drawLine( 150,y1,210,y1+10);
 g.setColor(Color.black);
 g.drawRoundRect (200,200, 120, 120, 90, 90);
 g.setColor(Color.red);
 g.fillArc ( 310, 310, 90, 90,-270,90 );
 }
}
```

Exercise12 . html

```
</html>
<head>
<title>
        Drawing -Exercise12
</title>
</head>
<body>
<applet code = ."Exercise12.class" width = 500 height = 370>
</applet>
</body>
</html>
```

Applet Exercise 12

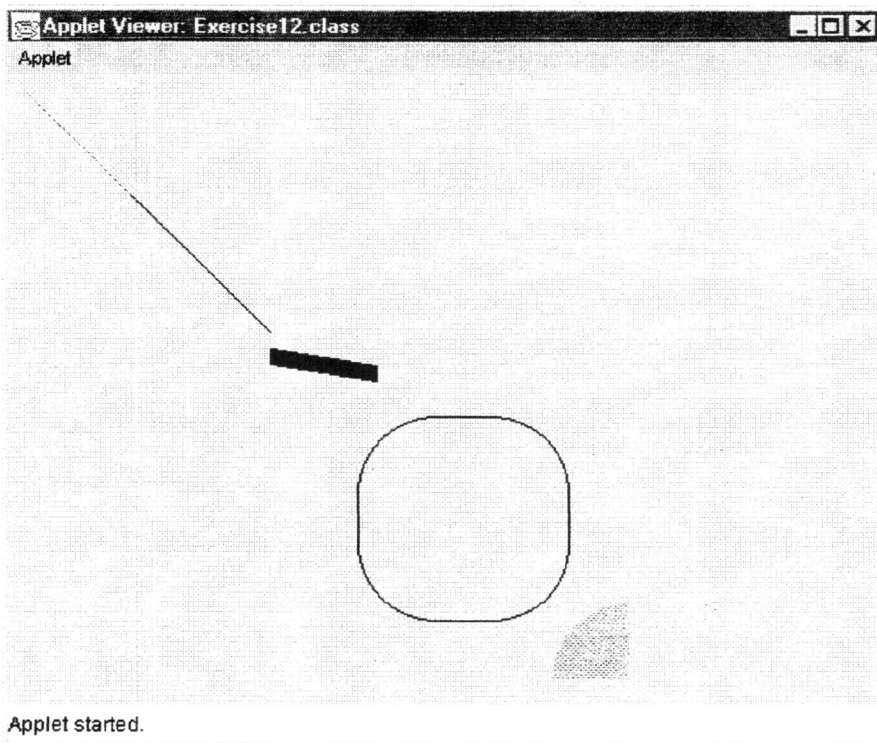

2.

```
                        DemoTC . java

import java.awt.*;
import javax.swing.*;
public class DemoTC extends JApplet
{
 double [ ] total   = new double [ 10 ];
 int     [ ] portion  =  new int    [ 10 ];
 Color [ ] col  = new Color      [ 10 ];
 public void init ( )
 {
      double sum = 0;
     total [ 0 ]  =  1500;
     total  [ 1 ] =  1500;
     total  [ 2 ] =  2000;
     total  [ 3 ] =  1200;
     total  [ 4 ] =  1900;
     total  [ 5 ] =  2500;
     total  [ 6 ] =  1800;
     total  [ 7 ] =  2400;
     total  [ 8 ] = 3000;
     total  [ 9 ] =  900;

     col  [ 0 ] = Color.red;
     col  [ 1 ] = Color.blue;
     col  [ 2 ] = Color.red;
     col  [ 3 ] = Color.red;
     col  [ 4 ] = Color.black;
     col  [ 5 ] = Color.gray;
     col  [ 6 ] = Color.yellow;
     col  [ 7 ] = Color.darkGray;
     col  [ 8 ] = Color. white;
     col  [ 9 ] = Color.green;
     for ( int counter = 0; counter <10; counter++ )
       sum +=  total [ counter ];
     for ( int counter = 0; counter <10; counter++ )
       portion [counter ] = ( int ) ( total [counter]/sum*360 );
 }
 public void paint ( Graphics g )
 {
   super.paint ( g );
   int begin = 0;
   for ( int counter = 0; counter <10; counter++ )
 {
 g.setColor (col [ counter ] );
 g.fillArc ( 100,100, 200, 200, begin ,portion [ counter ] );
 begin += portion [ counter ];
}} }
```

2.

Document: DemoTC . html

```
</html>
<head>
<title>
        Pie chart
</title>
</head>
<body>
<applet code= "DemoTC.class" width = 500 height = 350>
</applet>
</body>
</html>
```

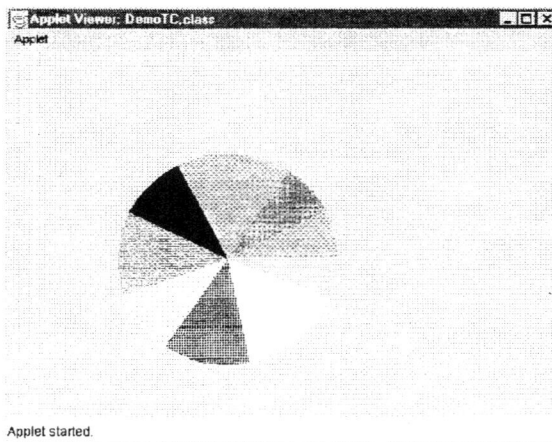

Applet DemoTC Displaying Pie chart

Chapter 12

See next page for answer 1.

2. It is true to say that circles and ellipses do not have corners. The constructor statement for creating an ellipse or a circle with 2D Graphics class is as follows.

Ellipse2D.Float cr = new Ellipse2D.Float (240, 40, 5, 5); - last two values are for width and height.

In this case both width and height are of 5 pixels each. Thus, it is a circle.In order to draw this object as oultine, you must call **draw (cr) method**. For drawing the filled circle, you must call **fill (cr) method**.

3. In order to change the current colour you must call **setColor ( ) method**.

1.

ClipShape1 .java (test it as java application)

```java
import java.awt.*;
import java.awt.geom.*;
import javax.swing.*;

public class ClipShape1 extends Frame
{

  public static void main ( String [  ] args )
{

  (new ClipShape1 (  ) ).setVisible ( true ); //
  }
  public ClipShape1 (  )
{
  super ( "Clipping" );
  setBackground ( Color.yellow );
  setSize ( 350, 350 );
}

public void paint ( Graphics screen )
{
  Graphics2D  screen2D = ( Graphics2D ) screen;
  RoundRectangle2D R = new RoundRectangle2D.Float ( 20, 20, 250, 250, 270, 90 );
  screen2D.setColor (Color.red );
  screen2D.clip (R );
  screen2D.fillRect (30, 60, 300, 300 );
  }
  }
```

Frame showing rectangular clip region

Chapter 13

1.

```
                    BlueMan . java ( continued on page 300)
import java . awt.*;
import javax. swing.*;
import java.awt.geom.*;        // for Graphicd2D
public class BlueMan extends JApplet
implements Runnable
{
Thread runner;
int xPosition;
public void init ( )
{
setBackground (Color.red);
}
public void start ( )
{
 if (runner == null)
  {
   runner = new Thread (this);
   runner.start ( );
  }
 }
 public void run ( )
 {
 Thread thisThread = Thread.currentThread ( );
 while (runner == thisThread )
  {
  repaint ( );
 try
   {
    Thread.sleep ( 1500);
  }
  catch
  ( InterruptedException e) { }
 }
 }

public void stop  ( )
 {
 if (runner != null)
 {
 runner = null;  .
 }
 }
```

Continued form page 299

```java
public void paint (Graphics screen)
{
 Graphics2D screen2D = (Graphics2D)screen;

  screen2D.setColor (Color.yellow);
  screen2D.fillRect(0,0,600,300);

                          // head
  screen2D.setColor (Color.blue);
  Ellipse2D head = new Ellipse2D.Float(20,20,150,150);
  screen2D.fill ( head);

// Left Eye
  screen2D.setColor (Color.white);
  Ellipse2D LE = new Ellipse2D.Float(75, 70, 10,10);
  screen2D.fill(LE);
                          // Right Eye
  screen2D.setColor (Color.white);
  Ellipse2D RE = new Ellipse2D.Float(95, 70, 10,10);
  screen2D.fill(RE);
                          // Mouth
  screen2D.setColor (Color.white);
  Rectangle2D MO = new Rectangle2D.Float ( 75,90,30,30);
  screen2D.fill(MO);

}
 public void update (Graphics screen)
  {
   paint (screen);
  }
}
```

BlueMan . html

```html
<HTML>
<HEAD>
<TITLE> < BlueMan>
</TITLE>
</HEAD>
<BODY>
<Applet CODE = "BlueMan.class" width= 300 height = 250>
</Applet>
</BODY>
</HTML>
```

Animated applet BlueMan

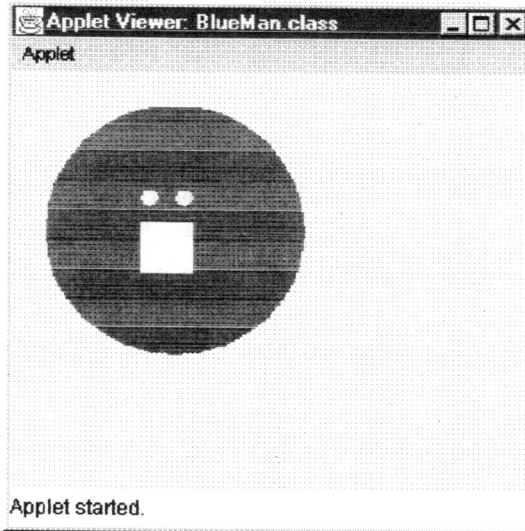

You can test it with the appletviewer. It works!

Chapter 14

An error is usually caused by virtual machine problems. These are not handled by the programmer.

A run time exception occurs during the normal execution of the program. These may be errors made by the programmer when writing the code.

Exceptions are circumstantial which are caused by things such as you have called a file in your code which does not exist on your system and thus your program failed. It is not strictly an error due to the programmers fault. It is a condition or a given circumstance of which the programmer is not aware (let's assume so).

You may be aware of the fact that in practice such a fine distinction is not usually made. The word error is most commonly used for errors and exceptions of all kinds.

Glossary of Terms

Abstract class - Abstract class cannot be instantiated.

Abstract Windowing Toolkit (AWT) - A collection of a huge number of Java classes. It enables you to develop Java programs by making use of enormously large number of classes and methods that are stored in this package.

Applet - A Java program designed to run on the Internet. It is usually much smaller in size than an application program.

Appletviewer - It is one of the Java Development Kit tools. It enables you to test your applet which is linked to the World Wide Web page (html document or page).

Application - A program designed to run on your computer or locally as opposed to the applet.

API - It is an abbreviation for Application Programming Interface. The Java language has a large number of class libraries, methods and interfaces to enable the programmer to develop Java programs by using any of these API components. This helps the programmer as he/she can use already tested pieces of software.

Argument - It is the same thing as the parameter. It is a value or information which is passed to a method during the program execution. In **int add (x),** x is a parameter of integer type.

Array - It is a set of the same type of data grouped together under a name called identifier. Arrays can be one-dimensional or multi - dimensional (two-dimensional). Each data item in an array is called an element. All elements are numbered in order to distinguish them from each other.

ASCII (or Ascii) code - acronym for American Standard Code for Information Interchange. It has been widely used since it was introduced in 1963. It has 128 different character values in the range 0 - 127.

ASCII text file - It does not have any special characters, such as **boldfaced** text.

Attribute - It is generally associated with the Object Oriented Programming in order to distinguish one object from the other. For instance, a car has a number of attributes, such as colour, number of doors etc.

AWT - See API.

Base class - see the superclass.

Baseline - It is an imaginary line on which characters are drawn. It is associated with the FontMetric class.

Bean (s) - A comparatively new development of re-useable Java software. See JavaBeans.

Bit - It stands for binary digit, which can be either 0 or 1.

Block - A group of statements within { }.

Boolean - (Boolean) A boolean variable can have only true or false values, such as small or large.

Browser - It is the software for viewing the World Wide Web pages. You need to have a browser software on your system to run your applet on the Net.

Buffer - It is a temporary storage area. A buffer is usually built into a disk drive or printer, so that it can hold data during the transfer of data from one device to another device.

Bug - In simple terms, it means an error.

Byte - It is a fixed number of bits for the computer to treat as a single unit. It consists of 8 bits.

Bytecode - It is the compiled Java source file. Bytecode invention has made Java World wide famous.

Case - It is the word used in switch-case statement.

Casting - It is the process of converting the value of an object or primitive type into another type.

Catch - This word is used in exception handling code, try ----catch. It implies to report exceptional errors.

Character - A single character, number or symbol. For instance " is a character.

Character stream - It is associated with input and output of characters. It means the handling of characters as a series of characters.

Check box - It is one of the Graphics user interface components. A check box can be either checked or unchecked.

Choice - A graphics user interface component. It consists of a drop-down list of choices.

Class - In Object Oriented Programming languages, such as Java, the class forms the basis of the concept of object. Java has many classes. For instance, your own Java program is also a class.

Class file - It is generated by the Java compiler. It is in fact the binary file that has Java bytecode.

Class library - A class library is a collection of similar type of classes, which the programmer can use. See API.

Class variable - It is a variable within a particular class. Class variable can only be used by the class itself. It is associated with the class objects.

Command line - You enter a command line at the prompt of the MS-DOS Prompt operating system. This is another way of entering your commands and communicating with the computer.

Comments - In a source file, one can add comments. These comments are purely for the benefit of humans.

Compiler - It translates the source file into a self self-contained program called object program that can be run.

Component - In a graphical User Interface (UGI), a component is an item such as a button, Combo Box and the like. For instance, you can click a button to communicate with the program. Component is also a class.

Concatenate - It means to join two strings together in order to display them as a single string.

Conditional statement - A conditional statement leads to a selective action, providing a specific condition is met. **If** and **switch** are conditional statements.

Constructor - It is a special method. It is used to create an object (instance) of the class.

Container - It is a component that can be used to contain other components in a UGI . It is also a class.

Debug - or debugging. The process of identifying and removing errors/ bugs from a program.

Default method - Java has many default methods. A default method is automatically called when no other method is supplied. You can override a default method by supplying your own method. For instance, the cause of animation flickering lies in the default update ( ) method. You can override this method by including your own update ( ) method in your program.

Double-buffering - It involves the use of two buffer areas. When working with animation, one buffer can be used for drawing to an **offscreen** buffer. The second buffer is then used to copy the drawing to the applet window. This can eliminate flickering from the animation.

Element - A data item in an array. See array.

Encapsulation -In object oriented programming the concept of encapsulation states that an object contains or encapsulates its own set of data and methods. In practical terms, its implication is that a class can be instantiated a number of times, creating a number of objects, each one having its own data and methods.

Event - When you press a key, click a mouse or do any other thing which makes the component react, this process is called an event.

Event -driven programming - see below.

Event handling - When a UGI component responds to the user event such as a button being clicked, it is called event handling. The program development techniques that deal with such external events as mouse clicks or the key presses and the like, is also called **event-driven programming**.

Exception - Any condition or occurrence that disrupts the normal flow of the program.

Extends - A keyword used when a subclass inherits a superclass. For instance your applet class extends the super class JApplet. This way, your applet is a subclass of JApplet class.

Finally clause - It is a code that is executed whether or not an exception was caught.

Floating-point numbers - These are real numbers. 12.34 is one such number.

Frame - It refers to the graphical outline of a window when dealing with graphical user interface. Frame is also a class. Frames are examples of containers.

GIF file - This is an image file. For instance, Anim .GIF is an image file. GIF format is most commonly used for viewing images on the World Wide Web.

GIF 89a file - It is GIF file that supports transparent colours.

Graphical user interface - The components such as buttons, text fields, combo box, and the like help the user to interact with the computer by using the mouse or the keyboard. For short GUI is often used.

GUI - as above.

Hierarchy of classes - In Java, classes are organised in the form of an Egyptian pyramid in which the superclass is at the top of the pyramid and all other classes are in their own hierarchical order below it.

HTML - Or html. Acronym for Hypertext Markup Language. In this language, Web page or document is written. An applet is embedded in HTML document.

HTTP - Acronym for Hypertext Transfer Protocol. The application protocol with the lightness and speed necessary for distributing Web documents.

Hypertext Markup Language - see HTML .

Identifier - A name given to a class, method, or variable in accordance with Java restriction on using leading characters as identifiers.

Inheritance - The ability of a new class to extend the definition of its superclass. The new class inherits both variables and methods of its superclass but it can override the behaviour which it inherits.

Inner class - An inner class is defined within another class , just like a method, which is defined within a class. It's function is to support the class that contains it.

Input stream - It is an object from which data can be read into a program

Instance - It is an object.

Instance variable - It is a variable within a class.

Instantiation - The way of creating an instance is called instantiation.

Integer - A whole number, such as 55.

Interface - An interface is a collection of methods. Interfaces can be added to classes in order to inherit methods, which are not inherited from the superclass. An interface can also provide additional methods that are not defined in a particular class.

Internet Explorer - It is one of the World Wide Web browsers on the market. It is a piece of software from Microsoft which may enable you to run your applet on the Web page.

Interpreter - It is a language processor. It reads a line of code, interprets it and then executes it. Thus, it does not produce any machine code to be executed at a later stage.

java - It is an interpreter, which is one of the tools in the Java Development Kit.

JavaBeans - A program which is designed with a view to re-using it in other programs. It is fairly a new Java technology.

Java Core API - It contains both the core language, and Java class libraries for tasks such as graphics.

Java Development Kit (JDK) - It is a set of Java development tools. It is available free of charge from Sun Microsystems. It enable you to write and test Java programs in a command-line environment.

Java Virtual Machine (JVM) - It is a software that executes the bytecode.

Javac - It is a compiler. It comes with the Java Development Kit.

JPEG file - Acronym for Joint Photographic Experts/Engineering Groups file. The **. JPG file** version is for presenting photographic images.

Keyword - A reserved word. Java has a set of keywords. Each keyword has a unique meaning to the Java compiler.

Layout Manager - It is an object that handles the arrangement of the graphical user interface (GUI) components. You can also write it as LayoutManager.

Logical Value - Some writers call boolean True and False values logical values.

Logical error - Logical errors are the result of poor program design. These errors are recognised when the program outputs the wrong result or it just does not generate the required output.

Loops - Loops are used for repeating execution of a block of code. These are also called iteration statements because of their repetition or cyclic nature. Examples of loops:
> *. while loop*   .   *do ..... while loop*   *. for statement*

Method - It is a procedure for performing a task in Java. A method's body is within the { }.

Multithreading - It is also called multitasking. When a program or an operating system can simultaneously perform more than one task, without interfering each other's operations, it is multithreading.

Navigator - It is one the Web browsers supplied by Netscape.

newline - the symbol **\n** for next line. It generates a new line on which text begins at the far left column.

Null - It is a keyword. It means no object. It is equivalent to zero. It is also called null object.

Object - Anything that has attributes and behaviour and can be distinguished from other objects.

Object variable - In order to access an object, you must define an object variable. It is thus a variable, which is associated with a particular object.

Object Oriented Programming (OOP) - The conceptual thinking that forms the basis of OOP is that of independent objects and their relationship with other objects. This thinking is formalised as a program design methodology, according to which a computer program is designed as a group of objects, in which each object has its own resources to perform a specific task.

Output stream - It is an object which can send data from a program to an output device. For instance, in **System . Out . println ("OK!") ; System . out** is an object which sends data to a screen.

Overriding - See default method.

Package - It is a collection of classes.

Parameter - See argument.

Parent class - It is another name for the superclass. It is the class which is at the top of the inheritance hierarchy. All classes below it are subclasses, which inherit its attributes and behaviour.

Platform - A computer system which has its own specific operating system and hardware making it different from all other computer systems.

Platform independent - In particular, it means that a Java program can run on any computer, which has installed a JVM.

Primitive type - It is a data type. There are eight primitive data types which handle integer, floating-point numbers characters and boolean values. Primitive types are not objects. They are built into the system.

Program - A program is a set of instructions arranged in a sequence for a computer. It tells a computer what to do and how to carry out a task step-by-step.

Protocol - It is a legal agreement between parties that exchange information between computer systems. It governs the rules and procedures for data communication between two computers. The World Wide Web uses a number of protocols. HTTP and FTP are most common with the Internet.

Scope - Broadly speaking, it means the same as in the English language - limits. In a Java program variables have their scopes within their block in which they are created. A variable cannot be used outside its own scope.

Signature - A declaration of method includes its name, arguments and return type. Some writers call it signature.

Source file - The program you write is a source file.

Standard RGB values - The 'Color class' defines standard color objects. The standard colours are red, green and blue. All other colour are specified by giving the percentage of red, green and blue.

Statement - A line of code which is an instruction to the computer. The end of a statement is marked by a semicolon (;).

Stream - It is an object that can read (input stream) and write (output stream) sequential and linear flow of input and output data.

Subclass - A subclass extends from the superclass. For instance, Your own applet class extends JApplet superclass.

A subclass inherits attributes and behaviour of all classes which are above it in the hierarchical structure of classes.

Superclass - See hierarchy of classes, and Parent class.

Swing - The Swing consists of classes for the graphical user interface handling. The Swing is extended by the AWT by providing a richer set of user interface components.

Switch statement - It is used when the program offers multiple choices.

Syntax error - An error which is due to violation of the rules of Java language for whatever reason. Syntax errors are detected by the compiler and reported as error messages.

Tag - In html document , tag is enclosed within < > marks.

Text area - It is one of the user interface components in the GUI system. It allows you to enter more than one line of text.

Text editor - Java programs are prepared by using a text editor, such as **WordPad**. It is a kind of word processor.

Text field - It is a user interface component. It can allow you to enter only one line of text.

Thread - It is a single flow of control of program execution. A program can have multithreads. In multithreading, each thread has its own resources, but also shares some common resources such as memory space.

Unicode - It is a 16-bit code. It is defined by the Unicode Consortium, as an international character - mapping system.

URL - An abbreviation for Uniform (or universal) Resource Locator. It is the address system which is used to specify the location of a document in the World Wide Web. For example **http:/ www. me.com.**

Virtual Machine - see Java Virtual Machine.

Web browser - See browser.

Zip file - A standard zip file uses some form of compression. This compression makes the file smaller and unrecognisable. It has to be unzipped before it can be used. For example, when you copy JDK, it is zipped.

Index

312

ADR Forthcoming Titles
in Year 2000

- Windows Programming

- Visual C++ Programming

- Designing Graphics for the Internet

ADR Student simplified text series comprises of slim books for students who may be studying at home or at an institution. A reader may be a professional programmer, who wishes to know the fundamental elements of a new language.

For a serious and enthusiastic reader, ADR books lay the foundation for mastering advanced programming skills, and launch a new career.

Prospective ADR Writers

You are invited to send your proposal for IT and computing related topics. You can send it to us now. This proposal should precisely describe your specific objective for the contents of your proposed book. You should also outline how your book will be organised to enable its readers to benefit from it. The relevant material must be up-to-date, concise, and exemplified with practical programming solutions to support the student, and tutor.

Send your proposal now

A.D.R. (London) Limited
24 St. Alban Road
Bridlington
YO16 7SS
England